Florence

D0071762

The Travellers' Companion series

General editor: Laurence Kelly

St Petersburg: a travellers' companion
Selected and introduced by Laurence Kelly (1983)

Moscow: a travellers' companion
Selected and introduced by Laurence Kelly (1984)

Naples: a travellers' companion
Selected and introduced by Desmond Seward (1986)

Edinburgh: a travellers' companion
Selected and introduced by David Daiches (1986)

Overleaf: Florence seen from Fiesole: engraving after J.M.W. Turner

FLORENCE

A Travellers' Companion

SELECTED AND INTRODUCED BY

Harold Acton and Edward Chaney

Atheneum · New York · 1986

Library of Congress Cataloging-in-Publication Data

Florence, a travellers' companion.

  (The Travellers' companion series)
  Bibliography: p.
  1. Florence (Italy)—History. 2. Florence (Italy)—
Description. 3. Historic buildings—Italy—Florence.
I. Acton, Harold Mario Mitchell, 1904–   .
II. Chaney, Edward.   III. Series: Travellers' companion
series (New York, N.Y.)
DG732.5.F56 1986   945′.51   86-7978
ISBN 0-689-70713-4

For Jessica and Olivia

Contents

FLORENCE

and Michael Faraday used Galileo's 'great burning glass' to explode the diamond); from Sophia Hawthorne's *Notes in England and Italy*

THE APPROACHES TO FLORENCE

LIFE, CUSTOMS AND MORALS

Illustrations

Acknowledgements

In compiling this anthology the major problem has been what to exclude. Much relatively esoteric material on Florence has been sacrificed in the cause of producing a more entertaining and broadly informative book, which focuses on those buildings and phenomena most likely to interest the discriminating tourist. In surveying the vast quantity of material available, we were struck by how much of the best documentary writing was published many decades, even centuries ago. This, at any rate, is our excuse for presenting numerous passages from sources such as Landucci, Vasari and Cellini. Where a greater claim to originality might be made is in the selection of several lesser-known travel accounts, which are no less vivid and usefully complement the merely factual. In this book, as in others in the series, we have adhered to the original spelling and punctuation used by different authors.

Most of the research for this book was completed at the Villa I Tatti, the exquisite Anglo-American creation which Bernard Berenson left to Harvard University as a research institute for Renaissance Studies, and was done during the last year in which that institute was presided over by Craig and Barbara Smyth, whose extraordinarily successful management of things both academic and domestic has earned them widespread praise and deeply felt gratitude. We warmly thank both them and their excellent staff, American, English, German and Italian, who made working there such a pleasant experience.

Of those who either volunteered or were recruited into helping with this anthology, we would like to thank Salvatore Camporeale, Bob Gaston, Bill Kent, Mark Roberts, Michael Rocke and Joe and Elayne Trapp. We are particularly grateful to Eve Borsook, Gene Brucker, John Fleming, Cecil Grayson, Rab Hatfield, Nicholas Havely, Iris Origo, and Nicolai Rubinstein for permission to quote from their works, or for translations done especially for this volume; and to Prudence Fay who did far more than a publisher's editor should have to do in order to create a coherent book out of an unwieldy manuscript.

We also wish to make acknowledgement to the following for extracts used from their editions, translations, or where copyright permission was needed:

Edward Arnold for *A Room with a View* by E.M. Forster; Penn State Press for *The Life of Brunelleschi* by Antonio Manetti, translated by Catherine Enggass and edited by Howard Saalman; Princeton University Press for *Florentine Art under Fire* by Frederick Hartt, and *A Documentary History of Art* by Elizabeth Holt; George Braziller for *Gothic versus Classic: Architectural Projects in Seventeenth Century Italy* by Rudolf Wittkower; Oxford University Press for John Ruskin's *Diaries*, edited by J. Evans and J.H. Whitehouse, for *Movements in European History* by D.H. Lawrence, for *The Mural Painters of Tuscany* by Eve Borsook, and for John Evelyn's *Diaries* edited by E.S. de Beer; Phaidon for *Fra Angelico* by John Pope-Hennessy; Macmillan for *Great Morning* by Osbert Sitwell; John Murray for *Robert Adam and his Circle* by John Fleming; Rupert Hart-Davis for *The Letters of Oscar Wilde*; Faber & Faber for *The Collected Letters of Dylan Thomas*, edited by Paul Ferris and the *The Italian Journal* of Samuel Rogers, edited by J.R. Hale; Prentice-Hall International for *Brunelleschi in Perspective* by Isabelle Hyman and for *Italian Art 1400–1500. Sources and Documents in the History of Art* by Creighton Gilbert; Phaidon for *Italian Painters of the Renaissance* by Bernard Berenson; Collins for *Civilisation and Capitalism: 15th–18th Century*, by Fernand Braudel; Little, Brown & Co for *Stories and True Stories* by Francis Steegmuller; Allen & Unwin for *People of Florence* by Joseph Macleod; Gollancz for *The Private Diaries of Stendhal*, edited and translated by Robert Sage; the Istituto Nazionale di Studi dal Rinascimento for Bastiano Arditi's *Diario*; Diana Editrice for *Reflections on Florence* edited by Simone Bargellini and Alice Scott; the trustees of the National Library of Scotland for permission to quote from Richard Lassels's 1654 manuscript *Description of Italy* (Advocates' MS 15.2.15); the British Institute of Florence for Susan Horner's manuscript travel journals; the Bodleian Library for *A Discourse of H. P. his travells* (Rawlinson MS D.83); McGill-Queen's University Press for Joseph Spence's *Letters from the Grand Tour*; and Hammond Hammond for *The Life and Death of Radclyffe Hall* by Lady Una Troubridge. We are also grateful to the Mansell Collection for their help with the illustrations, and to Patrick Leeson, who drew the map.

Introduction

At the turn of the century Florence was the only Italian city with a strong English accent. 'Useful information', the first chapter of Augustus Hare's and St Clair Baddeley's guide-book of that period, is studded with the names of English bankers, hotels, pensions, chemists, booksellers, dentists, and even artists (W. Spence, H. Teague, and W. Gould). For cups of tea the reader is advised to call on the Misses Macaulay, close to Vieusseux's Library. These havens have vanished with the original names of streets and squares. Concerning galleries readers are warned: 'These frequently undergo sectional re-arrangement, and the official catalogues are as defective as the guide-books.' While paintings such as Botticelli's 'Primavera' have undergone radical restoration, many of their attributions have been promoted or demoted. Tourists no longer make a bee-line for the 'Medici Venus' which was once the absolute cynosure of the Uffizi, yet Hare and Baddeley's little black book still reflects the enthusiasm of visitors for all that is characteristic of the jewel city.

When the Goncourt brothers arrived in the autumn of 1855 they exclaimed: '*ville toute anglaise* – an entirely English city, where the palaces have almost the gloomy darkness of London and everything seems to smile on the English, especially the *Tuscan Monitor* [*sic*], which is only concerned with the affairs of Great Britain.' They expatiated on their common Latin heritage and good reasons for Franco-Italian agreement with an astute Florentine lawyer. The latter smiled ironically, and after a while replied, 'I'm afraid you have illusions on the subject . . . To prove it, in the first salon you enter containing a Frenchman and an Englishman, an Italian would approach the Englishman instinctively.'

The British community in Florence had doubled since the Congress of Vienna, and the term *Inglese* was applied to foreigners in general. A hotel porter would say to his manager, 'Some *Inglesi* have arrived but I haven't yet discovered if they are Russians or Germans.' In 1825 Leigh Hunt wrote that Florence had 'more conveniences for us, more books, more fine arts, more illustrious memories, and a greater concourse of Englishmen, so that one might possess, as it were, Italy and England together.' Some two hundred English families were then resident in

Florence, consequently he wished to launch a magazine for them. And in April 1833 Emerson confided to his journal: 'It is pleasant to see how affectionately all the artists who have resided here a little speak of getting home to Florence. And I found at once that we live here with more comfort than in Rome or Naples. Good streets, industrious population, spacious, well-furnished lodgings, elegant and cheap caffés [*sic*]. The Cathedral, the Campanile, the splendid galleries and no beggars, make this city the favourite of strangers.'

The Industrial Revolution brought an increasing number of travellers, many of whom decided to settle there. The most famous of these were the poets, novelists and painters who basked in the aura of the Brownings. In fact one can scarcely think of a mid-Victorian Florence without that romantic couple whose writings served as eloquent propaganda for the cause of Italian independence. When he composed *The Italian in England* ('I would grasp Metternich until/ I felt his red wet throat distil/ In blood through these two hands . . .') Browning was obviously influenced by Mazzini who translated it. But Elizabeth surpassed her husband as a propagandist in *Poems before Congress* and *Casa Guidi Windows*. As Signora Artom Treves pointed out in her seminal book *The Golden Ring: The Anglo-Florentines 1847–1862*: 'There is a moving parallel between the passionate woman imprisoned by her frail health, tyrannized by her father, who was the prototype of the Victorian family despot, and Italy which in those same years was being restored to life and liberty.'

Mrs Browning worshipped Cavour; Jessie White Mario idolized Mazzini and followed Garibaldi's campaigns as a nurse; Margaret Fuller Ossoli, 'the Yankee Corinne', was equally devoted to Mazzini, who described her as 'a woman of the rarest, for her love and active sympathy for all that is beautiful, great and holy, and therefore for our Italy'.

Though Ruskin showed less interest in the Risorgimento, his aesthetic influence on the Brownings was reflected in Robert's rambling poem *Old Pictures in Florence*:

'But at any rate I have loved the season
Of Art's spring-birth so dim and dewy;
My sculptor is Niccolo the Pisan,
My painter – who but Cimabue?
Nor even was man of them, all indeed,

From these to Ghiberti and Ghirlandaio,
Could say that he missed my critic-meed.'

Ruskin, who never settled in Florence, changed the whole
attitude of visitors towards the fine arts they came to see. 'What a
bishop was lost in him,' his father used to sigh, and he might well
be called a bishop of aesthetic taste, for he preached that art
could never be divorced from Christianity, that 'things done
delightfully and rightly are always done by the help and in the
spirit of God'. For him the grace and purity of Giotto and the
original pre-Raphaelites, the so-called Primitives, evaporated
with the Renaissance, which he saw as the triumph of worldli-
ness, decadence and 'harlotry'. This was scarcely logical, for
while he damned Palladio he admired Veronese and Tintoretto,
who were surely consummate products of the High Renaissance.
And Florence was the birthplace of what we understand as
Renaissance. It was Filippo Brunelleschi who revived the spirit
of Greek and Roman architecture, and Cosimo de' Medici, *Pater
Patriae*, who recognized his genius, though he chose Michelozzo,
who had accompanied him into exile, to design his private
palace. A galaxy of Florentine architects was imbued with
Brunelleschi's refinement, and these imposed the solid character
on Florentine buildings which Ruskin considered forbidding,
though he made an exception for the rusticated masonry of the
Pitti palace, 'brother-heart to the mountain from which it is
rent'.

Legend blends with tradition in attributing the remote origin
of Florence to Etruscan Fiesole on the north-eastern hilltop.
After a severe siege Fiesole was forced to surrender to the Roman
invaders under Julius Caesar who destroyed it and built a new
city, Florentia, in the Arno valley below in 59 BC. Excavations
bear witness to a typical Roman *castrum*, or garrison town, and
the outlines of the medieval city follow the Roman pattern,
including a forum, a temple of Mars, public baths, and an
amphitheatre. Some derive its name from a Roman general
Florinus, slain during the siege of Fiesole; others from Fluentia,
confluence of the rivers Arno and Mugnone. But the popular
tradition is the most poetical: Florence remains the city of flowers
and its cathedral is known as Santa Maria del Fiore, for the *Iris
Florentia* is the Blessed Virgin's emblem and it has remained the
heraldic emblem of the city.

Myth prevails during the first ten centuries of the Christian era. The names of such barbaric invaders as Rhadagasius and Totila are about all we know of them, and no ancient chronicle is complete without Charlemagne, who is said to have rebuilt the ruined city in 786, but the miracles of certain saints are commemorated in lively scenes by the early Florentine painters. The column beside the Baptistery evokes the legend of the fifth-century bishop Zenobius, whose coffin touched a dead elm which burst into leaf. St Miniatus is commemorated by the sublime eleventh-century Romanesque basilica overlooking the city from the south. He was said to have been an Armenian prince martyred under the Emperor Decius in 254. After being beheaded he climbed the hill named in his honour, carrying his head in his hands, and was buried on the site of an old oratory, which reminds one of Madame du Deffand's famous remark to the prelate who told her that Saint Denis the Areopagite walked with his head under his arm all the way from Montmartre to the Church of St Denis, a distance of six miles: '*Ah, Monseigneur! dans une telle situation il n'y a que le premier pas qui coûte.*'

Saint Giovanni Gualberto, the Abbot of San Miniato who built the church, founded the Vallombrosan Order of reformed Benedictines and died in 1073. A painting by Lorenzo di Niccolò Gerini in the Metropolitan Museum of Art, New York, represents a scene from his legend. According to this, he was asked by his father to avenge the murder of his brother, but when he met the murderer in a narrow street he forgave him and spared his life. He then climbed to the hill of San Miniato, and while he prayed a painted crucifix leaned towards him as if to thank him for pardoning his enemy. While simony was rife, a Vallombrosan monk known as 'Peter Igneus' braved the ordeal by fire unsinged by the flames to convict Pietro of Pavia, then Bishop of Florence, of simony in 1068 – an ordeal that was avoided in the case of Savonarola.

All that we know of Willa, the mother of Ugo, Margrave of Tuscany, is that she founded the Florentine Badia in 978, where Ugo was buried in 1001, though his actual tomb was designed by Mino da Fiesole in the fifteenth century. Matilda, Countess of Tuscany, is reputed to have governed wisely from 1076 to 1115. She supported Pope Gregory VII against the Emperor Henry IV and appeared with a sword on battlefields. Her popularity was attested by the frequent use of 'Contessa' or 'Tessa' as a name for daughters. Dante was to praise Matilda in his *Divina Commedia*. Florence prospered under her beneficent rule, marred only by skirmishes between the Florentine burghers and the predatory barons of the countryside. Gradually their feudal castles were demolished and they were forced to live in the city. Dante glorified this period in his *Paradiso* when, as he wrote, Florence enjoyed 'such full repose she had no cause for lamentation'. After Matilda's death the struggle between Popes and Emperors for her legacy began and her counsellors became consuls of the republican Commune. The Teutonic barons backed the Emperor, the Latin burghers the Pope (rather from fear of foreign subjection than from religious motives), and there was constant friction between them.

Visitors to San Gimignano may picture medieval Florence, a labyrinth of narrow streets with towering fortress-like buildings surrounded by massive walls. At the end of the twelfth century the city bristled with 150 towers nearly 250 feet high, but in 1250 the Commune ordered those above 100 feet to be truncated. Family quarrels became party feuds identified with Guelph and Ghibelline – derived from 'Welf' and 'Waiblingen', which were war cries at a battle between the Bavarian allies of the Pope and the Hohenstaufen Emperor Conrad III respectively.

Ever since the tragic Easter Sunday of 1215 when young Buondelmonte dei Buondelmonti was murdered on the oldest bridge across the Arno, the Ponte Vecchio, the city had been divided into Guelph and Ghibelline factions. For the sake of peace Buondelmonte had agreed to marry a girl of the Amidei clan, but he broke his engagement when a widow of the rival Donati persuaded him to wed her more attractive daughter. The infuriated Amidei held a family council to decide what punishment to inflict. Mosca dei Lamberti said, 'Let him die. What is done is done with.' Consequently Buondelmonte, all in white on a white steed, was struck down and stabbed repeatedly by a gang of Amidei below an old statue of Mars by the Ponte Vecchio. The body was carried through the streets with its head on the bride's lap to excite the people's vengeance. The Ghibelline aristocracy were partisans of the Amidei; the burghers and a sprinkling of nobles of the Buondelmonti. The latter considered themselves Guelphs but they often changed sides.

The leading Guelphs were descended from wealthy merchants whereas most of the Ghibellines were descended from feudal barons, and the civil war between them continued for fifty years. In spite of this, two new bridges were built across the Arno, the Carraia (1220) and Rubaconte (1227), now alle Grazie from a tiny oratory on one of its piers; and a third circle of walls was begun, enclosing an area of 1,556 acres. The Ghibelline nobles gained control of the city in 1249 with the aid of Frederick II's German troops, but after the Emperor's death in 1250 a Guelph Constitution was established under a Captain of the People, to counterbalance the Podestà, a foreign noble appointed by the citizens as head of the Commune. The Constitution, called *Il Primo Popolo*, was comparatively democratic. From a white lily on a red field, the banner of the Commune was changed to a red lily on a white field and the Ghibellines were expelled. Pisa, Pistoia and Volterra were subjugated during the next decade but the Florentines were defeated in an attack against Ghibelline Siena on 4 September 1260, and the Guelph magnates fled to Lucca. Six years of Ghibelline despotism followed, during which in 1265 Dante Alighieri, the poet who was to celebrate the salient events of this turbulent period, was born.

Charles of Anjou entered Italy to seize the crown of Naples and Sicily at the invitation of Pope Urban IV, and Byron's hero Manfred, King of Sicily, was defeated and killed near Benevento in 1266, which signified the end of German rule in Italy. For the next ten years the new King of Naples and Sicily became suzerain of Florence.

Dante assailed the incessant constitutional changes in his *Purgatorio*. These make monotonous reading. The triumphant Guelphs soon split into Black and White factions. Fortunately civic pride was stronger than party conflict. The Church on one side, the trade guilds on the other, stimulated an efflorescence of painting and architecture. The trade guilds were organized into miniature republics, each with its own officers, councils and banners. The government was entrusted to the *Arti Maggiori* or Greater Guilds whose leading members, called 'priors of the arts', were appointed chief magistrates of the State though they only held office for two months. Thus Florence became an independent republic of merchants and bankers. (The gold coin called *fiorino*, first issued in 1252, bearing a lily on the obverse and the Latin name *Florentia* on the reverse, became accepted as international currency, and in England it was known as a 'florence'.) The Ghibelline nobility were replaced by Guelph magnates whose power was restrained by the Gonfalionere, or 'Standard-bearer of Justice', eventually the supreme head of the State with an armed force of 1,000 men at his disposal. The last hopes of the Ghibellines were shattered at the battle of Campaldino against the city of Arezzo in 1289, when Dante fought with the cavalry that lost.

The century from the battle of Benevento in 1266 to the return of the Popes from Avignon in 1377 is generally treated as the *trecento* by historians, and in spite of the great flood of 1333, the failure of banks in 1343, and the famine followed by plague in 1348, this was a period of extraordinary activity in literature and the visual arts. Dante's *Divine Comedy* soars above every other poem of the Middle Ages, and in the first half of the fourteenth century Petrarch and Boccaccio were far more than great precursors. Though Petrarch was a Tuscan born at Arezzo in 1304, his father, like Dante, belonged to the White faction of Guelphs and was expelled from Florence in 1302. His extensive missions between Avignon and Naples were more adventurous than those of his cosmopolitan successors.

Before the invention of printing, the fame of Dante, Petrarch and Boccaccio spread throughout Europe. Petrarch's sonnets in the vernacular were models for future sonneteers even in French and English. Deeply moved by the grandeur of surviving Roman monuments amid the squalor of their surroundings four centuries before Piranesi depicted them, Petrarch longed to see the glories of ancient Rome revived when he was crowned with laurel on the Capitol in 1341. But the French popes were deaf to his appeals to quit their 'Babylon' on the Rhône. He was the first humanist in that he collected Latin manuscripts, inscriptions and coins, and he inspired chosen pupils to follow his example. His younger friend Giovanni Boccaccio has been called 'the first modern novelist'. Born in Paris in 1313, he was brought by his father to Florence in his boyhood, and in the stories of his immortal *Decameron* we breathe the very air of the *trecento*. After Dante's death in exile at Ravenna in 1321, Boccaccio wrote his first biography. He was probably in Naples when the terrible plague known as the Black Death broke out in Florence, which he used as a sinister background for his fugitive group of storytellers. Alarmed by a monk's dire warnings of eternal damnation, he wished to destroy the *Decameron*, but Petrarch assured him that literature was not incompatible with religion. However, he abandoned creative writing for classical scholarship – a pity, for the naturalism of his style was quite original. Petrarch criticized the 'freedom' of his narrative and regretted its composition in the vernacular, but nevertheless he paid it the compliment of translating the story of patient Griselda into Latin. Chaucer owed him 'The Clerk's Tale', and his *Troilus and Criseyde* was based on Boccaccio's *Filostrato*.

During the summer of 1348 plague reduced the population of Florence from 90,000 to 45,000. Giovanni Villani was among the victims, but his *Chronicle* was continued by his brother Matteo and his nephew Filippo till 1364. The death of so many people, it was supposed, would create abundance, instead of which there was a dearth. 'The cost of labour,' wrote Matteo Villani, 'and the products of every trade and craft, rose in disorderly fashion beyond the double. Lawsuits, disputes and riots arose everywhere . . . by reason of legacies and successions. Special privileges were granted to artisans and such professional men as physicians, which encouraged immigration on a vast scale.' Newly rich tradesmen married into the impoverished upper class and became eligible for election to the priorate. Petrarch's *Triumph of Death* and the preface to Franco Sacchetti's *Trecento novelle* express the gloom that gathered over Tuscany. Sermons on the misery and brevity of human life were preached from pulpits and portrayed in frescoes of the Last Judgement and the tortures of Hell. At least the Church benefited from large bequests and donations. The Dominican prior of Santa Maria Novella, Jacopo Passavanti, terrified his congregations with prophecies of new calamities and, as Millard Meiss observed, 'his thought and his mood are closely related to contemporary painting in Santa Croce and Pisa's Camposanto. Man appears a perpetual sinner, hovering in the shadow of death and judgement.' Societies of Flagellants lashed themselves in penitential frenzy twice a day and once at night for thirty-three consecutive days – one day for each of Christ's years on earth. These depressing exhibitions shocked rather than edified the average citizen. Pope Clement VI tried to stop them but his authority was weakened by the 'Babylonian Captivity' at Avignon. St Catherine of Siena implored him to return to Rome. Meanwhile his bands of Breton mercenaries preceded him, committing appalling atrocities in the Papal States.

Cardinal de Noellet, the French legate in Italy, antagonized the Florentines by refusing their request for corn during a shortage. This led to an alliance with Bernabò Visconti, Duke of Milan, and a 'Board of Eight' was appointed by the *Signory* to wage war on the Church. Siena, Lucca, Cortona, Arezzo, Pisa and Bologna joined an anti-papal league; Church property was heavily taxed; and eighty towns rebelled against their French governors. Gregory XI retaliated by excommunicating the Florentine priors and State officials, and Florentine merchants in most Catholic countries were expelled and despoiled. The latter and the Guelph party, nominally the clerical faction, were eager for peace, but the unprovoked sack of Faenza by papal mercenaries under the English *condottiere* Hawkwood caused such general indignation that the Eight were encouraged to fight on. Eventually Hawkwood left the papal service for that of its opponents; the Signory ordered a sale of ecclesiastical property and defied the interdict. The last French Pope died during the final peace negotiations. His successor, Urban VI, elected on 8 April 1378, was the Italian Bishop Prignano of Bari, and three months after his election a peace treaty was signed at Tivoli. Florence had to pay an indemnity of 200,000 florins and restore the Church property it had expropriated, whereupon the interdict was removed.

Urban VI wished to restore the universality of the papacy which had suffered during exile at Avignon. Unfortunately his rough treatment of the French cardinals was to provoke the Great Schism (1378–1417) because they maintained he had been elected under duress. The ferocious Robert of Geneva was appointed the first anti-pope, with the title of Clement VII.

During the war with the papacy the beautiful Loggia dei Priori – later dei Lanzi – was built for public ceremonies, and the bulk of the Cathedral was completed in 1378 while the Guelph party were conspiring to usurp the government. Under the direction of the Albizzi clan the Guelphs had become as despotic as the Ghibellines of old. Their ambitions were frustrated by Salvestro de' Medici, the head of the rising family of bankers who was Gonfalonier of Justice. He supported the downtrodden artisans of the Arte della Lana or Wool Guild, who broke out in the rebellion known as that of the Ciompi or wool-carders. Their leader, Michele di Lando, stepped into Salvestro's shoes as Gonfalonier of Justice and a chaotic period of arson and pillage ensued when the minor guilds predominated in the government.

After three years of turbulence the Parte Guelfa regained supremacy. Their opponents were exiled or 'admonished' (excluded from office) and until 1414 Florence was practically ruled by Maso degli Albizzi, followed by his son Rinaldo. The names of their adherents were dropped into bags and constantly revised to bolster the party. Magnates became eligible for office by being declared *Popolani*, thus losing their aristocratic status. The opulent Alberti, enemies of the Albizzi, were dubbed magnates and banished. The nominal free republic of twenty-one guilds was in fact a government of autocratic merchants who were hated on account of the war taxes.

Between 1382 and 1434, either by sale or conquest, Florence acquired Arezzo, Pisa, Cortona, Livorno and Montepulciano, sops to civic pride but costly to the tax-payer. A war with Milan was purely defensive since Gian Galeazzo Visconti aimed at the conquest of Italy and hoped to be crowned in Florence. Fortunately he died in 1402 and Florence's other foe, King Ladislaus of Naples, died in 1414. Forced loans (*prestanze*) and indirect taxes (*gabelle*) had paid for these wars, but after the Milanese war a more equitable system was adopted in 1427. This was called the *catasto* from the register of assessments: every citizen was compelled to declare the value of his property in detail and omissions were liable to confiscation.

In 1419 Pope Martin V was invited to Florence by the Signory, and Guicciardini describes this as a halcyon period when great artists and scholars found enlightened patronage before the Medici rose to power. Since Salvestro de' Medici had supported the Ciompi no member of his family had been allowed to hold office in the State, but in 1421 the prosperous banker Giovanni di Bicci de' Medici was elected Gonfalonier of Justice against the advice of Niccolò da Uzzano, the most influential statesman of the Albizzi faction. Apart from his great wealth as papal banker with sixteen branches in Europe, Giovanni was popular for his wide benevolence and generosity. He died in 1429 when Florence was attempting to conquer its harmless rival Lucca, an attempt that failed. Rinaldo degli Albizzi was rightly blamed for its failure.

Giovanni di Bicci's eldest son Cosimo, more ambitious than his father, was the consolidator of his family's fortune. Before dying, Giovanni had urged him to avoid attracting attention and Cosimo remembered his advice. 'Envy', as he said, 'is a plant

one should never water,' and the Florentines were endemically
envious. In 1433 he had a narrow shave when he was suddenly
imprisoned by his Albizzi opponents in the tower of the Palazzo
Vecchio. During that dangerous month he might have been
poisoned or executed. Instead – so extensive was his popularity –
he was banished to Padua where he had loyal friends, as he had
in Venice and Ferrara, who intervened on his behalf. One year
later a pro-Medicean Signory, supported by his creditor Pope
Eugenius IV, recalled him to Florence. Thus quietly, without
ceremony or bloodshed, a middle-aged banker returned to
found the famous dynasty which provided Rome with two
eminent pontiffs, France with two flamboyant queens, and
Florence with one of the most versatile personalities of the
Renaissance and, eventually with a Grand-ducal government.

The family's history has often been related and it still
continues to fascinate scholars. In recent years Professor Nicolai
Rubinstein, Sir John Hale, and Professor Gene Brucker are
among the most illuminating experts on the subject in English; in
Italian their bibliography would fill many a stout volume before
and since Gaetano Pieraccini's encyclopaedic *La stirpe dei Medici
di Cafaggiolo*.

Cosimo became the virtual prince of a republic whose pattern
was preserved in the Palazzo Vecchio with subtle variations. He
had occasionally been elected Gonfalonier, otherwise he held no
public office. He pulled the strings of government, as it were,
from his private palace in the Via Larga (now Cavour).
Prematurely aged by gout, the family curse, he was a patriarch
who cherished the country of his farming ancestors (as the
bookseller Vespasiano da Bisticci recorded, he had an intimate
knowledge of agriculture and pruned his vines at Careggi as a
hobby), but he was also a voracious reader and collector of
manuscripts. His patronage of scholars, Greek as well as Tuscan,
enriched the monastic libraries of San Marco and the Badia of
Fiesole; his own library, now in the Laurenziana, is as distinguished for its design by Michelangelo as for the rarity of its
manuscripts, including early codices of Virgil, Tacitus, Greek
tragedies, Petrarch's *Horace*, and the unique *Pandects of Justinian*.
As Professor Hale wrote, Cosimo 'exemplified that blend of the
active and contemplative life which was a leading theme of
Florentine humanist discussion in the first half of the fifteenth
century'.

A financier of far-sighted acumen with a mystical streak, he encouraged Marsilio Ficino, the precocious son of his doctor from Figline, to translate the works of Plato and Plotinus and to found the celebrated Platonic Academy in 1462. 'Certainly I owe much to Plato,' Ficino wrote, 'but must confess that I owe no less to Cosimo, inasmuch as Plato only showed me the idea of courage, Cosimo showed it me every day.' More than any contemporary magnate he promoted the humanistic movement by welcoming the learned Greek refugees from Constantinople who whetted an appetite for their art and philosophy. It was mainly due to Cosimo's efforts that the council for the union of Greek and Latin Churches was transferred from Ferrara to Florence in 1439. Though it failed in its objective it was one of the three events, as Lord Acton pointed out, 'which determined the triumph of the Renaissance'. (The others were the fall of Constantinople and the election of Tommaso Parentucelli as Pope Nicholas V, the founder of the Vatican Library.)

Among the galaxy of Florentine architects Cosimo patronized, he commissioned Michelozzo to build his palace in the city, country houses at Careggi, Cafaggiolo, Il Trebbio, and the convent of San Marco; among sculptors he recognized the genius of Donatello, whose 'David' and 'Judith' once embellished his palace courtyard. His detractors have accused him of patronizing artists for propaganda purposes but he was a firm friend to the unworldly Donatello, and he appreciated the prestige conferred on Florence by so great an artist. He was by no means alone in this appreciation, for the humanist Cristoforo Landino, writing in 1481, specified Masaccio, Fra Angelico, Fra Filippo Lippi, Paolo Uccello and Andrea del Castagno as the outstanding painters of the fifteenth century; Brunelleschi, Ghiberti, Donatello and Desiderio da Settignano as the greatest sculptors. In the dedication of his treatise on painting to Brunelleschi, Leon Battista Alberti mentions Luca della Robbia and Masaccio as 'quite equal to the greatest artists of antiquity'.

Brunelleschi had completed the dome of the Cathedral in 1436, the first notable engineering achievement of Renaissance architecture, and while the dome was being built he laid the foundations of this architecture more profoundly in his less complicated works. His design for the Pazzi chapel was probably the first ecclesiastical building in a Renaissance style; Santo Spirito, the church and sacristy of San Lorenzo in the Medici

parish, the exquisite foundling hospital named after the Innocents massacred by Herod, and the centre of the Pitti Palace,
were other pioneering examples of his genius.

Considering the state of culture in Europe at this time,
Florence was far in advance of all other cities. Ficino wished to
reconcile Platonism with Christianity and though he was
ordained as a priest in 1473 and became a canon of the
Cathedral, he burned a lamp before a bust of Plato as before a
patron saint. But the real patron was Cosimo de' Medici, directly
responsible for the growth of Italian Hellenism. 'Too large a
house for so small a family!' he sighed in his palace after the death
of his favourite son Giovanni, little dreaming he had founded a
dynasty which, with republican intervals, was to last until the
eighteenth century. When he died on 1 August 1464, he was
buried in San Lorenzo with the simplicity he had requested, and
the Signory voted to honour his grave with the Roman
inscription *Pater Patriae*, a title that endures.

The short career of his only surviving legitimate son Piero was
overshadowed by Cosimo's glamour, but Piero was accepted as
heir to his figurative throne. In spite of chronic ill-health – he was
known as Piero the Gouty – he maintained his position with
dignity and distinction. Luca Pitti's conspiracy to overthrow
him was crushed without vengeful reprisals. From his dealings
with artists he appears to have been more fastidious than his
father. It was Piero who commissioned Benozzo Gozzoli's
delightful frescoes of the Journey of the Magi for his palace
chapel, as well as paintings by the Pollaiolo brothers, and Luca
della Robbia's glazed terracotta ornaments for his study. His
wife Lucrezia Tornabuoni was an intellectual more sophisti-
cated than her domestic mother-in-law Contessina de' Bardi,
and Luigi Pulci's dedication of his burlesque epic *Il Morgante
Maggiore* to Lucrezia commemorates their friendship. This
strange farrago of buffoonery and theology was to influence
Byron when he wrote *Beppo* and the *Vision of Judgement*;
Savonarola condemned it to the bonfire of vanities.

Their sons Lorenzo and Giuliano were carefully educated by
Cristoforo Landino, Marsilio Ficino and Gentile Becchi, the
crème de la crème of contemporary humanists. Under their tuition
Lorenzo 'lisped in numbers', and at the age of fifteen he was sent
on goodwill missions to the rulers of other Italian states,
acquitting himself with precocious urbanity. All the talent in

Florence was drawn to this genial, high-spirited youth, who was married to the Roman patrician, Clarice Orsini, with suitable festivity six months before his father died in 1469.

It is rare that a major poet, a statesman, and an arbiter of taste combine in a single temperament, and Lorenzo's was immensely versatile. The Florentines delighted in pageantry and he has been blamed for providing it in spectacular tournaments, as if they were a form of political corruption, but the people benefited from what Lord Asquith in a different context called 'the pervading influence of a commanding mind'. His younger brother Giuliano, to whom he was devoted, was blessed with the handsome features Lorenzo lacked, but Lorenzo's magnetic vitality compensated for his facial defects. Almost automatically he assumed the leadership of the regime at the age of twenty. 'The principal men of the city,' as he wrote, urged him to take charge of it as his grandfather and his father had done. Though he feigned reluctance on account of his youth, he accepted the responsibility 'for the sake of our friends and our possessions, since it is ill living in Florence for the rich unless they rule'.

The complexity of ruling a nominal republic while Italy was divided into so many bickering states was a formidable challenge to a youth of twenty, especially when the nepotistic Pope Sixtus IV decided to appropriate the Romagna, an important source of grain and a commercial highway to the Adriatic. Lorenzo's obstruction to the purchase of Imola antagonized the expansionist Pontiff, who borrowed money for the sale from the rival Pazzi bank. This led to the Pazzi conspiracy of 1478 when Lorenzo barely escaped being murdered with his brother at High Mass in the Cathedral. The aftermath was to confirm Lorenzo's popularity, for the papal interdict was disregarded and the Signory refused to surrender Lorenzo as a hostage. In the subsequent war with the Pope and his ally the King of Naples, the Florentine army, commanded by the Duke of Ferrara and the Marquis of Mantua (who came to blows over some loot), was defeated. During the truce before winter set in Lorenzo decided to sue for peace personally with King Ferrante of Naples, the less virulent of his enemies. It was a calculated risk, for Ferrante had previously murdered the *condottiere* Piccinino in spite of his safe-conduct. After three months of procrastination Ferrante was won over by Lorenzo's logical eloquence and a creditable peace was patched up before he returned to Florence in March 1480.

'If Lorenzo was great when he left Florence,' wrote Machiavelli, 'he returned much greater than ever; and he was received with such joy by the city as his fine qualities and his fresh merits deserved, having exposed his own life to restore peace to his country.' Lorenzo took advantage of this temporary euphoria to tighten control of the regime by a new council of seventy members, nominally for five years but actually permanent.

The Pope refused to withdraw his interdict and insisted that Lorenzo should risk his life again by going to Rome and imploring his forgiveness. Eventually twelve other Florentines went unwillingly in Lorenzo's stead and were tapped with a staff in token of chastisement and pardon. Meanwhile a Turkish attack on Otranto had caused a providential diversion: King Ferrante's son Alfonso of Calabria was recalled from his occupation of Siena to drive out the infidel intruders.

Lorenzo was eager for his son Giovanni to be raised to the Cardinalate but this was impossible while Sixtus IV was alive. When Cardinal Cibò succeeded Sixtus as Pope Innocent VIII, the thirteen-year-old boy was promised the red hat, vastly to his father's satisfaction. Having recovered the strongholds of Pietrasanta and Sarzana, lost during the war, Lorenzo was determined to keep on good terms with the new Pontiff, whose son Franceschetto married his daughter Maddalena. In the meantime he strained every nerve to pacify the warring Italian states. Apart from his subtlety as a statesman and the financial brilliance of his grandfather Cosimo, Jacob Burckhardt rightly pointed out that the charm the elder branch of Medici exercised over Florence and their contemporaries was due less to their political capacity than to their leadership of the culture of the age. In this view Edward Gibbon had preceded Burckhardt, inspiring William Roscoe of Liverpool to produce his popular biographies of Lorenzo the Magnificent and of his son Pope Leo X. These were eventually followed by Walter Pater's precious studies in art and poetry entitled *The Renaissance*, and John Addington Symonds's exuberant *Renaissance in Italy*. In our age of general belittlement, historians accentuate the Medici's manipulation of the Republic rather than their beneficial influence on European culture.

Among painters Botticelli seems to stand closest to Lorenzo: his 'Birth of Venus', his 'Primavera', his 'Mars and Venus', have a visual affinity with the poems of Lorenzo and Poliziano, the poet laureate of the Laurentian Age. His pictures reveal the Tuscanized Hellas of the Florentine humanists who formed Lorenzo's circle. Their portraits are vivid in Ghirlandaio's frescoes, especially in the Sassetti Chapel of Santa Trinità (circa 1483–6). Lorenzo asked Ghirlandaio to send his most promising pupils to work in the garden of San Marco, where he wished to form a school for sculptors under the supervision of Donatello's pupil Bertoldo. Among these was Michelangelo, who had caused his teacher to exclaim, 'This boy knows more than I do.' From 1490 till 1492 the fifteen-year-old genius lived in the Medici palace and was treated like a relation, associating with Marsilio Ficino, Pico della Mirandola, Luigi Pulci, and Poliziano who, as Ascanio Condivi related, 'recognizing the lofty spirit of Michelangelo loved him exceedingly, and little as he needed it, spurred him on in his studies, always explaining things to him and giving him subjects. One day amongst others, he suggested "The Rape of Deianira" and "The Battle of the Centaurs", telling him in detail the whole of the story.' The marble relief of the latter, now in Casa Buonarroti, is the earliest work by the master to which an exact date, 1492, can be given, and it shows already that 'power over rhythm of line in a crowded composition' which distinguishes his later groups.

In spite of his republican sentiments, Michelangelo was shattered when Lorenzo died. He was so upset that for a long time he was unable to work, and he was one of the few who survived from the golden age of the Medici until the establishment of the younger branch under Duke Cosimo. It is hard to realize that the dynamic Lorenzo had suffered from gout, now diagnosed as uricæmia, throughout his strenuous career. He succumbed to it on 8 April 1492 and it is extraordinary that he asked for Savonarola, who had fulminated against his tyranny, to grant him absolution. Savonarola's disciples left a garbled account of the occasion which several historians have swallowed. In fact his last moments were edifying. Probably the doctors hastened his death at the age of forty-three, for one of them prescribed a concoction of pulverized pearls and precious stones and another committed suicide. Even if Lorenzo was despotic, let us leave the last word on the subject to Guicciardini: 'Florence could not have had a better or more delightful tyrant.'

Lorenzo's eldest son Piero, who succeeded him in the undefined regency at the age of twenty, soon alienated his supporters by his arrogance and conceit, for which they blamed his Roman mother and wife, both members of the Orsini family. When Charles VIII of France brought a huge army to claim the throne of Naples in 1494 Piero rushed to surrender the principal Florentine fortresses as well as Pisa and Livorno without consulting the Signory. Consequently he was expelled by a popular rising. He made three attempts to return before he was drowned at the battle of Garigliano in 1503.

Savonarola's prophecies of chastisement seemed to be fulfilled when Charles VIII entered Florence with his army, and in 1495 the friar from Ferrara was entrusted with organization of the State. Under his influence there was an anti-humanistic return to the Middle Ages. Street urchins were encouraged to act as moral police, collecting 'luxuries' such as feminine ornaments and decorative bric-à-brac, profane literature such as the writings of Boccaccio and Pulci, portrayals of sinful nudities and pagan deities, for the virtuous 'bonfire of vanities' on the Piazza della Signoria. It was the reign of militant puritanism, and again the city was divided as in the time of Guelphs and Ghibellines. The revulsion of the public was ferocious when it came in 1498. 'Prophet! now is the time for a miracle!' the mob shouted, when Savonarola was hanged from the gibbet and a fire was kindled beneath his tortured body. The Florentines were weary of penitence and fasting. So the nude returned to favour, and in virginal innocence Adam and Eve reappeared without fig-leaves.

In Rome the young Cardinal Giovanni kept the Medicean party together with the help of his younger brother Giuliano. When he was elected Pope Leo X in 1513, six months after the family returned from a second period of exile, the Florentines celebrated the event with spectacular festivities, adorned by such artists as Andrea del Sarto and Pontormo. Most of the leading Florentine families congregated in Rome to gather the papal fruits of office distributed with too liberal a hand. Raphael's portrait of Leo seated between Cardinal Giulio de' Medici and Luigi de' Rossi in the Uffizi, for all its solemnity, reminds us of the saying attributed to him: 'Let us enjoy the papacy since God has given it to us.' Like his father, he cultivated literature and the fine arts, and we are indebted to him for his patronage of Raphael in particular. But it was his first cousin, Giulio, the illegitimate son of the murdered Giuliano, who paved the way for the Medici's return to Florence after he was elected Pope Clement VII in 1523.

The interregnum between the expulsion of the Medici in 1494 and their return to power under Cosimo of the younger branch of hereditary Grand Dukes has been romanticized by republican sympathizers, but in spite of exhilarating moments it was a period of constant upheavals against a background of warfare in Italy. Liberty regained brought neither happiness nor prosperity, though Piero Soderini, who was elected Gonfalonier for life in 1502, was an honest patriot, as was also Niccolò Machiavelli, his chief mentor. Perhaps these years were most memorable because Michelangelo and Leonardo da Vinci were both in Florence working for the vast council hall of the Palazzo Vecchio. Their frescoes disappeared from its walls, but Michelangelo's more permanent 'David' was completed in 1504. None of his works have been so admired by the citizens of Florence, who placed it in front of the Palazzo della Signoria as a symbol of the victory of the republic over tyrants. What we see there now is a copy: the original dominates the Accademia museum. The Medici Chapel or New Sacristy in San Lorenzo was a later work (1520–24 and 1530–33) commissioned by Clement VII as a mausoleum for his father and uncle and his recently deceased cousins Giuliano, Duke of Nemours and Lorenzo, Duke of Urbino. The statues are purely allegorical. Reams have been written about them and the architectural scheme. 'The two Dukes are not portrayed as the dead up to this time had been, reclining on their sarcophagi, but as seated men, watching the Virgin. Thus a spiritual unity links all the figures in the Chapel.' (Charles de Tolnay.)

Alessandro, the first Medici duke, was probably an illegitimate son of Lorenzo, Duke of Urbino, and he is best known for his lurid murder by his cousin Lorenzino, dramatized by Alfred de Musset, than for such accomplishments as building the Fortezza da Basso. The murder was hushed up while his successor was chosen with the approval of the Emperor Charles V. The son of the gallant *condottiere* Giovanni delle Bande Nere, descended from the elder Cosimo's brother Lorenzo, and Maria Salviati, half a Medici of the senior line, eighteen-year-old Cosimo grabbed the reins of government in 1537. Here was a resolute exemplar of Machiavelli's *Prince*, who conjured order out of anarchy 'regardless of the reproach of cruelty'. His government was severe and absolute but he administered strict justice. The new roads and fortifications, the canal between Pisa and Livorno, as well as the militia he raised, were advantageous to Tuscany. He obtained his ducal title from the Emperor Charles V and was created Grand Duke of Tuscany by Pope Gregory XIII. His marriage to Eleonora, the only child of Don Pedro of Toledo, the powerful Viceroy of Naples, increased his wealth and influence. Contrasting in every respect with his venerated namesake, he proclaimed his sovereignty by settling in the former Palace of the Priors, a stout bastion of authority since Arnolfo di Cambio had built it in 1298; and he commissioned Giorgio Vasari to enlarge and redecorate its rooms.

Vasari, Bronzino, Ammannati, and Benvenuto Cellini were the most prominent exponents of Florentine taste at this period – and of Cosimo's taste, since he was the supreme arbiter. Cosimo's patronage of artists was practical: it encouraged competition and stimulated other grandees to buy their work. The buildings Vasari designed deserve higher praise than his overcrowded frescoes; and his *Lives of the Italian Painters, Sculptors, and Architects* will always be invaluable to students, pithy as prose and still valid as criticism. His devotion to Michelangelo was unstinted, and it was according to Michelangelo's plan that he completed the vestibule and staircase of the Laurentian Library. The Uffizi was his masterpiece: here he availed himself of the limited space at his disposal with elegance and ingenuity, in sober harmony with the adjacent Palazzo Vecchio. The covered passage over the Ponte Vecchio connecting the Pitti Palace with the Uffizi is another example of his skill. It was finished in five months and, as he complacently observed, 'anyone who examines its great length would suppose that it must have taken as many years'. Vasari was also largely responsible for the first academy of fine arts, which was founded under Cosimo's patronage in 1563 'to perpetuate the traditions of a glorious past as well as more recent doctrines and techniques'. Though originality may be inhibited by academic training this institution served successfully as a barometer of refined taste. Vasari told Michelangelo that its every member was indebted to him, and in fact it was dominated by the master's style, especially by his muscular distortions, which gave birth to so-called Mannerism.

Angelo Bronzino was the first and oldest of the academicians, a close friend of Vasari and a pupil-collaborator of the

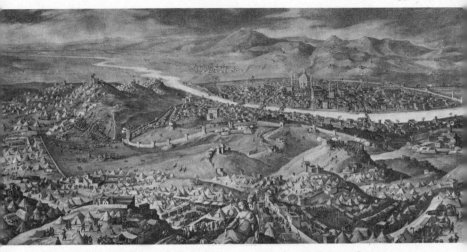

Panorama of Florence during the siege of the Prince of Orange;
by Giorgio Vasari

powerfully imaginative Pontormo. Cosimo's choice of this
painter to portray his family was brilliantly justified, for he has
stamped the Duke's proud features on our visual memory even
more effectively than Cellini in his busts. Eleonora of Toledo and
the children were painted at the same time, *circa* 1545, and as
Berenson observed, these portraits were to determine the
character of court painting all over Europe.

After the birth of seven children, the ducal apartments in the
Palazzo Vecchio became too cramped. Cosimo purchased and
enlarged the massive Pitti Palace with his wife's money, together
with the hillside behind it, which was gradually transformed into
the grandiose Boboli Gardens. Tribolo designed the first plans,
which were carried out after his death by Bernardo Buontalenti
and his pupils. Bartolomeo Ammannati mitigated the severity of
Brunelleschi's frontal façade by inserting arched windows, but it
did not assume its present form with additional wings until the
middle of the seventeenth century. Nearly all the stone used was
quarried on the spot. The garden façade was embellished with a
deep, paved courtyard and a spacious grotto beneath the
retaining-wall whence water gushes as from the hillside. An
elaborate fountain stands on a level with the first-floor windows
and a vast amphitheatre with six tiers of stone seats surmounted
with statues in niches and clipped laurel hedges, merges into the

slopes of the upper garden which ends in a miniature lake amid balustrades of potted lemons. This was a suitable setting for Medicean pageantry on a monumental scale. The palace remained the main seat of the Medici Grand Dukes until their line was extinguished in 1737, yet it continued to bear the surname of its first owner, an opponent of the elder branch of the family.

Ammannati was prodigiously active in designing other palaces and country houses, stately and restrained in comparison with such buildings elsewhere, but his masterpiece was the Santa Trinita bridge. This was rebuilt after a flood, and again after its destruction in the Second World War, a pious labour beyond praise when we consider the technical difficulties, including the recovery of the drowned fragments and the quarrying of stone to match them. So perfect are the proportions of this bridge that it has been attributed to Michelangelo.

As a sculptor, Ammannati was inferior to his rival Cellini, yet there is much to admire in his fountain of 'Neptune' in the Piazza della Signoria, especially the nude tritons and nereids surrounding it, flaunting their outstretched limbs with the serenity of sunbathers on a beach. The nereids remind one of Cellini's 'Nymph of Fontainebleau' and have been attributed to Giambologna, a native of Douai but a Florentine by adoption, whose flying 'Mercury' has become world-famous through myriad reproductions.

The devastation caused by the flooded Arno in 1557 incited Cosimo to restore and beautify the city. The graceful Loggia dei Lanzi, named after Cosimo's Swiss lancers from the neighbouring barracks, became an open-air sculpture gallery where Cellini's bronze 'Perseus' was given pride of place: its feverish creation is dramatically described in his autobiography. Eventually it was joined by Giambologna's marble 'Rape of the Sabines', a remarkable group of figures in violent action. Excavations for Etruscan antiquities were started at Arezzo and Chiusi, the products of which, including the 'Minerva' and 'Chimaera', were to form the nuclei of the Etruscan Museum. Botanical gardens were laid out in Florence and Pisa; a more scientific attention was paid to agriculture; learned academies flourished; and a semi-religious Order of Santo Stefano was founded to protect the coast against Algerian pirates (but they were accused of being Christian pirates by the Turks whose ships they attacked). Porto Ferraio on Elba was made a fine fortified port, and a harbour was begun at Livorno. The charge that Cosimo destroyed the remnants of Florentine liberty was scarcely felt at the time. The sudden death of his wife and two sons Giovanni and Garzia from malarial fever caught in the Maremma caused gruesome tales of murder to be spread by his enemies. This domestic tragedy seems to have weakened his fibre: he sought consolation in the arms of a morganatic wife and allowed his son Francesco to govern in his stead. He was only fifty-five when he died at Castello in 1574.

Francesco, who was even more maligned than his father on account of his liaison with and ultimate marriage to the voluptuous Venetian Bianca Cappello, inherited his flair as a collector and patron of the arts, and it was under his aegis that the Uffizi began to be converted into a picture gallery. He bought the estate of Pratolino on the high road to Bologna, to escape from the summer heat with his adored Bianca. Fantastic grottoes and extraordinary water-powered mobile sculpture were the speciality of these pleasure-grounds, which have been copiously described by Montaigne, Fynes Moryson and Richard Lassels, and engraved by Stefano della Bella. Now Giambologna's gigantic statue of the 'Apennine' is almost all that remains of the garden's original splendour.

Both Francesco and Bianca were rumoured to have been poisoned by Cardinal Ferdinando, Francesco's younger brother, whose hatred of his Venetian sister-in-law – '*la pessima Bianca*' as he called her – was an open secret. But it has been proved that this devoted couple died from natural causes within a short time of each other – luckily for Bianca, whose life as a detested widow would not have been worth living. Francesco had always dabbled in chemical research and probably hastened his end by swallowing one of his own medicinal potions.

Ferdinando, who renounced his cardinalate to succeed him, continued to collect works of art and enlarge the Uffizi gallery. While in Rome he had built the Villa Medici on the Pincio (which later became the French Academy), and filled it with some of the finest examples of Greek and Roman sculpture. The gems of this collection, including the 'Medici Venus', were eventually brought to Florence, and Buontalenti was commissioned to build the octagonal Tribuna for them, with its ceiling of inlaid mother-of-pearl and its pavement of coloured marble, the *sanctum sanctorum* of this temple of taste as it was called. Zoffany was to depict it crammed with British Grand Tourists in the eighteenth century.

Ferdinando's filial piety is attested by many monuments to his father, but he also raised a few to himself, such as Giambologna's equestrian statue in front of the Santissima Annunziata. Moreover, he started building the costly family mausoleum in San Lorenzo, about which opinions have always differed. 'A splendid piece of nonsense which has never been completed,' wrote Henry Matthews in 1817. Though its ground-plan was based on that of the Baptistery, it suffers from comparison with Michelangelo's New Sacristy. But the sarcophagi of polished oriental granite, the slabs of porphyry, and the profusion of polychromed marbles inlaid with the arms of subject cities, have a pompous gloom that is suitably sepulchral.

Excepting the bigoted Cosimo III, the last Medici were munificent patrons of the arts with a pronounced interest in science. Galileo's discoveries had wide repercussions and the number of his followers increased from year to year. Hobbes and Milton are both supposed to have visited him in the 1630s. Florence took the lead in scientific research. The Accademia del Cimento or Academy of Experiment, founded in 1657, used to forgather in the Pitti Palace where there was a well-equipped laboratory. Ferdinando II and his brother Cardinal Leopoldo were invariably present at these meetings and bore the expense of experiments in magnetism, electricity, the velocity of sound and light, etc. Thanks to their initiative, great progress was made in the manufacture of telescopes, microscopes, and other instruments; they also formed a curious natural history and anatomical waxwork collection. English exiles who returned home after the Restoration were inspired by the Cimento to help found the Royal Society. The private art collections of Cardinals Gian Carlo and Leopoldo were merged with those in the Pitti and Uffizi Palaces; Vittoria della Rovere, however incompatible with her husband, at least brought him her family treasures from Urbino.

The court painter Justus Sustermans has left us realistic portraits of these seventeenth-century princes, so similar in physique yet so unlike their fifteenth-century forebears. The gross Habsburg and Bourbon features overwhelmed the spare and alert Tuscan.

The Medici died out owing to a disastrous series of arranged marriages which brought them neither health, wealth, nor happiness. Cosimo III's marriage to Marguerite-Louise d'Orléans was a bed of Procrustes; both his hedonistic sons escaped from their plain Teutonic wives; and his corpulent younger brother's demise was hastened by matrimonial mortification. After two centuries of Medicean rule the Florentines regretted their tyrants, who had preserved an oasis of culture in a war-torn Europe. And the last female member of the Medici, the Electress Anna Maria Luisa, who died in 1743, secured all the treasures of her family for Florence by her generous will.

Tuscany became an apanage of Austria owing to the Empress Maria Theresa's marriage to Francis Stephen, Duke of Lorraine, whose own duchy was ceded to France via the King of Poland in exchange, but its independence was guaranteed by the Treaty of Aachen in 1748. The Lorrainers were overbearing and unpopular; the new Grand Duke was an absentee; and as Président de Brosses wrote in 1739: 'The Tuscans would give two-thirds of their property to have the Medici back, and the other third to get rid of the Lorrainers. They hate them as the Milanese hate the Piedmontese. The Lorrainers ill-use, and what is worse, despise them.' But the arrival of Pietro Leopoldo, younger son of Francis and Maria Theresa, was warmly welcomed and he did not disappoint them. He was interested in science and philosophy, and sincerely anxious for the welfare of his people. Like his brother Joseph, he was keen on reform in the civil, criminal, and ecclesiastical laws, and in theory he was an ardent progressive. Florence settled down to a period of placid provincialism, of which the British envoy Sir Horace Mann has left a graphic record in his letters to Horace Walpole. The famous views engraved by Giuseppe Zocchi (1740–44) show that externally the city had changed little since the sixteenth century. A few Baroque buildings had sprung up, but Tuscan Baroque was sedate and restrained: it never boomed as in Rome or trilled as in Naples or Sicily.

The eighteenth-century Grand Tourists saw Florence as it had been under the Medici. They enjoyed the social functions and picturesque pageantries but they did not respond to early Renaissance architecture and painting. The term 'Gothic' was used pejoratively by Président de Brosses, who failed to appreciate Giotto. An occasional collector or dealer like Ignatius

Hugford showed a historical interest in the Tuscan pre-
Raphaelites, but Domenichino and Guido Reni were still the
most admired, even by Horace Walpole, who was original in
considering Gothic architecture 'at once magnificent and
genteel'. Many of the families mentioned in his correspondence
with Mann still occupy their ancestral palaces and produce wine
which is sold in Piccadilly.

Now it is the Renaissance nucleus of the city, the piazzas –
open spaces rather than squares – of the Signoria, Santissima
Annunziata, Santo Spirito, and Santa Croce, the noble simplicity and elegance of the palaces, which reflect the great age of
humanism and enable us to enjoy its harmony.

The city's expansion when it became the provisional capital of
unified Italy in 1865 was accompanied by the regrettable
destruction of the historic centre, with a few exceptions, to make
way for the present Piazza della Repubblica, and the ancient
walls were torn down to be replaced by the Viale dei Colli, the
carriage drive winding towards Piazzale Michelangelo and San
Miniato al Monte. Charles Richard Weld, in *Florence, the New
Capital of Italy* (1867) wrote: 'The improvements are confined at
present to the north bank of the Arno. The new boulevard,
which will be planted with trees, will include in its course all the
old gates, which will be like flies in the amber of modern
civilization.' The few scattered gates retain their solid medieval-
ism, but the amber of modern civilization has cracked pretty
often since the ancient city walls were demolished. The Viale dei
Colli has its charm as a town-planning reform, though the walls
need not have obstructed the surrounding avenues. Giuseppe
Poggi's visual climax, the Piazzale Michelangelo, provides every
visitor with a stupendous panorama of the city.

The cruellest cracks in the amber were caused by the
devastation of 4 August 1944 when all the bridges save the Ponte
Vecchio were blown up, and, more recently, by the catastrophic
flood of 4 November 1966 which damaged innumerable arte-
facts and buried half the city under 500,000 tons of mud mixed
with crude petroleum. Young students, native and foreign, the
so-called 'angels of the mire', volunteered to clear up the débris,
a back-breaking process. The zone round Santa Croce was the
worst victim. Not even Ghiberti's 'Gates of Paradise' were
spared, five of whose exquisite panels were torn out by the raging
torrent. But such is the technical skill of modern restoration that

recent visitors would hardly believe how battered and soiled these were at the time. Families were marooned on roofs and top floors without food or electricity; cellars and furnaces were drowned in a dense blackish bog. Shops were reduced to shambles; metal shutters were twisted like tinfoil, and the wrecks of motor cars were countless. The stench of it lingered long after the mess had been swept away. But the atavistic resilience and enterprising spirit of the Florentines were not defeated by this last calamity. Far from it! They were strengthened by an exhilarating sense of international solidarity, and their *campanilismo* (attachment to the bell-tower) became more intense.

Such rivers of ink have flowed on the subject since the nineteenth century that it is not easy to say anything new about Florence, but from the majority who have recorded their impressions and opinions we have selected those extracts which form a mosaic of its long history and illustrate changes of taste. It is still intensely alive as a capital of the arts and crafts.

The English accent has become less noticeable, but English words have invaded the Tuscan language. 'Self-service' is visible all too often. Many shops have English names and advertisements: one in particular is called 'Old England', and it is old in the sense that it sells such national products as plum puddings. While in England we may seek in vain for Allen and Hanbury's delectable blackcurrant lozenges, I was surprised to find them here like relics from Pompeii. The tranquil tea-shops have been replaced by noisy discothèques, but even there the words of the pop songs are a sort of Anglo-American.

The British community, so large at the turn of the century, has dwindled since the last World War, but latterly there has been a new wave of emigration to the hospitable countryside of what is nicknamed Chiantishire. The ancient farms of Greve and Castellina have been converted into cosy cottages, a bit more spacious than those in an English shire, and owing to the Common Market the local shops provide comestibles dear to the English palate, which soon adapts to Tuscan fare. Excepting the hilly landscape and the stony soil where smooth lawns for tennis and croquet are difficult to cultivate, the emigrants have imported an atmosphere of week-end Surrey. Swimming-pools abound; the vineyards and groves of olives are full of flowers, but the music of cathedral bells is far away.

Harold Acton
Florence, 1985

**Map of the city locating
the places described**

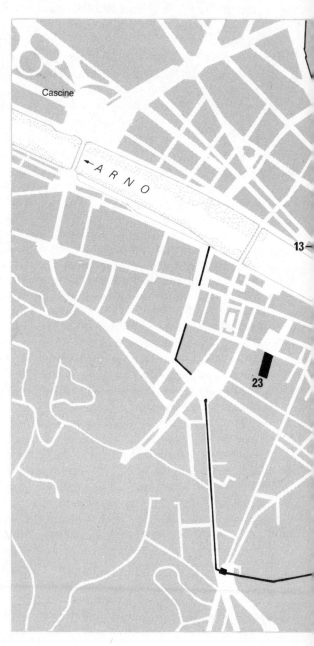

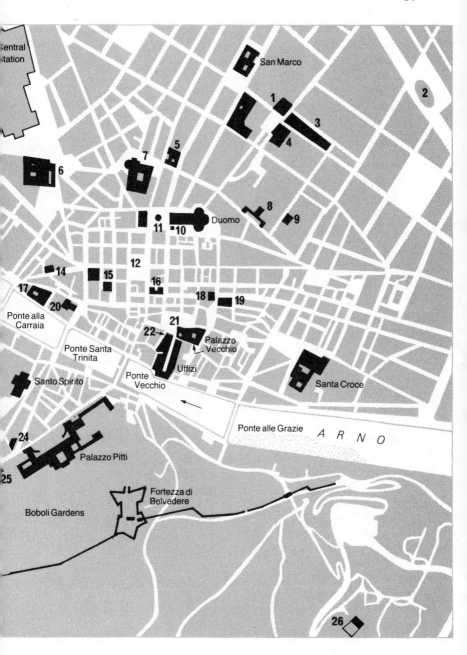

Central Station

San Marco

1

2

3

4

5

6

7

8

9

Duomo

11 10

12

14 15

16

17 20

Ponte alla Carraia

18 19

Ponte Santa Trinita

21

22

Palazzo Vecchio

Uffizi

Santo Spirito

Ponte Vecchio

Santa Croce

24

Ponte alle Grazie

ARNO

25 Palazzo Pitti

Fortezza di Belvedere

Boboli Gardens

26

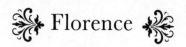# Florence

Rise of the city

[1] The destruction of Fiesole by the Florentines in the early eleventh century; from Giovanni Villani's *Croniche Fiorentine*.

(Giovanni Villani (1280–1348) was the son of a well-to-do Florentine merchant who belonged to that class which helped establish the democratic priorate system of government toward the end of the thirteenth century. In 1300, the year of the Great Jubilee, the twenty-year-old Villani was inspired by the ancient Roman historians to become his native city's chronicler. He died of the plague during the Black Death.)

In the said times [1010] when the Emperor Henry I was reigning, the city of Florence was much increased in inhabitants and in power, considering its small circuit, especially by the aid and favour of the Emperor Otho I, and of the second and third Otho, his son and grandson, which always favoured the city of Florence; and as the city of Florence increased, the city of Fiesole continually decreased, they being always at war and enmity together; but by reason of the strong position, and the strength in walls and in towers which the city of Fiesole possessed, in vain did the Florentines labour to overcome it; and albeit they had more inhabitants, and a greater number of friends and allies, yet the Fiesolans were continually warring against them. But when the Florentines perceived that they could not gain it by force, they made a truce with the Fiesolans, and abandoned the war between them; and making one truce after another, they began to grow friendly, and the citizens of one city to sojourn in the other, and to marry together, and to keep but little watch and guard one against the other. The Florentines perceiving that their city of Florence had no power to rise much, whilst they had overhead so strong a fortress as the city of Fiesole, one night secretly and subtly set an ambush of armed men in divers parts of Fiesole. The Fiesolans feeling secure as to the Florentines, and not being on their guard against them, on the morning of their chief festival of S. Romolo, when the gates were open, and the Fiesolans unarmed, the Florentines entered into the city under cover of coming to the festival; and when a good number were within, the other armed Florentines which were in ambush secured the gates of the city; and on a signal made to Florence, as had been arranged, all the host and power of the Florentines came on horse and on foot to the hill, and entered into the city of Fiesole, and traversed it, slaying scarce any man, nor doing any harm, save to those which opposed them. And when the Fiesolans saw themselves to be suddenly and unexpectedly surprised by the Florentines, part of them which were able fled to the fortress, which was very strong, and long time maintained themselves there. The city at the foot of the fortress having been taken and overrun by the Florentines, and the strongholds and they which opposed themselves being likewise taken, the common people surrendered themselves on condition that they should not be slain nor robbed of their goods; the Florentines working their will to destroy the city, and keeping possession of the bishop's palace. Then the Florentines made a covenant, that whosoever desired to leave the city of Fiesole, and come and dwell in Florence, might come safe and sound with all his goods and possesions, or might go to any place which pleased him; for the which thing they came down in great numbers to dwell in Florence, whereof there were and are great families in Florence. Others went to dwell in the region round about where they had farms and possessions. And when this was done, and the city was devoid of inhabitants and goods, the Florentines caused it to be pulled down and destroyed, all save the bishop's palace and certain other churches, and the fortress, which still held out, and did not surrender under the said conditions. And this was in the year of Christ 1010, and the Florentines and the Fiesolans which became citizens of Florence, took thence all the ornaments and pillars, and all the marble carvings which were there, and the marble war chariot which is in San Piero Scheraggio in Florence.

Badia Fiorentina

[2] The origin of the Badia in the tenth century; from Giovanni Villani's *Croniche Fiorentine.*

With Otho III there came into Italy the Marquis Hugh; I take it this must have been the marquis of Brandenburg, forasmuch as there is no other marquisate in Germany. His sojourn in Tuscany liked him so well, and especially our city of Florence, that he caused his wife to come thither, and took up his abode in Florence, as vicar of Otho, the Emperor. It came to pass, as it pleased God, that when he was riding to the chase in the country of Bonsollazzo, he lost sight, in the wood, of all his followers, and came out, as he supposed, at a workshop where iron was wont to be wrought. Here he found men, black and deformed, who, in place of iron, seemed to be tormenting men with fire and with hammer, and he asked what this might be: and they answered and said that these were damned souls, and that to similar pains was condemned the soul of the Marquis Hugh by reason of his worldly life, unless he should repent: who, with great fear, commended himself to the Virgin Mary, and when the vision was ended, he remained so pricked in spirit, that after his return to Florence, he sold all his patrimony in Germany, and commanded that seven monasteries should be founded: the first was the Badia of Florence, to the honour of S. Mary; the second, that of Bonsollazzo, where he beheld the vision; the third was founded at Arezzo; the fourth at Poggibonizzi; the fifth at the Verruca of Pisa; the sixth at the city of Castello; the last was the one at Settimo; and all these abbeys he richly endowed, and lived afterwards with his wife in holy life, and had no son, and died in the city of Florence, on S. Thomas' Day, in the year of Christ 1006, and was buried with great honour in the Badia of Florence.

[3] How the office of Priors was first created, and housed in the Badia; from Giovanni Villani's *Croniche Fiorentine.*

In the year of Christ 1282, the city of Florence being under government of the order of the fourteen good men as the Cardinal Latino had left it, to wit eight Guelfs and six

Ghibellines, as we afore made mention, it seemed to the citizens that this government of fourteen was too numerous and confused; and to the end so many divided hearts might be at one, and, above all, because it was not pleasing to the Guelfs to have the Ghibellines as partners in the government by reason of the events which were come to pass (such as the loss which King Charles had already sustained of the island of Sicily, and the coming into Tuscany of the imperial vicar, and likewise the wars begun in Romagna by the count of Montefeltro on the Ghibelline side), for the safety and welfare of the city of Florence they annulled the said office of the fourteen and created and made a new office and lordship for the government of the said city of Florence, to wit, the Priors of the Arts; the which name, Priors of the Arts, means to say 'the first,' chosen over the others; and it was taken from the Holy Gospel, where Christ says to His disciples, "Vos estis priores." And this invention and movement began among the consuls and council of the art of Calimala, to which pertained the wisest and most powerful citizens of Florence, and the most numerous following, both magnates and popolani, of those which pursued the calling of merchants, seeing the most part of them greatly loved the Guelf party and Holy Church. And the first priors of the Arts were three, whereof the names were these: Bartolo di M. Jacopo de' Bardi, for the sesto of Oltrarno and for the art of Calimala; Rosso Bacherelli, for the sesto of San Piero Scheraggio, for the art of the exchangers; Salvi del Chiaro Girolami, for the sesto of San Brancazio and for the woollen art. And their office began in the middle of June of the said year, and lasted for two months, unto the middle of August, and thus three priors were to succeed every two months, for the three greater Arts. And they were shut up to give audience (sleeping and eating at the charges of the commonwealth), in the house of the Badia where formerly, as we have aforesaid, the Ancients were wont to assemble in the time of the old Popolo, and afterwards the fourteen.

The Baptistery

[4] Why the Pisans gave Florence the two porphyry columns which now flank Ghiberti's 'Gates of Paradise' at the Baptistery; from Giovanni Villani's *Croniche Fiorentine*.

In the year of Christ 1117, the Pisans made a great expedition of galleys and ships against the island of Majorca, which the Saracens held, and when the said armada had departed from Pisa and was already assembled at Vada for the voyage, the commonwealth of Lucca marched upon Pisa to seize the city. Hearing this, the Pisans dared not go forward with their expedition for fear that the Lucchese should take possession of their city; and to draw back from their emprise did not seem for their honour in view of the great outlay and preparation which they had made. Wherefore they took counsel to send their ambassadors to the Florentines, for the two commonwealths in those times were close friends. And they begged them that they would be pleased to protect the city, trusting them as their inmost friends and dear brothers. And on this the Florentines undertook to serve them and to protect their city against the Lucchese and all other. Wherefore the commonwealth of Florence sent thither armed folk in abundance, horse and foot, and encamped two miles outside the city, and in respect for their women they would not enter Pisa, and made a proclamation that whosoever should enter the city should answer for it with his person; and one who did enter was accordingly condemned to be hung. And when the old men who had been left in Pisa prayed the Florentines for love of them to pardon him, they would not. But the Pisans still opposed, and begged that at least they would not put him to death in their territory; whereupon the Florentine army secretly purchased a field from a peasant in the name of the commonwealth of Florence, and thereon they raised the gallows and did the execution to maintain their decree. And when the host of the Pisans returned from the conquest of Majorca they gave great thanks to the Florentines, and asked them what memorial they would have of the conquest – the metal gates, or two columns of porphyry which they had taken and brought from Majorca. The Florentines chose the columns, and the Pisans sent them to Florence covered with scarlet cloth, and some said that before they sent them they put them in the fire for envy. And the said columns are those which stand in front of San Giovanni.

[5] A pro-Brunelleschian view of how Lorenzo Ghiberti won the competition to produce the bronze reliefs on the north doors of the Baptistery; from Antonio Manetti's *Life of Brunelleschi*.

(Antonio di Tuccio Manetti (1423–1491) was competent in mathematics and astronomy as well as architecture, in which latter capacity he came to know Brunelleschi in his old age and to complete some of his major works. His remarkable eulogistic account of the great architect provides the basis for all subsequent biographies.)

In the year of Our Lord 1401 when he [*Filippo Brunelleschi*] was a young man of twenty-four, working at the goldsmith's art, the *operai* of the building of the temple of San Giovanni had to commission the making of the second bronze doors (which are today on the north façade) for the embellishment of the aforesaid church. While considering the reputation of the masters of figure casting – including the Florentine masters – in order to assign them to the one who was best, they decided, after many discussions amongst themselves and after counsels with the citizens and artisans, that the two finest they could find were both Florentines . . . Those two were the aforementioned Filippo and Lorenzo di Bartolo. The latter's name is inscribed on the doors as Lorenzo di Cione Ghiberti as he was the son of Cione. At the outset of this affair of the doors Lorenzo was a young man also. He was in Rimini in the service of Signor Malatesta when he was called to Florence for this event. The following method was employed to choose the best one: they selected the shape of one of the compartments from the bronze doors that had been made by non-Florentine masters in the last century (although the design of the wax modeled figures was by the painter Giotto) containing the story of St John. Each of them was given a scene to sculpt in bronze within such a form with the principal intention of commissioning the doors to the one who came out the best in the aforesaid test.

They made those scenes and they have been preserved to this day. The one in the Audience Hall of the Guild of the Merchants is by Lorenzo and the one in the dossal of the sacristy altar of San Lorenzo in Florence is by Filippo [*both the reliefs are now in the Bargello*]. The subject of both is Abraham sacrificing his son. Filippo sculpted his scene in the way that still may be seen today. He made it quickly, as he had a powerful command of the art. Having cast, cleaned, and polished it completely he was not eager to talk about it with anyone, since, as I have said, he was not boastful. He waited for the time of confrontation. It was said that Lorenzo was rather apprehensive about Filippo's merit as [*the latter*] was very apparent. Since it did not seem to him that he possessed such mastery of the art, he worked slowly. Having been told something of the beauty of Filippo's work he had the idea, as he was a shrewd person, of proceeding by means of hard work and by humbling himself through seeking the counsel – so that his work would not fail at the confrontation – of all the people he esteemed who, being goldsmiths, painters, sculptors, etc. and knowledgeable men, had to do the judging. While making [*his scene*] in wax he conferred and – humbling himself a great deal – asked for advice constantly of people of that sort and, insofar as he could, he tried to find out how Filippo's work was coming along. He unmade and remade the whole and sections of it without sparing effort, just as often as the majority of the experts in discussing it judged that he should. The *operai* and officials of the church were advised by the very people Lorenzo had singled out. They were in fact the best informed and had been around Lorenzo's work many times: perhaps there was no one else [*to consult*].

Since none of them had seen Filippo's model they all believed that Polycletus – not to mention Filippo – could not have done better [*than Lorenzo*]. Filippo's fame was not yet widespread as he was a young man and his mind was fixed on deeds rather than on appearances. However, when they saw his work they were all astonished and marveled at the problems that he had set himself: the attitude, the position of the finger under the chin, and the energy of Abraham; the clothing, bearing, and delicacy of the son's entire figure; the angel's robes, bearing, and gestures and the manner in which he grasps the hand; the attitude, bearing, and delicacy of the figure removing a thorn from his foot and the figure bending over to drink – how complex these figures are and how well they fulfill their functions (there is not a limb that is not alive); the types and the fineness of the animals as well as all the other elements and the composition of the scene as a whole.

Those deputized to do the judging changed their opinion when they saw it. However, it seemed unfeasible to recant what they had said so persistently to anyone who would listen to them, though it now seemed laughable, even though they recognized the truth. Gathering together again they came to a decision and made the following report to the *operai*: both models were very beautiful and for their part, taking everything into consideration, they were unable to put one ahead of the other, and since it was a big undertaking requiring much time and expense they should commission it to both equally and they should be partners. When Filippo and Lorenzo were summoned and informed of the decision Lorenzo remained silent while Filippo was unwilling to consent unless he was given entire charge of the work. On that point he was unyielding. The officials made the decision thinking that certainly they would in the end agree. Filippo, like one who unknowingly has been destined for some greater tasks by God, refused to budge. The officials threatened to assign it to Lorenzo if he did not change his mind: he answered that he wanted no part of it if he did not have complete control, and if they were unwilling to grant it they could give it to Lorenzo as far as he was concerned. With that they made their decision. Public opinion in the city was completely divided as a result. Those who took Filippo's side were very displeased that the commission for the whole work had not been given to him. However, that is what happened, and in view of what was awaiting Filippo experience proved that it was for the best.

[6] The victor's view of how he won the competition to execute the north doors of the Baptistery in 1402; from Ghiberti's *Commentarii*, edited by Isabelle Hyman in *Brunelleschi in Perspective*.

(Lorenzo Ghiberti (1378–1455) was born in Florence and started his career as a painter and goldsmith. As well as the two Baptistery doors which occupied him almost continuously from 1403 to 1452, Ghiberti completed two statues for Orsanmichele, bronze reliefs for the baptismal font at Siena, and designs for stained glass at the Duomo.)

As the trial piece the committee and the governors of that temple wanted each of us to make one narrative panel for the door. The story they selected was the Sacrifice of Isaac, and each of the contestants had to make the same story. The trial pieces were to be executed in one year and he who won would be given the prize. The contestants were these: Filippo di ser Brunellesco, Simone da Colle, Nicolò d'Arezzo, Jacopo della Quercia of Siena, Francesco di Valdambrina, Nicolò Lamberti. There were six[1] taking part in this contest, which was a demonstration of the various aspects of the art of sculpture. To me was conceded the palm of victory by all the experts and by all those who competed with me. Universally I was conceded the glory without exception. At that time it seemed to all, after great consultation and examination by the learned men, that I had surpassed all the others without any exception. The committee of the governors wanted the opinion of the experts written by their own hand. They were highly skilled men among painters, goldsmiths, silversmiths, and marble sculptors. There were thirty-four judges from the city and other places nearby. From all came the declaration of the victory in my favour by the consuls and the committee and the entire body of the Merchants' Guild which is in charge of the temple of S. Giovanni. It was conceded to me and determined that I should make the bronze door for this temple. This I carried out with great diligence. . . .

[7] Ghiberti's autobiographical account of how he completed what Michelangelo was to call 'The Gates of Paradise', the gilt bronze east doors of the Baptistery, between 1424 and 1452; from Ghiberti's *Commentarii*, edited by Elizabeth Holt in *A Documentary History of Art*.

I was commissioned to do the other door, that is, the third door, of S. Giovanni. The commission gave me permission to execute it in whatever way I believed would result in the greatest perfection, the most ornamentation, and the greatest richness. I began the work in frames one and a third *braccia* in size. The stories, which had numerous figures in them, were from the Old

---

[1] Ghiberti neglected to include himself in the count.

Testament. With every proportion observed in them, I strove to imitate nature as closely as I could, and with all the perspective I could produce [*to have*] excellent compositions rich with many figures. In some scenes I placed about a hundred figures, in some less, and in some more. I executed that work with the greatest diligence and the greatest love. There were ten stories all [*sunk*] in frames because the eye from a distance measures and interprets the scenes in such a way that they appear round [*plastic*]. The scenes are in the lowest relief and the figures are seen in the planes; those that are near appear large, those in the distance small, as they do in reality. I executed this entire work with these principles.

There are ten scenes. The first is the creation of man and woman and how they disobeyed the Creator of all things. Also in the same scene is shown how they were driven from paradise for the sin they committed; thus in that panel four stories – that is scenes – are given. In the second panel, Adam and Eve beget Cain and Abel, who appear as small children. Then there is [*shown*] how Cain and Abel offered [*their*] sacrifices. Cain sacrificed the worst and vilest thing he had. Abel sacrificed the best and noblest. Abel's sacrifice was very acceptable to God, and that of Cain was entirely the opposite. There was [*shown*] how Cain slew Abel in envy. In that scene Abel was watching the animals and Cain was tilling the soil. Also there was [*shown*] how God appeared to Cain and demanded of him the brother he had slain. Thus in each panel are scenes of four stories. In the third panel is [*shown*] how Noah came out of the ark with his sons, his daughters-in-law, his wife, and all the birds and animals; and how with all his company he offered sacrifice. There is [*shown*] how Noah planted the vine and became drunk and Ham, his son, mocked him; and how his other two sons covered him. In the fourth panel is [*shown*] how three angels appear to Abraham and how he worshipped one of them; and how the servants and the ass remain at the foot of the mountain and how he stripped Isaac and wanted to sacrifice him, and the angel seized the hand with the knife and showed Abraham the ram. In the fifth frame is [*shown*] how Esau and Jacob were born to Isaac; how Esau was sent to hunt; how the mother instructed Jacob, gave him the kid, and fastened the skin at his neck and told him to ask the blessing of Isaac; and how Isaac searched for his neck, found it hairy, and gave him his benediction. In the sixth panel is [*shown*] how

Joseph is placed in the cistern by his brothers; how they sold him and how he is given to Pharaoh, the king of Egypt, and it was revealed through a dream that there would be a great famine in Egypt, and the remedy Joseph gave, and all the country and the provinces were spared, for their needs were met; and how he was greatly honoured by Pharaoh. [*Also is depicted*] how Jacob sent his sons, and Joseph recognized them; and how he told them to return with Benjamin, their brother, otherwise they would receive no grain. They returned with Benjamin and Joseph gave them a feast and had a cup placed in Benjamin's sack. [*There is shown*] how the cup was found and Benjamin was led before Joseph and how he made himself known to his brothers. In the seventh panel is [*shown*] how Moses received the tables on the mountain top, and how Joshua remained half way up the mountain, and how the people wondered at the earthquake, lightning and thunder, and how the people at the foot of the mountain were amazed. In the eighth panel is [*shown*] how Joshua went to Jericho, came and crossed the Jordan, and placed [*there*] twelve tents; how he went around Jericho sounding the trumpets, and how at the end of seven days the walls fell and Jericho was taken. In the ninth panel is [*shown*] how David slew Goliath and how the people of God destroyed the Philistines, and how David returned with the head of Goliath in his hand and how the people came to meet him making music and singing and saying, 'Saul destroyed one thousand, David ten thousand.' In the tenth panel is [*shown*] how the Queen of Sheba came with a large company to visit Solomon. The scene is rich and contains many people.

There are twenty-four figures in the frieze that surrounds the stories. Between one frieze and the other is placed a head. There are twenty-four heads. Executed with the greatest study and perseverance, of all my work it is the most remarkable I have done and it was finished with skill, correct proportions, and understanding. In the outer frieze on the doorjambs and the lintel is a decoration of leaves, birds, and little animals as is suitable to such ornamentation. There is also an architrave of bronze. On the inside of the doorjambs is a decoration in low relief made with the greatest skill. And likewise the threshold, at the base, that decoration is of fine bronze.

[8] How the Baptistery was transformed in honour of the birth of the future Francesco I, and how Vasari got a job which no one else wanted; from Vasari's *Lives* . . .

(Giorgio Vasari was born in Arezzo in 1511 but spent most of his life based in Florence working for the Medici. Though he was a practising painter and architect of considerable talent, he is now chiefly remembered as the author of the pioneering *Vite de' piu eccellenti Pittori, Scultori, e Architettori*, first published in 1550.)

When Don Francesco [*Cosimo I's*] eldest son, was born, Tribolo had charge of the decoration of S. Giovanni at Florence for the christening, with an apparatus to contain the hundred youths who walked in procession from the palace to the church. Together with Tasso [*the engineer*] he made that ancient and beautiful building look new and modern, surrounding it with seats richly adorned with pictures and gilding. Under the lantern he made a large octagonal wooden vessel, carved, approached by four steps. At the angles were large vine-stems starting from the ground, where lions' claws are represented, and at the top are large cherubs in various attitudes, holding the mouth of the vase and supporting festoons on their shoulders forming a garland about. Tribolo also made a wooden pedestal, in the middle of the vase, decorated with beautiful fancies, surmounted by Donatello's St John the Baptist from the house of Gismondo Martelli. Only the principal chapel escaped decoration, containing an old tabernacle with figures in relief by Andrea Pisano. But this seemed to detract from the grace of the rest, everything [*else*] being renewed. So one day, when the Duke went to the spot and praised Tribolo's arrangements, for his good judgement showed him how well Tribolo had adapted himself to this site and in other ways, he blamed him for not touching the principal chapel. At once, like a man of judgement, Tribolo decided that it should be covered with a large canvas painted in grisaille, representing St John the Baptist baptising Christ, with people looking on, and being baptised, some undressing and others dressing, in various attitudes. From above God sends down the Holy Spirit, and two springs, the JOR and the DAN, unite to form the Jordan. When M. Pier Francesco

Riccio, then the Duke's majordomo, wanted Jacopo da
Pontormo to do this work, he refused, because he only had six
days, and he did not think it sufficient. Ridolfo Ghirlandajo,
Bronzino and many others also declined. Giorgio Vasari
returned from Bologna at this time . . . He was not in much
consideration, although he was friendly with Tribolo and Tasso,
because those who were not of the party favoured by M. Pier
Francesco Riccio did not enjoy the favour of the court, however
skilful they might be, so that many who might have excelled if
assisted by the prince were neglected, Tasso directing everything, being architect of the palace and a merry fellow who
exercised complete dominion over Tribolo. Being suspicious of
Giorgio, who laughed at their vanity and folly, and sought to
gain more by study of his art than by favour, they did not think of
him, when the Duke ordered him to do that canvas. He
completed it in six days, in grisaille, gracefully decorating that
part of the church which most needed such an adornment.

[9] Richard Lassels remembers St Zenobius and the elm
which miraculously came into leaf when the Bishop's body
was translated from San Lorenzo to Santa Reparata (the
original Duomo) in the ninth century; from *The Voyage of
Italy* (1670) by Richard Lassels.

(Richard Lassels was born in Yorkshire in 1603. He became a
Roman Catholic priest after being sent secretly to Flanders for
his education, and spent most of his adult life in France,
teaching, working for Cardinal Richelieu and as a travelling
tutor to the sons of English Catholics and Royalist exiles. When
he died, in 1668, on his way to Italy for what would have been his
sixth tour, he left the most detailed version of a long series of
manuscript accounts of that country, to be published posthumously as *The Voyage of Italy*.)

I cannot omit here to take notice of a little *round pillar* in the
Piazza, neare this *Baptistery*, with the figure of a *tree* in iron nayled
to it, and old words engraven upon it importing, that in this very
place stood anciently an *Elmetree*, which being touched casualy
by the *hearse* of S. Zenobius, as they carried it here in procession,

the tree presently hereupon budded forth with green leaves of sweet odour though in the month of *Ianuary*. In memory of which miracle, this pillar was set up in the same place for a memorial.

The courtyard of the Bargello

The Bargello

[10] The translation of a thirteenth-century inscription still to be seen on the Bargello, originally the Palazzo del Popolo; from Nicolai Rubinstein's 'The Beginnings of Political Thought in Florence'.

Both Florentine and non-Florentine sources show that the Roman idea had a considerable bearing on political ideology in the period of intense military expansion which began with the establishment of the Popular government and ended with the crushing defeat of Montaperti in 1260.

During these years the Palazzo del Popolo, the first monumental public building in Florence, was being erected. It was intended both to manifest and to protect the power of the Republic. Shortly after the foundation was laid, an inscription was set on the façade which gives a good illustration of the political atmosphere of that time, and which, moreover, may be taken as an expression of the official attitude of the government. It reads as follows:

> Florence is full of all imaginable wealth,
> She defeats her enemies in war and in civil strife,
> She enjoys the favour of fortune and has a powerful population,
> Successfully she fortifies and conquers castles,
> She reigns over the sea and the land and the whole of the world,
> Under her leadership the whole of Tuscany enjoys happiness.
> Like Rome she is always triumphant.

[11] A mishap in the Via del Proconsolo; from Franco Sacchetti's *Trecentonovelle*.

(Franco Sacchetti (c.1333–1400) was the son of a Florentine merchant and held a number of public offices both in Florence and elsewhere. His best-known work is the collection of stories, the *Trecentonovelle* (1392–7?), many of which vividly portray

Florentine life and contemporary Florentine personalities. The
following street scene forms the opening of one of his most famous
stories – No 17.)

In the city of Florence there was once a man called Piero
Brandani who used to spend his whole time on litigation. He had
a son who was eighteen years old, and one morning when he had
amongst other things to go to the Palazzo del Podestà [*Bargello*]
to contest a case he gave this son of his some papers, telling him to
go on ahead with them and wait for him outside the Badia. The
boy did just as he was told, went along there and settled down to
wait for his father with the papers. All this took place during the
month of May – and it so happened that whilst the boy was
waiting it began to pour with rain. A countrywoman who had
come to sell fruit was passing by with a basket of cherries on her
head, and the basket overturned, spilling the cherries all over the
street, where the gutter because of all the rain was already
flowing like a stream. This boy, who, like the rest of them, had an
eye for this sort of thing, eagerly joined in the free-for-all over the
cherries, and he and the others went chasing after them all the
way to the edge of the gutter. However, when all the cherries
were finished and he had returned to his post he suddenly
discovered that the papers he had been holding under his arm
were no longer there – for whilst his mind had been on other
things they had dropped into the stream and immediately been
swept away down to the Arno. He began rushing hither and
thither, desperately asking if anyone had seen them, but all in
vain – by that time the papers were sailing on towards Pisa.

The Campanile

[12] The building of the Campanile; from the life of Giotto
in Vasari's *Lives* . . .

After these things, in the year 1334, on the ninth day of July,
[*Giotto*] began work on the campanile of S. Maria del Fiore, the
foundations of which were laid on a surface of large stones, after
the ground had been dug out to a depth of 20 braccia, the
materials excavated being water and gravel. On this surface he
laid 12 braccia of concrete, the remaining 8 braccia being filled
up with masonry. In the inauguration of this work the bishop of
the city took part, laying the first stone with great ceremonial in
the presence of all the clergy and magistrates. While the work
was proceeding on its original plan, which was in the German
style in use at the time, Giotto designed all the subjects comprised
in the ornamentation, and marked out with great care the
distribution of the black, white and red colours in the arrangement of the stones and friezes. The circuit of the tower at the base
was 100 braccia, or 25 braccia on each side, and the height 144
braccia. If what Lorenzo di Cione Ghiberti has written be true,
and I most firmly believe it, Giotto not only made the model of
this campanile, but also executed some of the marble sculptures
in relief, which represent the origin of all the arts. Lorenzo asserts
that he had seen models in relief by the hand of Giotto, and
particularly those of these works, and this may readily be
credited, since design and invention are the father and mother of
all fine arts, and not of one only. According to Giotto's model, the
campanile should have received a pointed top or quadrangular
pyramid over the existing structure, 50 braccia in height, but
because it was a German thing, and in an old-fashioned style,
modern architects have always discountenanced its construction, considering the building to be better as it is. For all these
things Giotto received the citizenship of Florence, in addition to
a pension of one hundred gold florins yearly from the commune
of Florence, a great thing in those days. He was also appointed
director of the work, which was carried on after him by Taddeo
Gaddi, as he did not live long enough to see its completion.

[13] Giotto's Campanile; from Hippolyte Taine's *Italy*.

(Hippolyte Adolphe Taine (1828–1893) made his reputation as
a literary critic when still in his twenties, but soon turned to
philosophy and aesthetics, in 1864 becoming Professor of the
History of Art and Aesthetics at the École des Beaux Arts in
Paris.)

The more we contemplate architectural works the more do we
find them adapted to express the prevailing spirit of an epoch.
Here, on the flank of the Duomo, stands the Campanile by
Giotto, erect, isolated, like St Michael's tower at Bordeaux, or
the tower of St Jacques at Paris; the mediæval man, in fact, loves
to build high; he aspires to heaven, his elevations all tapering off
into pointed pinnacles; if this one had been finished a spire of
thirty feet would have surmounted the tower, itself two hundred
and fifty feet high. Hitherto the northern architect and the
Italian architect are governed by the same instinct, and gratify
the same penchant; but whilst the northern artist, frankly gothic,
embroiders his tower with delicate mouldings and complex
flower-work, and a stone lace-work infinitely multiplied and
intersected, the southern artist, half-latin through his tendencies
and his reminiscences, erects a square, strong and full pile, in
which a skilful ornamentation does not efface the general
structure, which is not a frail sculptured bijou but a solid durable
monument, its coating of red, black and white marble covering it
with royal luxuriance, and which, through its healthy and
animated statues, its bas-reliefs framed in medallions, recalls the
friezes and pediments of an antique temple. In these medallions
Giotto has symbolized the principal epochs of human civilization; the traditions of Greece near those of Judea, Adam, Tubal-
Cain and Noah, Dædalus, Hercules and Antæus, the invention of
ploughing, the mastery of the horse, and the discovery of the arts
and the sciences; laic and philosophic sentiment live freely in him
side by side with a theological and religious sentiment. Do we not
already see in this renaissance of the fourteenth century that of
the sixteenth? In order to pass from one to the other, it will suffice
for the spirit of the first to become ascendant over the spirit of the
second; at the end of the century we are to see in the adornment
of the edifice, in these statues by Donatello, in their *baldness* so
expressive, in the sentiment of the real and natural life displayed

among the goldsmiths and sculptors, evidence of the transform-
ation begun under Giotto having been already accomplished.

Giotto's Campanile

[14] The 21-year-old Ruskin climbs the Campanile for the
first time in November 1840; from *The Diaries of John
Ruskin*.

(In recent years an outpouring of literature of all kinds has been
devoted to the life and works of John Ruskin (1819–1900). After
an over-protected youth he emerged as a brilliant, moralizing
and highly influential arbiter of taste but lapsed into insanity
and silence in his old age.)

Out immediately after breakfast to climb the Campanile.
Funeral in the cathedral; black and white festooned draperies at
all the doors, behind the high altar a square space enclosed with
black cloth, with a coffin, or something like it, covered with black
velvet, richly inwoven with gold, and a skeleton at each corner,
and a manservant, alive, one in tears, and all in cocked hats and
livery; the sword, cap, and something very like the shirt of the
deceased chevalier lying on the pall, all surrounded by very
handsome silver candlesticks. It had rather a good effect; as the
cathedral is always very dark, the candlelight did not look
tallowy or consumptive; but it was all sham; the chevalier had
been buried the day before. Then hard work up 418 steps in the
Campanile, the marble columns of the windows very exquisite
seen near, twisted, with rosettes; the gallery round the top of very
beautiful snow white marble. Tiled flat roof; protection from the
wind, which was keen, but, curiously enough, not so cold here as
below. Several splendid peaks of Apennine, quite alpine in form,
to the west, rising above a long range slightly sprinkled with
snow; then thirty miles of most lovely plain, but a great deal cut
up by the white houses. The town looks well from here – rather
large, and all its public buildings show well; very little of the
river. Went down with regret, though I had looked as long as I
cared, thinking how often, in the monotony of English scenery, I
shall remember that panorama of snow and marble, with the
wild, sick yearning – the desire of the moth for the star, of the
night for the morrow.

Casa Guidi

[15] Robert Browning's account of the death of Elizabeth Barrett Browning at Casa Guidi near the Palazzo Pitti; from *William Wetmore Story and his Friends* edited by Henry James.

(William Wetmore Story (1819–1895) was the son of an eminent Massachusetts jurist. He was admitted to the bar but in 1843 went to Italy to become a sculptor, author and poet. Here he records Browning's account.)

At about three o'clock he was startled by her breathing and woke her, but she said she was better, and reasoned so quietly and justly about her state that his fears were again subdued. She talked with him and jested and gave expression to her love for him in the tenderest words; then, feeling sleepy, and he supporting her in his arms, she fell into a doze. In a few minutes, suddenly, her head dropped forward. He thought she had fainted, but she had gone for ever. She had passed as if she had fallen asleep, without pain, without thought of death. After death she looked, as Browning told me, like a young girl; all the outlines rounded and filled up, all traces of disease effaced, and a smile on her face so living that they could not for hours persuade themselves she was really dead.

   We [*the Storys*] went immediately to Florence, and it was a sad house enough. There stood the table with her letters and books as usual, and her little chair beside it, and in her portfolio a half-finished letter to Mme [*Jessie White*] Mario, full of noble words about Italy. Yes, it was for Italy that her last words were written; for her dear Italy were her last aspirations. The death of Cavour had greatly affected her. She had wept many tears for him, and been a real mourner. This agitation undoubtedly weakened her and perhaps was the last feather that broke her down. 'The cycle is complete,' as Browning said, looking round the room; 'here we came fifteen years ago; here Pen was born; here Ba wrote her poems for Italy. She used to walk up and down this verandah in the summer evenings, when, revived by the southern air, she first again began to enjoy her out-doors life. Every day she used to walk with me or drive with me, and once even walked to

Bellosguardo and back; that was when she was strongest. Little by little, as I now see, that distance was lessened, the active outdoors life restricted, until walking had finally ceased. We saw from these windows the return of the Austrians; they wheeled round this corner and came down this street with all their cannon, just as she describes it in "Casa Guidi." Last week when we came to Florence I said: "We used, you know, to walk on this verandah so often – come and walk up and down once. Just once," I urged, and she came to the window and took two steps on it. But it fatigued her too much, and she went back and lay down on the sofa – that was our last walk. Only the night she went away for ever she said she thought we must give up Casa Guidi; it was too inconvenient and in case of illness too small. We had decided to go away and take a villa outside the gates. For years she would not give up this house, but at last and, as it were, suddenly, she said she saw it *was* too small for us and too inconvenient. And so it was; so the cycle was completed for us here, and where the beginning was is the end. Looking back at these past years I see that we have been all the time walking over a torrent on a straw. Life must now be begun anew – all the old cast off and the new one put on. I shall go away, break up everything, go to England and live and work and write.'

. . . The funeral was not impressive, as it ought to have been. She was buried in the Protestant cemetery where Theodore Parker lies; many of her friends were there, but fewer persons than I [*Story*] expected and hoped to see. The services were blundered through by a fat English parson in a brutally careless way, and she was consigned by him to the earth as if her clay were no better than any other clay. I did what I could, but I had arrived too late to assume the arrangements. . . . So I carried two wreaths – it was all I could do – one of those exquisite white Florence roses, and the other of laurel, and these I laid on her coffin.

The Cascine

[16] The Cascine gardens in December 1732; from Joseph
Spence's *Letters from the Grand Tour*.

(Joseph Spence (1699–1768) was appointed Professor of Poetry
at Oxford at the age of 29 and then earned his living
accompanying young men on foreign tours. In 1742 he was given
as a sinecure the Regius Professorship of Modern History at
Oxford. He is chiefly remembered for his literary *Anecdotes*, most
of which were published posthumously.)

A little way out of the gate that we live next to (and Florence I
can assure you is worth no less than ten gates) is a place made for
the pleasure of the Great Duke and his good subjects. You go to it
through a range of vast Scotch fir-trees: on your left hand is a
long run of groves and pretty artificial islands full of arbours, and
on the right lie the vineyards and cornfields interspersed, which
is the manner all about Florence (as in Lombardy). This leads
into a large beautiful meadow. The walk of firs is continued on,
all the length of it; the groves and wood, with a variety of a
thousand different walks on the left, beyond which, all along,
runs the river Arno. These woods are at last brought rounding to
join the fir-walk, and so terminate the meadow. This meadow all
our autumn was almost as fresh a green as we have in England (a
very uncommon thing here), and was all sprinkled with wild
crocuses as thick as the stars in heaven. Many of the trees in the
woody part wanted to show another crop of leaves, and the wild
vines that are very frequent in it hung over your head from tree to
tree with their glistening black bunches of grapes, that were left
there for the happiness of the birds that inhabit those woods very
plentifully. In short, all the autumn this place was the most like a
paradise of anything I ever met with . . .

[17] The young Duke of Hamilton and his tutor, Dr John
Moore, encounter the 56-year-old Bonnie Prince Charlie
and his young wife on an evening promenade; from *A View
of Society and Manners in Italy* by John Moore.

(The Scottish physician (and later novelist), John Moore (1729–1802), acted as travelling tutor to Douglas, eighth Duke of Hamilton and his own son (who became the famous General Sir John Moore) between 1772 and 1778.)

On the evenings on which there is no opera, it is usual for the genteel company to drive to a public walk immediately without the city, where they remain till it begins to grow duskish. Soon after our arrival at Florence, in one of the avenues of this walk we observed two men and two ladies, followed by four servants in livery. One of the men wore the insignia of the garter. We were told this was the Count of Albany, and that the Lady next to him was the Countess. We yielded the walk, and pulled off our hats. The gentleman along with them was the Envoy from the King of Prussia to the Court of Turin. He whispered to the Count, who returning the salutation, looked very earnestly at the Duke of Hamilton. We have seen them almost every evening since, either at the opera or on the public walk. His Grace does not affect to shun the avenue in which they happen to be; and as often as we pass near them, the Count fixes his eyes in a most expressive manner upon the Duke, as if he meant to say – our ancestors were better acquainted.

You know, I suppose, that the Count Albany is the unfortunate Charles Stuart, who left Rome some time since on the death of his father, because the Pope did not think proper to acknowledge him by the title which he claimed on that event. He now lives at Florence, on a small revenue allowed him by his brother [*Henry, Cardinal Duke of York*]. The Countess is a beautiful woman, much beloved by those who know her, who universally describe her as lively, intelligent and agreeable.

[18] The monument to the Maharajah of Kolhapur in the Cascine; from *Cook's Handbook to Florence*, 1924.

The *Cascine* is the Hyde Park, the Champs-Elysées, of Florence. It is two miles long, and a delightful resort in the intervals of sight-seeing. . . . On Ascension Day the people troop here to catch grasshoppers and so secure good luck throughout the year. The insects are imprisoned in tiny cages and fed on lettuce-leaves. At the extreme point where the waters of the Mugnone fall into the Arno, is the *Monument to the Rajah of Kolapore* (dell' Indiano). On the night of 1st Dec., 1870, the spot on which it stands was the scene of a strange and lugubrious ceremony. Numbers of officials in the picturesque costume of Hindustan were busily occupied in preparing the funeral pyre of their Prince. Rajah Ram Chuttraputti, Mahararajah of Kolapore, a young man of twenty years, the last of his line, ruling over one of the most extensive of the provinces of India, when returning from England to his native country, attended by his numerous suite, died, after a short illness, at one of the Florence hotels. In a space amidst the fine oaks and beeches of park they prepared the wood with large quantities of camphor and odorous ointments; and upon this pile, robed in the most splendid of his vestments, and surrounded by his most precious and favourite personal ornaments, they laid the body of the Rajah. The pile was lit about midnight, and continued to burn until near daylight; the venerable Brahmin, meanwhile, who directed the ceremonies, offering his prayers, and with the other faithful servants, at times, making the groves echo with their lamentations. At break of day the ashes of the Prince were collected with the greatest care into a golden vase, which now rests in the temple erected to his memory on the banks of the Punchgunga, but all the remaining ashes were thrown into the Arno. In June, 1874, on the same spot, was unveiled a monument, singularly beautiful and appropriate, designed by *Major Charles Mant, R.E.*, who was an intimate friend of the late Rajah. The style is thoroughly Indian; the canopy and base are of a grey local stone, beautifully carved; the columns are of bronze, elaborately chased; and the whole, including the bust, which is the central object, forms a most complete and successful specimen of polychromatic decorative art. . . . The cost of the work was borne by the British Government of India in conjunction with the family of the deceased.

Certosa di Galluzzo

[19] An Elizabethan Protestant visits the Certosa di Galluzzo; from Fynes Moryson's *An Itinerary* . . .

(Fynes Moryson was born in Lincolnshire in 1566. He became a Fellow of Peterhouse, Cambridge which gave him 'leave to travell' from 1589 to 1600. He travelled first in Europe and then in the Levant. After diplomatic service in Ireland, Moryson settled in London where he wrote his *Itinerary* and died in 1630.)

The next day wee went out on foote by the South Gate, to the stately Monastery of the Carthusians, called la Certosa, having in our company Italian Gentlemen, who caused us to bee well entertained there, and invited to dinner in their publique Refectory, where we had great cheare of fish, Pastry, and Sallats, but no flesh, which those Friers never eate, at least not publikely. I made mention of this Monastery in my journey from Sienna to Florence, at which time those that did pennance about Easter, flocked thither in great troopes, and now our Italian Consorts gave us the meanes to view the same. The Church is stately built, and the seates of the Chauncell are of Nut-tree. They did shew us the statua of Saint Chrisostome to the middle of silver, whose relikes also they keepe, and they shewed us one of the pots in which they said Christ turned water into Wine in Cana of Galily, (whereof the Papists shew many.) Also a statua of Saint Dennis Arcopagita, of silver, and like relikes kept there. These Friers professe great austeritie in Religion, and are tied to keepe silence, not Pithagoricall for some yeeres, but perpetuall, the lay-brethren excepted, who doe the manuall workes of the house. They never eate flesh, for such is their rule, which if they breake, yet they doe it not in the publike place of eating. The Priest having sung Masse, doth after it many times bow downe his head, and then falles prostrate on his face, praying. Each Frier hath foure cells or chambers, and his private Garden planted with fruit trees, and therein a private well. They have no beds, but sleep upon straw, and eat privately in their owne Celles, only eating together in the publique roomes on the feast dayes, so as they may easily in private breake this vow of not eating flesh, if they list.

The Duomo

[20] With great difficulty Brunelleschi persuades the authorities that his plan for building the cupola without any internal support is feasible; from Antonio Manetti's *Life of Brunelleschi*.

He repeated constantly that it could be vaulted without centering. After many days of standing firm – he in his opinion and they in theirs – he was twice angrily carried out by the servants of the *operai* and of the Wool Merchants Guild, the consuls, and many others present, as if he were reasoning foolishly and his words were laughable. As a consequence he was later often wont to say that during the period in which that occurred (some days elapsed between the first and second occasion) he was ashamed to go about Florence. He had the feeling that behind his back they were saying: Look at that mad man who utters such nonsense. However, he persevered in his judgment with great prudence, caution, and incredible patience, constantly praising others when he could do so in fairness and rendering honor to those who merited it, holding the esteem of the *operai* and the other citizens – except in this case – for the valiant, prudent, ingenious man that he was.

Seeing his persistence, some people began to heed him, especially because of the difficulty and almost impossibility demonstrated generally, in one way or another, by all the others: one, for example, said that he wanted to vault it by filling up the space inside with earth which would hold it up like formwork; another said that a tower should be constructed in the middle and the centering suspended from it. Others proposed various diverse methods until everyone was almost desperate. . . .

Thus, on returning home some heed began to be paid to him in certain quarters. They began to accept the reasons he had outlined and to ask whether he might not be trusted in the great undertaking if he could provide some confirmation in a small undertaking, stating that since Schiatti Ridolfi had to have a chapel constructed in San Jacopo di Borgo Oltrarno and since Filippo [*Brunelleschi*] knew about it he could show them what he could do in that chapel. And so he did. It was the first in Florence to be vaulted in that form which is still called 'with crests and sails.' Fixed at the lowest side is a cane or pole that circles upward, gradually narrowing as the cane or pole presses constantly on the bricks – or to be exact, *mezzane* – on the unfixed side until it is enclosed. That chapel, which is open on two sides, is at one side of the main chapel and the bell-tower. Because of this test, [*people*] partly began to trust his words, although not completely, since the chapel was a small undertaking and the other a great one which, as far as is known, was without precedent.

Finally after other experiments – although in small undertakings – in addition to that one, he was asked about the procedure [*for vaulting*] such a great thing without centering, with a double vault and a lantern appropriate to such a large building, since it seemed to them that the lantern of San Giovanni suggested one [*for the cupola*]. Filippo reasoned orally with great conscientiousness and precision, and finally he was requested to put down in writing the method of keeping it steady and firm so that it would not slip. He did not make any difficulty about this [*request*], and the written detailed information was handed over to them.

[21] The consecration of the Duomo by Pope Eugenius IV in 1436; from *The Vespasiano Memoirs* by Vespasiano da Bisticci.

(Vespasiano da Bisticci (1421–1498) was one of the most famous and successful booksellers and producers of manuscripts of his time, the early English humanists and patrons of humanism being among his customers. His *Vite di uomini illustri del secolo XV* records the lives of contemporary Popes, cardinals, statesmen and writers, and as such is a major source on the period.)

He consecrated with much pomp the Church of Santa Maria del Fiore in Florence; the bridge, which was built from one church to the other, being hung with draperies of blue and white, the colours of the Pope, and the woodwork which supported these decked with myrtle, laurel, pine and cypress. The hangings were stretched from one side to the other and heavy curtains hung all the way between the churches, carpets also and benches on both sides, a sight marvellous to behold. Along this gallery came the Pope and all the court of Rome, the Pope in full pontificals and

The Piazza del Duomo; from a German eighteenth-century
engraving

mitre, all the cardinals, in damask mitres; the bishops in mitres of
calimanco with the cross borne before them according to pontifical
usage, the apostolic subdeacons in their regular surplices, and
the whole court of Rome duly arrayed. At this time there was in
Florence a splendid gathering of prelates and ambassadors from
all parts; the Pope and all the court of Rome went in procession
along the gallery, and the people on foot made up a great
gathering of the citizens of Florence from within and without.
When the Pope and his court entered Santa Maria del Fiore they
found the church nobly adorned and filled with curtains and
ornaments fitting for such a solemn occasion. Round the altar
had been contrived a fine level space, covered with carpet, where
were stationed the College of Cardinals and the prelates, the
Pope's seat was covered with damask of white and gold, and
about it were benches for the cardinals. The Pope's seat stood on
that side where they read the Gospel, and on the other side were
the singers; the ambassadors according to rank and the College

of Cardinals were near the Pope, and on the other side the bishops, archbishops and prelates. The Pope sang the pontifical mass in due order, and the ceremony was of the finest.

[22] Verrocchio's bronze ball and cross on the summit of Brunelleschi's cupola; from Luca Landucci's *Diario Fiorentino*.

(Luca Landucci (1436–1516) was an apothecary whose conventional, somewhat timid nature is shown by his withdrawal of open support for Savonarola following the latter's excommunication.)

27th May [*1471*]. A Monday, the gilt copper ball was put up on the lantern of the cupola of *Santa Maria del Fiore*.
30th May. They placed the cross on the said ball, and the canons and many other people went up and sang the *Te Deum* there.

[23] Paolo Uccello's cenotaph to Sir John Hawkwood in the Duomo; from Eve Borsook's *The Mural Painters of Tuscany*, and 'L'Hawkwood d'Uccello et la "Vie de Fabius Maximus" de Plutarque', in *Revue de l'Art*, translated by the author.

(After forming a band of mercenary soldiers in France, Hawkwood, a tanner's son from Essex, eventually became the most feared and respected general in Italy. He married a daughter of the Duke of Milan, and died in 1394 in the pay of the Florentine republic. The year before he died the Signoria voted him a memorial in the Cathedral, along with seven other famous Florentines including Dante and Boccaccio.)

The idea of an actual monument gradually gave way to that of a painted substitute. For their designs for both monuments Gaddi and Pesello were to receive 30 florins – or 15 florins for each cenotaph. This is the same amount Uccello received for his mural of the same subject forty years later.

By 13 July 1433, the *operai* of the Cathedral revived the idea of carrying out Hawkwood's marble monument according to the terms of the original communal *provvisione* of forty years earlier. Notices of a competition were posted in the Baptistery, Orsanmichele, and S. Reparata, asking for models or designs. Nothing further happened for almost three years, and, in the interim, the long regime of the Albizzi had been replaced by that of Cosimo de' Medici. But on 18 May 1436, the *operai* deliberated again on the matter; declaring that Hawkwood's figure be repainted in the manner and form in which it was painted or represented earlier. . . . Eight days later they decided to get on with the work and finally on 30 May, we learn that Paolo Uccello is to paint Hawkwood on the wall. . . . Evidently, the *operai* had simulated bronze in mind – not only because this happened to be the *dernier cri* in Florence for monumental statuary, but also because according to Plutarch this was the medium used for the equestrian monument honouring Fabius Maximus with whom Hawkwood was compared. Plutarch's life of this ancient Roman military hero had just been translated in Florence by Lapo di Castiglionchio the Younger and two of his friends further influenced Uccello's fresco. Bartolomeo di ser Benedetto Fortini supplied the inscription taken from a recently unearthed marble tablet honouring Fabius Maximus. Leon Battista Alberti had just finished his treatise on painting which claimed that its principal aim should be to create relief. This is exactly what Uccello's fictive monument achieves. Furthermore, Alberti described the use of squaring for pantographic enlargement and Uccello's fresco is the earliest example of its practical application.

The comparison between Hawkwood and Fabius Maximus was a political as well as an archaeological exercise because Plutarch and contemporary Florentines compared these heroes to Hercules – one of the legendary founders of Florence. Hawkwood figured as a second Hercules, with his foe, the many-headed Hydra, personified by the Visconti of Milan (whose device was the viper). Florence at this time was still engaged in a long war with Milan. Therefore, Uccello's Hawkwood combines civic patriotism with the latest developments in Florentine humanism, antiquarianism, and art theory.

[24] A sixteenth-century Irish traveller notices Uccello's fresco of Sir John Hawkwood in the Duomo; from Henry Piers's manuscript *Discourse of H.P. his Travelles.*

(Henry Piers (1568–1623) was the son of one of Elizabeth's captains in the Irish wars. Inheriting lands granted to his father, he became a Catholic and in 1595 left his wife and children to go on a pilgrimage-cum-study-trip to Rome.)

There is a tombe in our Ladies Churche of an Englisheman, whoe as it is thought came by Chance into the Contrye, when the gothes and vandales weare subduinge of them, he beinge a good soldiour helped them to wynn manye battles; whereupon at his Deathe that monum^t was bestowed upon him; there are Differente opinions held Conserninge his Right Sirename, some saie that his name was Hawkwoode and that the Italians not knowinge the pronunciation of Englishe called him accutus, others saide his name was Sharpe and therefor termed accutus.

[25] Murder in the Cathedral: the Pazzi Plot and its aftermath in the spring of 1478; from Luca Landucci's *Diario Fiorentino*.

26th April. At about 15 in the forenoon [*11 a.m.*] in *Santa Maria del Fiore*, whilst high mass was being celebrated and the Host elevated, Giuliano, son of Piero, son of Cosimo de' Medici, and Francesco Nori were killed, near the choir of the said church towards the door which goes to the *Servi*; and Lorenzo de' Medici was wounded in the neck, and fled into the sacristy and escaped. They were killed in consequence of a certain conspiracy made by Messer Jacopo de' Pazzi and Franceschino de' Pazzi and Guglielmo de' Pazzi, the which Guglielmo was the brother-in-law of Lorenzo de' Medici, his wife being a sister of theirs, called Bianca. And the sons of Messer Piero de' Pazzi were also there, that is, Andrea and Renato and Niccolò; and of the house of Salviati, there were Francesco, Bishop of Pisa, and Jacopo Salviati, who was son-in-law to Filippo Tornabuoni, and another Jacopo also a Salviati, and Jacopo, son of Messer Poggio, Bracciolini and Bernardo Bandini of the house of Baroncegli, and Amerigo Corsi, and many others. The conspirators brought Cardinal di San Giorgio here, who was a young man; he entered Florence on the day above-mentioned, and they all came together in *Santa Maria del Fiore*, and, as I have said, at the elevation of the Host seized their swords, and it is said that Francesco de' Pazzi struck Giuliano, and Bandini the other. And having killed Giuliano they wanted to kill Lorenzo, but did not succeed, as he fled into the sacristy. Meantime the Bishop de' Salviati, with Jacopo, son of Messer Poggio, and two of his relatives who were both called Jacopo, went to the *Palagio*, with several priests, feigning to desire to speak to the *Signoria*, and they spoke to the *Gonfaloniere*, and became somewhat confused. The *Gonfaloniere* perceived the treachery, and he and his companions shut themselves up here and there, and ordered the doors to be closed, and the bell rung for a *parlamento*. And what with the rumour which came from *Santa Maria del Fiore* of Giuliano's death and the bell ringing at the *Palagio*, the city was immediately in arms. And Lorenzo de' Medici was taken to his house. Meantime Messer Jacopo de' Pazzi rushed on horseback to the Piazza de' Signori, crying '*Popolo e libertà!*' (The People and Liberty!), wishing to take the *Palagio*, but the bishop not having succeeded in getting possession of it, Messer Jacopo was not able to enter. He then went towards his own house, and was advised to take to flight; and he fled by the *Porta alla Croce*, together with many men-at-arms and with Andrea de' Pazzi. Meantime all the city was up in arms, in the Piazza and at Lorenzo de' Medici's house. And numbers of men on the side of the conspirators were killed in the Piazza; amongst others a priest of the bishop's was killed there, his body being quartered and the head cut off, and then the head was stuck on the top of a lance, and carried about Florence the whole day, and one quarter of his body was carried on a spit all through the city, with the cry of: 'Death to the traitors!' That same evening the cardinal was taken to the *Palagio*, barely escaping with his life, all his companions being captured without exception.

And the bishop remained in the *Palagio* with all the rest. And that evening they hung Jacopo, son of Messer Poggio, from the windows of the *Palagio de' Signori*, and likewise the Bishop of Pisa, and Franceschino de' Pazzi, naked; and about twenty men besides, some at the *Palagio de' Signori*, and others at the *Palagio del Podestà* and at the *Casa del Capitano*, all at the windows.

The next day [*the 27th*] they hung Jacopo Salviati, son-in-law of Filippo Tornabuoni, and the other Jacopo, also at the windows, and many others of the households of the cardinal and of the bishop. And the day after that [*the 28th April, 1478*], Messer Jacopo de' Pazzi was captured at Belforte. And that evening of the 28th, about 23 in the evening [*7 p.m.*], Messer Jacopo de' Pazzi and Renato de' Pazzi were hung at the windows of the

Palagio de' Signori, above the *ringhiera*; and so many of their men with them, that during these three days the number of those killed amounted to more than seventy. The cardinal remained a prisoner in the Palagio, and no harm was done him, except that he was made to write to the Holy Father, with his own hand, all that had happened. . . .

20th May. Guglielmo de' Pazzi gave his word to keep within fixed boundaries; and he was sent to his own estate and there limited to a distance of from five to twenty miles from Florence.

[26] A Romantic vision of the Pazzi conspiracy and the murder in the Cathedral; from Joseph Severn's *Life and Letters*.

(Joseph Severn (1793–1879) accompanied the dying Keats to Rome in 1820 and nursed him in what is now the Keats-Shelley Museum on the Piazza di Spagna. It is thanks to this rather than to his painting – the quality of which one can surmise from the following – that he is remembered.)

I have painted nineteen pictures (copies) here in Florence, and made sixty drawings, for I have been blessed with real health during this summer, which is all sun and heat. The great part of these pictures are preparations for my large picture, which I begin on the 1st of January [*1823*]. The subject is 'Lorenzo di Medici rescued from Assassination by his Friends.' This Lorenzo was the great Florence merchant about the time of our Henry VIII. He revived the arts, literature, &c.; everything is owing to him. This picture represents an attempt on his life by some enemies who were jealous of his greatness; he was saved by his friends, who devoted their lives to him. Why I take this subject is – first, I am, and everybody is, sick of sacred ones; next, I am fond of Gothic architecture, times, and people, and in the picture I shall show what is the feeling of my own heart – a human being, who has raised himself to such a pitch of goodness and greatness, that his friends devote their lives to save him. The scene is in the Gothic cathedral of Florence; Lorenzo is encircled by friends, his wife and son clinging round him; his brother is just dying from the assassins' wounds, who rush forward to finish their deed; but they are stopped, and Lorenzo's life is saved. Among the large group of friends I introduce the portrait of Raphael, the greatest painter that ever lived; Michael Angelo, Leonardo da Vinci, and many others of this great time – as Lorenzo's friends, for they were 'protected' by him. The assassins chose the time when the High Priest raised the Host, and the people were all praying. This subject is well known and admired by the English nobility. It is found best told in Roscoe's 'Life of Lorenzo di Medici,' which is read and admired by everybody. It is a subject quite new and very splendid in the dresses; the background is from the actual spot. My picture is 12 feet by 18, and I hope it will quite establish my fame. I shall be all next year at work upon it.

[27] The mob responds violently to an anti-semitic sermon in 1488, causing the Commune to deal firmly with the preacher; from Tribaldo de' Rossi's *Ricordanze*, in *The Society of Renaissance Florence*, by Gene Brucker.

Today, March 12, 1488, I record the following event. There was a Franciscan preacher by the name of Fra [*Bernardino da Feltre*] who preached in S. Maria del Fiore [*the Duomo*]. Since he had a reputation as an excellent man, a large crowd gathered to hear him. On several occasions, he had discussed the problem of the Jews, saying that they should not suck the blood of Christians by engaging in usury in this city and *contado*. He repeatedly told his audience that the government should establish a Monte di Pietà [*municipal pawnshop*] so that poor people in need of cash could borrow money on their property. He urged children and youths to come to his sermons, and this morning when he was preaching on the subject, he appealed to them to serve as his soldiers, in the following manner. Every morning, they should all go to the chapel in the cathedral where the body of Christ is exhibited, to pray that the citizens would remember that they had promised to expel the Jews and to establish the Monte di Pietà. These children should all kneel and recite three Paternosters and three Ave Marias, so that through the prayers which they addressed to our Lord, he hoped – between that day and Sunday – to have them expelled. Many had come [*to the sermon*] and there was a large crowd – between two thousand and three thousand boys – who came out [*of the cathedral*], and they ran to the pawnshop in the Vacca and with loud shouts they planned to sack it. The police official came with all of his men, but they weren't sufficient, so that two of the Eight [*on Security*] came in person. With the police official, they issued a proclamation that fathers would be banned as outlaws for their sons' crimes.

Finally, after an hour and with great difficulty, they subdued the tumult. They took away a boy who had struck an official in the face with a pipe; but in the square a crowd of factors from the silk guild released him.

The Signoria and the Eight sent for the preacher . . . and held him in the palace and had many discussions with him. Apparently, he demanded complete freedom to preach from the pulpit, and he said that it was necessary for the salvation of souls. So, after a time, he departed and returned to his affairs; and later . . . the Signoria and the Eight sent two or three citizens to his home, accompanied by two servants of the Eight with a torch. And they took him to the city gate and expelled him and forbade him to return again to preach in the city. . . .

[28] Less than a decade later the preaching of Savonarola produces happier results; from Luca Landucci's *Diario Fiorentino*.

15th August [*1496*]. Fra Girolamo [*Savonarola*] preached in *Santa Maria del Fiore*, and on account of the great crowd, one of the wooden stands for the boys, towards the door of San Giovanni, broke, but no one was hurt. It was considered a miracle. You must know that there were four stands: two against the walls facing the chancel; the other two, one above by the men, and the other below by the women, in the body of the church. The number of boys had so increased that it had been necessary to make these stands. And observe that there was such a feeling of grace in this church, and such sweet consolation in hearing these boys sing, now above, now below, now from the side, all in turn, quite modestly and low, as if to themselves; it seemed impossible that it was done by boys. I write this because I was present, and saw and heard it many times, and felt much spiritual comfort. Truly the church was full of angels.

[29] The excommunicated Savonarola continues to preach, and burn vanities, but abandons preaching in the Duomo; from Luca Landucci's *Diario Fiorentino*.

24th February [*Saturday 1497*]. Fra Girolamo preached in *Santa Maria del Fiore*, continuing to show that he took no heed of the excommunication; and observe that all the said sermons have been written down and published by a young notary, whose name is Ser Lorenzo Vivioli, who has achieved a superhuman feat, as we may say, having written down things that this *Frate* never said in the pulpit, and epistles and other things written and spoken during many years. You could not find anything more marvellous in the world, and no other miracle can be required in this work than the fact of the very least word and act being inscribed exactly, without a single iota wanting, which may well seem impossible, but it was done by divine permission, as is thought by righteous men.

27th February [*the Carnival*]. There was made on the *Piazza de' Signori* a pile of vain things, nude statues and playing-boards, heretical books, Morganti, mirrors, and many other vain things, of great value, estimated at thousands of florins. The procession of boys was made as the year before; they collected in four quarters, with crosses and olive-branches in their hands, each quarter arranged in order with tabernacles in front, and went in the afternoon to burn this pile. Although some lukewarm people gave trouble, throwing dead cats and other dirt upon it, the boys nevertheless set it on fire and burnt everything, for there was plenty of small brushwood. And it is to be observed that the pile was not made by children; there was a rectangular woodwork measuring more than 12 *braccia* each way, which had taken the carpenters several days to make, with many workmen, so that it was necessary for many armed men to keep guard the night before, as certain lukewarm persons, specially certain young men called *Compagnacci* wanted to destroy it. The *Frate* was held in such veneration by those who had faith in him, that this morning, although it was Carnival, Fra Girolamo said mass in *San Marco*, and gave the Sacrament with his hands to all his friars, and afterwards to several thousand men and women; and then he came on to a pulpit outside the door of the church with the Host, and showing it to the people, blessed them, with many prayers: *Fac salvum populum tuum Domine*, etc. There was a great crowd, who had come in the expectation of seeing signs; the lukewarm laughed and mocked, saying: 'He is excommunicated, and he gives the Communion to others.' And certainly it seemed a mistake to me, although I had faith in him; but I never wished to endanger myself by going to hear him, since he was excommunicated.

28th February (the first day of Lent). He preached, and said that the wicked had their hide full, having indulged in every sort of evil, especially at night, when certain suppers were given by the *Compagnacci*, all lukewarm persons who considered that they took a more broadminded view, not being so hard upon sin, and condoning the life of an epicure.

1st March. Fra Girolamo preached in *Santa Maria del Fiore*, and took his leave, saying that a ban had come from the Pope; and this being so, he took leave and would only preach in *San Marco*. One of his friars preached in *Santa Maria del Fiore* in the evening; and after this the number of people at *San Marco* kept increasing . . .

[30] A Welshman introduces the word 'cupola' into the English language in 1549; from William Thomas's *Historie of Italie* . . .

(William Thomas (c. 1507–1554) was a hot-blooded Welsh humanist who fled to Venice after stealing from his Catholic patron. He stayed in Italy for four years, and then returned home to become Clerk to the Privy Council and personal adviser to Edward VI. He was executed for treasonable opposition to the marriage of Mary to Philip II of Spain.)

Within the citee are manie goodlie temples and other edefices, amongest the whiche the cathedrall churche [*the Duomo*] is an excellent faire buildyng. For the walles without are all covered with fine white and blacke marble, wonderfullie well wrought, and over the quere is an whole vaulte called *Cupola*, faceioned [*fashioned*] like the halfe of an egge, risyng betwene .iii. iles and the body of the churche: so artificially made, that almost it semeth a miracle. For it is so high, that the pomell on the toppe beyng able to conteigne .vii. persons, seemeth a verie small thyng to theim that stande by lowe. And the compasse of it by the base,

is about .160. paces. Besides that the floors under this vaulte
rounde aboute the quiere is laide with fine marble of divers
colours so faire, that it yeldeth a delite to theim that walke upon
it.

The steple standyng besides the churche, is likewyse of fine
marble a verie faire and square tower, equall in height to the
circute of the base, with divers stories and thynges graven in it, so
artificiall and costlie, that it deserveth singuler praise.

[31] The Duomo; from Hippolyte Taine's *Italy*.

Desirous of seeing the beginnings of this renaissance we go from
the Palazzo-Vecchio to the Duomo. Both form the double heart
of Florence, such as it beat in the middle ages, the former for
politics, and the latter for religion, and the two so well united
that they formed but one. Nothing can be nobler than the public
edict passed in 1294 for the construction of the national
cathedral. 'Whereas, it being of sovereign prudence on the part
of a people of high origin to proceed in its affairs in such a manner
that the wisdom no less than the magnanimity of its proceedings
be recognized in its outward works, it is ordered that Arnolfo
master architect of our commune, prepare models or designs for
the restoration of Santa Maria Reparata, with the most exalted
and most prodigal magnificence, in order that the industry and
power of men may never create or undertake anything whatsoever more vast and more beautiful; in accordance with that
which our wisest citizens have declared and counselled in public
session and in secret conclave, to wit, that no hand be laid upon
the works of the commune without the intent of making them
correspond to the noble soul which is composed of the souls of all
its citizens united in one will.' In this ample period breathes the
grandiose pride and intense patriotism of the ancient republics.
Athens under Pericles, and Rome under the first Scipio
cherished no prouder sentiments. At each step, here as elsewhere, in texts and in monuments, is found, in Italy, the traces,
the renewal and the spirit of classic antiquity.

Let us, accordingly, look at the celebrated Duomo, – but the
difficulty is to see it. It stands upon flat ground, and, in order that
the eye might embrace its mass it would be necessary to level
three hundred buildings. Herein appears the defect of the great

mediæval structure; even to-day, after so many openings effected
by modern demolishers, most of the cathedrals are visible only on
paper. The spectator catches sight of a fragment, some section of
a wall, or the façade; but the whole escapes him; man's work is no
longer proportioned to his organs. It was not thus in antiquity;
temples were small or of mediocre dimensions, and were almost
always erected on an eminence; their general form and complete
profile could be enjoyed from twenty different points of view.
After the advent of christianity men's conceptions transcended
their forces, and the ambition of the spirit no longer took into
account the limitations of the body. The human machine lost its
equilibrium; with forgetfulness of the moderate there was
established a love of the odd. Without either reason or symmetry
campaniles or bell-towers were planted, like isolated posts, in
front or alongside of the Duomo, and this change of human
equipoise must have been potent, since even here, among so
many latin traditions and classic aptitudes, it declares itself.

In other respects, save the ogive arcades, the monument is not
gothic but byzantine, or, rather, original; it is a creature of a new
and mixed form like the new and mixed civilization of which it is
the offspring. You feel power and invention in it with a touch of
quaintness and fancy. Walls of enormous grandeur are devel-
oped or expanded without the few windows in them happening
to impair their massiveness or diminish their strength. There are
no flying buttresses; they are self-sustaining. Marble panels,
alternately yellow and black, cover them with a glittering
marquetry, and curves of arches let into their masses seem to be
the bones of a robust skeleton beneath the skin. The Latin cross,
which the edifice figures, contracts at the top, and the chancel
and transepts bubble out into rotundities and projections, in
petty domes behind the church in order to accompany the grand
dome which ascends above the choir, and which, the work of
Brunelleschi, newer and yet more antique than that of St. Peter,
lifts in the air to an astonishing height its elongated form, its
octagonal sides and its pointed lantern. But how can a
physiognomy of a church be conveyed by words? It has one
nevertheless; all its portions appearing together are combined in
one chord and in one effect. If you examine the plans and old
engravings you will appreciate the bizarre and captivating
harmony of these grand Roman walls overlaid with oriental
fancies; of these gothic ogives arranged in byzantine cupolas; of

these light Italian columns forming a circle above a bordering of Grecian caissons; of this assemblage of all forms, pointed, swelling, angular, oblong, circular and octagonal. Greek and Latin antiquity, the Byzantine and Saracenic orient, the Germanic and Italian middle-age, the entire past, shattered, amalgamated and transformed, seems to have been melted over anew in the human furnace in order to flow out in fresh forms in the hands of the new genius of Giotto, Arnolfo, Brunelleschi and Dante.

Here the work is unfinished, and the success is not complete. The façade has not been constructed; all that we see of it is a great naked, scarified wall similar to a leper's plaster. There is no light within: a line of small round bays and a few windows fill the immensity of the edifice with a gray illumination: it is bare, and the argillaceous tone in which it is painted depresses the eye with its wan monotony. A 'Pieta' by Michael Angelo and a few statues seem like spectres; the bas-reliefs are only vague confusion. The architect, hesitating between mediæval and antique taste, fell only upon a lifeless light, that between a pure light and a coloured light.

[32] The story behind the Duomo's nineteenth-century façade; from Rudolf Wittkower's *Gothic versus Classic.*

The new Florentine Cathedral was begun by Arnolfo di Cambio in the last decade of the thirteenth century, just about a hundred years before Milan Cathedral and S. Petronio [*Bologna*]. At first the building advanced rapidly, and a start was made on the west façade. After an interruption of more than a century the façade was continued, but never finished. The appearance of this façade is known from various representations, best of all through a drawing that can probably be dated in 1587. You see that this Gothic façade was only half finished; it consisted of three canopied portals and, in the fields between them, of niches in several tiers richly decorated with statuary. One can hardly doubt that Varignana took his bearings for his S. Petronio façade design of 1518 from the Gothic façade of Florence Cathedral. In 1587 Grand Duke Ferdinand I decided that the time had come to pull down the antiquated Gothic façade and replace it by a modern one. Although the barbarous act of destruction was carried out with Florentine efficiency there were voices of disagreement: a contemporary diarist, for instance, recorded with utter dismay the destruction of what he called the rich and beautiful old façade and regarded its loss as an eternal disgrace. . . .

Five renowned Florentine architects were commissioned to represent their ideas for a new façade in wooden models. These models survived in good condition in the Museo dell'Opera del Duomo and only suffered damage in the recent disastrous Florentine flood. The competing architects were Buontalenti, Dosio, Cigoli, Giovanni Bologna, and Don Giovanni de'Medici. The attribution of these models to the names of architects has caused some confusion which has not yet been entirely cleared up. The most Mannerist and the most classical of these models are by Buontalenti and Dosio and both are documented as being from 1589. Buontalenti's model, in three tiers and a high attic over the first, displays a confusing welter of motifs and relationships; Dosio's, by contrast, is utterly simple: it is concentrated in two tiers, has a giant order of Corinthian pilasters below, and telling horizontal breaks. This was the most successful project and once again the comparison with Pellegrini's contemporary project for Milan Cathedral offers itself.

The question whether or not a small model with the inscription 1596 in the frieze is also by Buontalenti (according to some sources he had made two models) or by the painter Cigoli, who studied architecture under Buontalenti, has not been decided satisfactorily. In any case, there are Buontalentiesque Cigoli drawings for the façade in the Uffizi and from them to the wooden model is not an easy but a possible step.

Giovanni Bologna's participation in the competition, testified to by various seventeenth-century sources, is now generally accepted. His model is akin to Dosio's and shares in the classicizing taste around 1600, while Don Giovanni de'Medici's model is closely related to Giovanni Bologna's. This Medici prince, Grand Duke Cosimo I's natural son, was a distinguished amateur practitioner who supervised most of the large Florentine architectural undertakings at the beginning of the seventeenth century.

Despite some considerable differences in style between all these models they have that much in common that they do not take the slightest account of the Gothic body of the church. The hasty destruction of Arnolfo di Cambio's medieval façade had been a sort of overture to these anti-Gothic and implicitly antiuniformity models, none of which was destined to be executed. For well over thirty years nothing happened at all. Then from 1630 onward things began to move again, and in 1633 Grand Duke Ferdinand II came back to Dosio's model, had it slightly modernized and proposed its execution to a committee of experts. Seven of them favoured execution, two liked the model but regarded it as unsuitable for the cathedral, and five turned against it: the result was a draw. Among the critics were Coccapani, now practically forgotten, and Gherardo Silvani, Florence's greatest seventeenth-century architect. These two were the only ones who considered the lack of unity between the old building and the new façade a serious shortcoming. Thus in Florence, too, the seventeenth century saw a return to the central question of the Gothic problem. The Grand Duke was impressed and ordered an examination by the prestigious Accademia del Disegno. After protracted planning and replanning the academicians produced a counterproject, of which a wooden model was constructed, and concurrently, in 1635, Gherardo Silvani, Ferdinand II's favourite architect, produced a model of his own.

Opinion favoured the Academy project, and the Grand Duke therefore ordered its execution. On 22 October 1636 the foundation stone for this façade was laid. Paradoxically, Silvani was appointed executing architect. Since the Academy project had been preferred to his own, it was only to be expected that he would soon discover so many technical and aesthetic faults in the Academy project that the Grand Duke gave the order to discontinue construction. . . .

It is, however, more interesting and important to note that, in the heat of the many discussions, the academicians once again dropped any reference to the Gothic style and presented a purely classical design – while Silvani made an attempt, albeit a scarcely successful one, to introduce a Gothic element in his façade model with the octagonal side towers, which were inspired by Giotto's Campanile, but they are not really integrated into the façade design. Silvani paid no more than lip service to the principle of conformity. It would be worth speculating on why Milan and Bologna had far outpaced Florence in progressing toward a positive historicizing attitude in relation to the Gothic style.

When, after two and a half centuries, the Florentines returned to their cathedral façade, it was a foregone conclusion that it had to be built in harmony with the rest of the church. Ninety-two Gothic projects were under consideration between 1861 and 1868; the one by De Fabris, chosen for execution, was built between 1875 and 1887. Obviously this façade spelled the victory of historicism: everything down to the minutest detail is amply supported by Tuscan precedent.

[33] The 'Scoppio del Carro' on Easter day at the turn of the century; from Janet Ross's *Italian Sketches*.

(Janet Ross (1842–1927) married a banker and lived in Egypt for six years, where she became a correspondent for *The Times*. Settling in Tuscany in 1867, she began a series of books on all aspects of Italian life and history which deserve to be better known.)

Mass was now said at the high altar, but everyone's attention seemed to be concentrated on an unsightly high white post close to the marble balustrade which surrounds the altar. To this post was fixed a cord, which, suspended in mid-air far above the heads of the people, disappeared out of the great front door, and was fastened to the chariot outside the Duomo. A small white speck was seen on the cord, fastened to the pillar, which we were informed was the famous dove. When the *Gloria* had been sung, a man went up a ladder with a lighted taper, which he applied to the dove. There was a great spitting and hissing, and all at once she shot forward down the cord, a streak of fire and sparks. There was a stir and hum in the crowd, and a few little screams from some of the women; the dove vanished out of the door, and then there was a series of explosions from outside, while the dove returned as fast as she had gone, and went back to the pillar of wood, where she remained still fizzing for a few seconds.

Then all the bells of Florence, which had been silent since twelve o'clock on Thursday, began to ring merry chimes, and the great organ pealed out a triumphal melody. We made our way out of the Duomo as fast as we could, and were in time to see the last of the fire-works on the chariot; they made a tremendous

The nineteenth-century façade of the Duomo

noise, but as the sun shone brightly, there was not much to see. The fireworks were piled up some twenty feet high, and arranged in such a manner that only half of them go off in front of the Duomo, the other half being reserved for the corner of Borgo degli Albizzi, where the house of the Pazzi family is situated, in whose honour this custom was originally instituted. When all the squibs and crackers were finished, four magnificent white oxen, gaily decked with ribbons, were harnessed to the car, which moved off slowly with many creaks and groans round the south side of the cathedral towards the Via del Proconsolo. The crowd was immense, so we took some short cuts down the tortuous narrow streets in this old part of Florence, each of which has some passionate love-story or some dark tale of blood attached to it, and took up a favourable position opposite the entrance to the street of Borgo degli Albizzi, which is too narrow to admit the car.

The four white oxen were unharnessed and taken away, and a cord being put from the door of the Pazzi Palace to the car, another dove again flew to the fire-works, and the popping and fizzing was renewed, to the intense delight of the crowd.

The dove had flown swiftly and well this year, so the *contadini* returned home joyfully, spreading the glad tidings as they went – '*La colonada e andato bene*' (The dove has flown well).

The English Cemetery

[34] Inmates of the English Cemetery; from *People of Florence* by Joseph Macleod.

(Joseph Macleod, twentieth-century Scots playwright, poet and broadcaster, spent the latter part of his life with his Italian wife and children in a modern studio-house overlooking Florence.)

I wandered into the 'English' Cemetery, not knowing why. Cemeteries smell of autumn damp. This one was very autumnal and distinctly damp, an island knoll in a lake of roaring and swishing traffic. Such measures as the italian government has taken to reduce traffic noise by silencers and other devices had not yet been taken: the din of Florence's narrow streets was unendurable. But most italians love noise. More is paid for the roar of a car than for its horse-power; and the lowest gears are used to produce the highest quantity of phons and decibels . . .

There is no guide nor plan to the graveyard. I heaved on an old iron bell-pull, beneath which there is now an electric buzzer, and was admitted to solitude. I walked up one of the two small lanes between waist-high box hedges, and soon came upon The Grave [*of Elizabeth Barrett Browning*]. Its greying white casket stood before three cypresses among cherry trees, an entablature of wet blobby semibreves. The lassitude of the coarse grass was lank. I did not know that in spring it would be full of wild tuscan anemones.

The rod-surround was rusty.

Lord Leighton's smudged casket proved unexpectedly pleasant, with inlaid black classical figures which suggested De Chirico's set for *Le Bal*. Some were greek lyres supported by olive branches. On the grave below, a real olive branch had been laid, shaped as a wreath.

There was also a bunch of plastic lily-of-the-valley.

One of the cypresses creaked in the dreich wind. The cry seemed to come from an unquiet tomb.

I was not a great admirer of Elizabeth Barrett Browning's poetry, but I was fond of the Brownings and loved *The Ring and the Book* when I was young. . . .

Next to E.B.B. lies Fanny, wife of Holman Hunt. She died in

Florence in december 1866 'in the first year of her marriage'.
That year Holman Hunt painted *Isabella and the Pot of Basil*, one
of the saddest of Pre-raphaelite pictures, the theme from
Boccaccio or Keats; for Keats drew much of his narrative poem
from the story in the *Decameron*, though he placed it in Florence
not Messina, and altered the heroine's name to Isabella from
Lisabetta, as it is in my edition anyway. However she was called,
this girl's lover was murdered by her brothers; and she dug up his
grave and reburied his head in a pot of basil, which she wept over
till she too died. I was sad for Holman Hunt and his pretty young
wife.

But it was not these graves which interested me, nor that of
A.H. Clough nearby. I passed on. Many solid-looking super-
structures of graves were smashed like chocolate easter eggs. The
more recent inscriptions, cut too lightly, had all but vanished.

At last I came on a slab of more white and greying marble, and
was standing higher than the bones of my turbulent hero.
Landor's famous quatrain is patently untrue in its first line; he
strove with nearly all – though very likely few of the bureaucrats
were worth his strife. This makes one wonder if the last line is any
truer. Was that old lion, who threw his cook out of the window
and yet was gentle with children, really ever ready to depart?
How many such lovers of life are? Would I be? For to stand by
a grave is to have one foot already in it. For everybody at all
graves . . .

The Lungarno

[35] 'A fine day in October' experienced by an American in 1834 from his hotel room on the Lungarno; from *Letters of a Traveller; or, notes of things seen in Europe and America* by William Cullen Bryant.

(William Cullen Bryant (1794–1878) was born in Cummington, Massachusetts, and published poetry (including the blank verse *tour de force, Thanatopsis*) whilst pursuing his career at the bar. Turning increasingly to journalism and politics, as editor of the *Evening Post* he played some part in forming the Republican Party in 1856.)

But let me give you the history of a fine day in October, passed at the window of my lodgings on the Lung' Arno, close to the bridge Alla Carraja. Waked by the jangling of all the bells in Florence, and by the noise of carriages departing, loaded with travellers for Rome and other places in the south of Italy, I rise, dress myself, and take my place at the window. I see crowds of men and women from the country . . . driving donkeys loaded with panniers, or trundling hand-carts before them, heaped with grapes, figs, and all the fruits of the orchard, the garden, and the field. They have hardly passed when large flocks of sheep and goats make their appearance, attended by shepherds and their families, driven by the approach of winter from the Apennines, and seeking the pastures of Maremma. . . . The men and boys are dressed in knee-breeches, the women in bodices. . . . They carry staves in their hands, and their arms are loaded with kids and lambs too young to keep pace with their mothers. . . . A little after sunrise I see well-fed donkeys, in coverings of red cloth, driven over the bridge, to be milked for invalids. Maidservants, bareheaded, with huge high carved combs in their hair; waiters of coffee-houses carrying the morning cup of coffee or chocolate to their customers; bakers' boys with a dozen loaves on a board balanced on their heads; milkmen with rush baskets filled with flasks of milk – are crossing the streets in all directions. A little later the bell of the small chapel opposite my window rings furiously for a quarter of an hour, and then I hear mass chanted in a deep, strong, nasal tone. As the day advances, the English, in white hats and white pantaloons, come out of their lodgings, accompanied sometimes by their hale and square-built spouses, and saunter stiffly along the Arno, or take their way to the public galleries and museums. . . .

But what is that procession of men in black gowns, black gaiters, and black masks, moving swiftly along, and bearing on their shoulders a litter covered with a black cloth? These are the Brethren of Mercy [*see Misericordia*], who have assembled at the sound of the cathedral bell, and are conveying some sick or wounded person to the hospital.

As the day begins to decline, the number of carriages in the streets, filled with gaily-dressed people attended by servants in livery, increases. The Grand Duke's equipage, an elegant carriage drawn by six horses, with coachmen, footmen, and outriders in drab-coloured livery, comes from the Pitti Palace and crosses the Arno. . . . The Florentine nobility with their families and the English residents, now throng to the cascine, to drive at a slow pace through its thickly-planted walks of elms, oaks, and ilexes. As the sun is sinking, I perceive the quay, on other side of the Arno, filled with a moving crowd of well-dressed people, walking to and fro, and enjoying the beauty of the evening. . . . Night at length arrives – the time of spectacles and funerals. The carriages rattle to the opera-houses. Trains of people, sometimes in white robes and sometimes in black, carrying blazing torches and a cross elevated on a high pole before a coffin, pass through the streets chanting the service of the dead. . . .

I return to my bed, and fall asleep amid the shouts of people returning from the opera, singing as they go, snatches of the music with which they had been entertained during the evening.

[36] The colours of the Lungarno; from *Italian Hours* by Henry James.

(The American novelist Henry James (1843–1916), after his permanent removal to Europe, travelled to Italy almost yearly from his base in London. He became a British subject in 1915.)

My room at the inn looked out on the river, and was flooded all day with sunshine. There was an absurd orange-coloured paper on the walls; the Arno, of a hue not altogether different, flowed beneath; and on the other side of it rose a line of sallow houses, of extreme antiquity, crumbling and mouldering, bulging and protruding over the stream. All this brightness and yellowness was a perpetual delight; it was a part of that indefinably charming colour which Florence always seems to wear as you look up and down at it from the river, from the bridges and quays. This is a kind of grave brilliancy – a harmony of high tints – which I know not how to describe. There are yellow walls and green blinds and red roofs, and intervals of brilliant brown and natural-looking blue; but the picture is not spotty or gaudy, thanks to the colours being distributed in large and comfortable masses, and to its being washed over, as it were, by some happy softness of sunshine. The river-front of Florence is, in short, a delightful composition.

The Lungarno near the Ponte Santa Trinita; by Giuseppe Zocchi

Mercato Vecchio

[37] The Mercato Vecchio in the fourteenth century; from Antonio Pucci's *Proprietà di Mercato Vecchio*, translated by Nicholas Havely.

(Antonio Pucci (c.1310–1388) served the Commune for more than thirty years, as bell-ringer, auditor and town-crier. As well as verse-narrative *cantari* he also wrote a number of descriptive poems in *terza rima* such as the following, which celebrates the old market that was demolished to make way for the late nineteenth-century Piazza della Repubblica).

There's many a market-place I've been to see
In many a town, but here let me just tell
Of those nearby – we'll let the others be.
Perugia has a square that I could dwell
A while upon – its's finely enough laid out
And here in Florence it's admired as well.
But don't go praising other market-places here about,
For if you're asked to show just what's so fine in these,
The lack of witnesses will leave your claims in doubt.
As for that place called Campo by the Sienese –
It's more like a pan, where in summer you fry
And in winter are left to keep cool or to freeze.
But, if I'm honest now and really try
To tell the truth about produce and place
And how they serve their city – well then, I
Must now admit I'm glad to have the space
To praise *our* Market. I first saw the light
Here in the town of which it's the chief grace
(I mean in Florence), and I'm surely right
To say the Mercato Vecchio is our chief source
Of life – no other square gives such delight.
  And so I'll let these verses run their course,
Describing for you features you might please
To know, and making only claims one can endorse
About our market-place – which, to be brief, are these:
In each of its four corners a church stands
Which you can reach by several streets with ease.

Craftsmen and dealers of all sorts have stands
Stocked with all kinds of things I'll let you know
About, now, as this scene of ours expands.
Sovereign remedies for all ills here below
Can be obtained; wool and cloth dealers abound;
Apothecaries and grocers put their wares on show;
Traders in pots and pitchers can be found –
As well as those who offer bed and board
To tramps who'd otherwise doss on the ground.
Nearby stand massive vaults, where goods are stored,
And splendid butchers' stalls, where they display
What are the primest cuts in Florence, we're assured.
'Always be closing' seems the rule of the day
For traders here – especially that band
Of hucksters and sharp-practisers who make hay
While the florin shines – I mean, dealers in second-hand
Clothes, lenders and changers of money, lords of the game
(These last two sit at boards, and all their moves are planned).
Stalls elsewhere, though, deal in much fairer game
And they are richly laden all the year
With hares, wild boars and goats, fowl (wild and tame),
Partridges, pheasants and huge capons which they rear
Along with other birds for the gourmet's delight –
And if you want to hunt, buy hawks and falcons here.
   The women who sell fruit here might give some a fright:
Tough as they are, they surely know their parts
And, just for two dried chestnuts, morning to night
They'll bawl and brawl and call each other tarts –
Though you'll still find as much fruit as you please
(If it's in season) piled up on their carts.
Other women here sell eggs and cheese
For making vegetable flans and pies
Or ravioli or any dish like these.
Next to them, keeping close watch on who buys
What, are women selling herbs and mustard-seeds
To charm the nose or else bring water to the eyes.
   Thus women from the farms as each new day succeeds
Bring fresh supplies in, and the good cook bears
Home again all that the kitchen needs.
And when the time comes for fruit to be sold at fairs
Girls from the country pack their baskets high

With ripe round figs and grapes, peaches and pears.
If you try repartee with them, they won't be shy,
And some of them, brighter than florins, shine
With flowers from gardens that they tend nearby.
No garden, though, ever looked half as fine
As the Mercato Vecchio does when spring is here.
It feeds the eye and taste of every Florentine
And in this world it can't be matched – that's clear
To all who care to read this verse of mine
And all who've eyes to see or ears to hear.

[38] The Mercato Vecchio in the late fifteenth century;
from George Eliot's *Romola*.

(The novelist George Eliot, *vere* Mary Ann Evans (1819–1880),
was inspired by a summer visit to Florence in 1860 to write a
novel set in the period of Savonarola. She returned the following
spring and, with the help of her common-law husband George
Lewes, conducted detailed research in the Florentine libraries.
She was paid £10,000 for the novel, which appeared in
instalments in *The Cornhill Magazine*.)

They had now emerged from the narrow streets into a broad
piazza, known to the elder Florentine writers as the Mercato
Vecchio, or Old Market. This piazza, though it had been the
scene of a provision-market from time immemorial and may
perhaps, says fond imagination, be the very spot to which the
Fesulan ancestors of the Florentines descended from their high
fastness to traffic with the rustic population of the valley, had not
been shunned as a place of residence by Florentine wealth. In the
early decades of the fifteenth century, which was now near its
end, the Medici and other powerful families of the *popolani grassi*,
or commercial nobility, had their houses there, not perhaps
finding their ears much offended by the loud roar of mingled
dialects, or their eyes much shocked by the butchers' stalls,
which the old poet Antonio Pucci accounts a chief glory, or
dignità of a market that, in his esteem, eclipsed the markets of all
the earth beside. But the glory of mutton and veal (well attested
to be the flesh of the right animals; for were not the skins, with the
heads attached, duly displayed, according to the decree of the

Signoria?) was just now wanting to the Mercato, the time of Lent not being yet over. The proud corporation, or 'Art', of butchers was in abeyance, and it was the great harvest-time of the market-gardeners, the cheese-mongers, the vendors of macaroni, corn, eggs, milk, and dried fruits, – a change which was apt to make the women's voices predominant in the chorus. But in all seasons there was the experimental ringing of pots and pans, the chinking of the money-changers, the tempting offers of cheapness at the old-clothes stalls, the challenges of the dicers, the vaunting of new linens and woollens, of excellent wooden-ware, kettles, and frying pans; there was the choking of the narrow inlets with mules and carts, together with much uncomplimentary remonstrance in terms remarkably identical with the insults in use by the gentler sex of the present day . . .

And high on a pillar in the centre of the place, – a venerable pillar, fetched from the church of San Giovanni, – stood Donatello's stone statue of Plenty, with a fountain near it, where, says old Pucci, the good wives of the market freshened their utensils, and their throats also; not because they were unable to buy wine, but because they wished to save the money for their husbands.

The Misericordia

[39] The Misericordia, founded, according to tradition, in 1240; from Janet Ross's *Old Florence and Modern Tuscany*.

Most visitors to Florence have seen the brethren of the Misericordia bound on some mission of mercy, gliding silently – black ghosts carrying a black catafalque – through the city. All heads are uncovered as they pass, and the most ribald and uncouth carter draws his mules on one side to give more room.

No wonder the Florentines are proud of their Confraternity, the finest charitable institution that ever was founded. Anyone can give money, but the brethren give personal fatigue, and are often exposed to infection. Neither winter snow nor burning summer sun stops the devoted band. Three times a day the bell of the Misericordia Chapel, in the Piazza del Duomo, rings to call those of the Confraternity whose turn it is to carry sick poor to the hospital. Ten brethren usually go with each litter, under the orders of a Capo di Guardia, who is distinguished by a bag tied round his waist containing brandy, cough lozenges, and the key of a drawer under the litter in which is a drinking-cup, a stole, a crucifix, the ritual, and some holy water, in case the sick person should die on the way. The long overcoat and the cowl with two holes for the eyes are made of black cotton, and black gaiters are worn so that the brethren may not be recognized by the colour of their trousers. The cowl may only be thrown back outside the city gates and in certain specified streets, and if it rains hard or the sun is powerful, a black felt hat is worn over it. Four brethren carry the litter, which weighs about 180 lbs., and the reserve men keep one hand under the poles in case a bearer should stumble or fall. A slight tap on the pole is the signal for changing bearers, and this is so skilfully done that the sick or wounded are never shaken. The fresh men say as they relieve the others, 'May God reward you!' and the answer is: 'Go in peace!'

If they have to go some distance, sixteen brethren are told off for service, and should the case be a very bad one, a brother walks on either side of the litter to watch the invalid's face or feel his pulse.

Should the door of the house be too small to admit the litter, the Capo di Guardia and six brethren go to the sick-room.

Tenderly and carefully they carry the invalid on a thick quilted coverlid to the litter, and the arched top is opened against the street so that curious passers-by should not see the sick person. Before leaving the room, the Capo di Guardia leaves a small sum on the table, in obedience to a legacy left for that purpose to the Confraternity by two pious citizens in long past days, and if the invalid is the bread-winner, or the poverty of the family is evident, the Capo di Guardia begs the brethren to do yet another charity, and holding his hat together like a bag he goes from one to another to collect alms. He asks the sick person to whom the money is to be given, and, without counting, pours the contents of his hat into their hands. The members of the Misericordia take it by turn to go at stated hours to the houses of sick people to change their linen, or to sit up at night with those who are too poor to pay a nurse. In maladies like rheumatic fever, when the slightest touch is agony, they are often called by rich folk to lift an invalid – so gentle and sure from long habit is their touch. No brother is allowed to accept anything – money or food – save a glass of water, in any house.

Someone is always on guard at the Misericordia Chapel, and if an accident occurs a message is sent there to call a litter. Then the great bell of Giotto's Tower, just opposite the chapel, is tolled in a peculiar way – twice for an accident, three times for a death – to call the brethren who are on the list for that day.

Twice it has happened to me that a shopman has left his wife to serve in the shop, while he hastily threw on his cloak and ran out of the door. The first time, being new to Florence, I thought the man had gone mad. My face, I suppose, showed my surprise, for one of the customers said, 'Eh, signora, don't you hear the bell? – an accident.'

Museo Archeologico

[40] The 20-year-old Oscar Wilde enthuses over the Etruscans in the old Archaeological Museum when it was in the Via Faenza; from *The Letters of Oscar Wilde*, edited by Rupert Hart-Davis.

Then to the Etruscan Museum, which is in the suppressed monastery of San*[t']* Onofrio and most interesting. You come first to a big tomb, transplanted from Arezzo; cyclopean stonework, doorway with sloping jambs and oblong lintel, roof slightly conical, walls covered with wonderfully beautiful frescoes, representing first the soul in the shape of young man naked, led by a beautifully winged angel or genius to the two-horsed chariot which is to convey them to Elysium – and then represents the banquet which awaits him. The same idea of the resurrection of the soul and a state of happiness after death pervades the whole system of Etruscan art. There were also wonderful sarcophagi which I have roughly drawn for you. On the top the figure of the dead man or woman holding a plate containing the obol for paying the ferryman over Styx. Also extraordinary jars with heads and arms – funeral of course – I have drawn them. The sarcophagi are sculptured with the achievements and adventures of the dead man, mostly in bas-relief which are sometimes coloured. There were some with frescoes instead of sculpture, beautifully done. Of course urns and vases of every possible shape, and all painted exquisitely.

A great collection of coins, from the old *as*, a solid pound weight of metal about as big as a large bun and stamped with a ship on one side and a double-faced Janus on the other, down to tiny little gold coins the same size as gold five-franc pieces. The goldsmith's work for beauty of design and delicacy of workmanship exceeded anything I have ever seen. As I was kept there for a long time by an awful thunderstorm I copied a few which I send you. I cannot of course give you the wonderful grace and delicacy of workmanship, only the design. Goblets and bowls of jasper and all sorts of transparent pebbles – enamelled jars in abundance. Swords of the leaf shape, regular torques but somewhat same design, metal hand-mirrors, and household utensils of all kinds, and every thing, even the commonest plate or jug, done with greatest delicacy and of a beautiful design. They must have been a people among whom artistic feeling power was most widely spread. There is also a museum of Egyptian antiquities, but their devices and frescoes appeared to me grotesque and uncouth after the purity and sentiment of the Etruscan. You would have been much interested in all the Etruscan work: I spent two delightful hours there.

Orsanmichele

[41] The miraculous origins of the Church of Orsan-michele; from Giovanni Villani's *Croniche Fiorentine*.

In the same year [*1292*] on 3 July, there began a series of great and visible miracles in the city of Florence connected with a figure of Our Lady painted on one of the pillars of the open gallery of Orto San Michele, where grain is sold. The sick were healed, the lame walked again, and the possessed were liberated in large numbers for all to behold. But out of envy or for some other reason the preaching friars and minor orders refused to believe this and consequently fell into ill repute with the Florentines. In the place where Or' San Michele stands today there was formerly the church of San Michele in Orto, under the jurisdiction of the Abbey of Nonantola in Lombardy but since demolished to make way for the piazza. Every evening hymns were sung for laymen, habitually in devotion for the aforesaid figure, and the fame and merits of Mary grew to such an extent that people came there on pilgrimage from all over Tuscany for her anniversary, bringing divers wax images to record the miracles wrought. Whence a great part of the loggia before and around the holy figure was crowded and the congregation, including many of the best citizens, so increased that copious charities, alms, and bequests to the poor have been offered to this very day, the whole being distributed among the poor without any personal reward.

[42] Guild rivalry behind the beauty of the exterior of Orsanmichele; from Creighton Gilbert's *Italian Art 1400–1500. Sources and Documents*.

Resolution of April 20, 1406

For the completion of the decorations of the oratory of San Michele in Orto: they resolved . . . that whatever guild among the guilds of the city of Florence that has a place in the wall or columns of the oratory or palace of the Garden of San Michele on the exterior, is required to and must within the next ten years from now have made, in the place assigned to it, one figure or

Orsanmichele, and the sculptures on the exterior

sculptured marble image, large and honourable, of that saint whose feast is celebrated by it each year. And that whatever such place in which, beyond the said time, the said figure or image was not placed, completed, and perfected, is understood to be taken from that guild, and priors of the guilds [*City Council*] can and shall assign any such place whatsoever to any other guild that does not have a place.

[43] An English Catholic admires the sculpture on Orsanmichele in the mid-seventeenth century; from Richard
Lassels's *Voyage of Italy* (1670).

(The St George, St Mark and perhaps the St Peter are by
Donatello, whom Lassels eulogizes elsewhere in the *Voyage*.)

Going from the Piazza [*Signoria*] towards the *Domo*, we were
presently stopt by the *Church* of *S. Michael* a square flat Church
whose outside is adorned with rare statues, if not of gold, yet
worth their weight in gold. The best are, that of *S. Matthew* in
brasse made by *Laurentius Cion* [*Ghiberti*]: that of *S. Thomas* in
brasse touching the side of our *Saviour* with great demonstration
of diffidence in his lookes, is of *Andrea Varrochios* hand. That of
S. Peter in marble is excellent for the *Drappery* of it. That of
S. George in marble, is compared to the best in Rome, and hath
been praysed both in *Prose* and *verse*: that of S. *Marke* hath so
grave and honest a countenance, that *Michel Angelo* (a competent
iudge) stopping one day to behold it, and being asked what he
thought of it, answered: if S. *Marke* had such a countenance as
this, as its likely he had, a man might almost, for lookes sake,
beleeve all that he wrott: for never did I see (sayd hee) any man
have more the lookes of a good man, then this.

Ospedali (hospitals)

[44] The Silk Guild petitions the Commune for official recognition of their sole patronage of the Ospedale degli Innocenti; from Luigi Passerini's *Storia degli stabilmenti di beneficenza e d'istruzione gratuita della città di Firenze*, in *The Society of Renaissance Florence* by Gene Brucker.

[*October 20, 1421*] . . . This petition is presented with all due reverence to you, lord priors, on behalf of your devoted sons of the guild of Por Santa Maria [*the silk guild*] and the merchants and guildsmen of that association. It is well known to all of the people of Florence that this guild has sought, through pious acts, to conserve . . . and also to promote your republic and this guild. It has begun to construct a most beautiful edifice in the city of Florence and in the parish of S. Michele Visdomini, next to the piazza called 'Frati de' Servi.' [*This building is*] a hospital called S. Maria degli Innocenti, in which shall be received those who, against natural law, have been deserted by their fathers or their mothers, that is, infants, who in the vernacular are called *gittatelli* [*literally, castaways; foundlings*]. Without the help and favour of your benign lordships, it will not be possible to transform this laudable objective into reality . . . nor after it has been achieved, to preserve and conserve it.

And since [*we*] realized that your lordships and all of the people are, in the highest degree, committed to works of charity, [*we have*] decided to have recourse to your clemency, and to request, most devotedly, all of the things which are described below. So on behalf of the above-mentioned guild, you are humbly petitioned . . . to enact a law . . . that this guild of Por Santa Maria and its members and guildsmen – as founders, originators, and principals of this hospital – are understood in perpetuity to be . . . the sole patrons, defenders, protectors, and supporters of this hospital as representatives of, and in the name of, the *popolo* and Commune of Florence. . . .

[45] The building and growth of the Innocenti; from *Old Florence and Modern Tuscany* by Janet Ross.

In 1421 the guild of Silk Merchants of Por Santa Maria began building the actual 'Hospital of the Innocents' in Piazza dei Servi, and the Signoria named the Guild 'inventor, founder and master of the said hospital with full powers to elect the governor and other officials, granting at the same time such privileges and exemptions as were enjoyed by the hospital of Santa Maria Nuova'. Filippo Brunelleschi was the architect employed, and his pupil Francesco della Luna directed the works; but probably for want of funds, the building was only finished in 1445, when the Consuls of the Guild invited the commune and the people of Florence to be present at the ceremony of inauguration on the 24th January. The Patriarch of Jerusalem was then Papal Legate in Florence, and he accompanied the Bishop of Fiesole in solemn procession from the Duomo, followed by the Consuls of the Guild and much people. But the church was only consecrated six years later by St Antonino, the pious Archbishop of Florence, who placed under the altar stone a leaden box containing relics, which was found when the church was repaired in 1615. It was with a feeling of reverence that I took up the little box, still containing the relics enveloped in discoloured cotton wool, which had been touched by the hands of the saintly Archbishop . . .

The number of 'innocents' increased so rapidly that in 1448 the guild of Silk Merchants decreed that one soldo in every lira paid for winding silk, and two soldi in every lira paid for weaving damask, should be set aside, after one third of the total sum had been deducted for the Congregation of Weavers, for the benefit of the hospital. At the same time the Signoria ordered that all merchandise of whatsoever description, saving wheat and building materials, should pay one soldo for every horse, mule, or donkey-load, brought into the town, to the hospital, and exempted it from the tax on salt and on eatables . . .

Still the 'family', as the old records call it, grew so rapidly, that in 1463 the hospital of San Gallo was incorporated with the new Foundling Hospital in order to increase its revenues; and three years later the Consuls of the Guild petitioned the Signoria to remit certain arrears of taxes on house property, saying 'if ever this hospital was in need of help, it is so now, with 700 mouths to feed: 400 of them being out at nurse, and fifty being girls of a marriageable age.' In a later petition we find that the number of children was so large, and the debts were so pressing, that the wet-nurses could not be paid, and some of the babies died of hunger, 'a thing that cannot be tolerated by men of gentle and kindly nature, as are the Florentines, or heard tell of without horror and tears.' In 1513 the number of 'mouths' had increased to 1,320 when Leo X. bestowed spiritual privileges on anyone who maintained a foundling for one year, and many of the great Florentine families made handsome donations.

When Cosimo I. became Grand Duke, he ordered that the Governor, or as he was then called the Prior, should be elected for life, and not only live in the hospital, but have his meals with the other officials, a rule that was only abolished in 1742. An edict was also passed that the hospital should have a soldo in the lira out of every fine, three golden florins for every sentence of death, and one for all amputations or bodily punishments, but if the sentence was remitted, the claims of the hospital were to be satisfied before the remission took effect.

The small remuneration given to the wet-nurses made it difficult to place out the 'innocents', so that many died, and it was not until the Grand Duke Francesco, in 1577, told the Prior that in Spain cow's milk was often given to children, that 'the doctors consulted together and a cow was bought, whose milk was given to the babies in certain glasses with nozzles, and it suited them well.' This is the first record of bringing up children by hand in the city of Florence.

The first experiment of inoculating smallpox in Florence was also made in the Innocenti hospital in 1756 with good results, but it does not appear to have found much favour with the public in general. The Prior must have had enough to do, as the family numbered 3,855; but many children, instead of being taken back into the hospital, were left with their foster-mothers for a very small annual payment, and brought up as peasants. In 1801 vaccination was attempted by a doctor of the Innocenti . . .

In Florence the surnames 'Innocenti', 'Degli Innocenti' , 'Nocentini', are often met with, as until the beginning of the last century the children only received a Christian name when they were baptised, and the name of 'Innocent' was often added to distinguish them. The Grand Duke Ferdinand III. then ordered that to every child should be given a surname in order to remove the slur of illegitimacy. In 1903 the 'family' belonging to the hospital numbered 4,949 including the sisters, nurses, servants, etc., so the office of Governor is no sinecure.

[46] An architect's view of what happens when you don't stick closely to the original plans of a fellow-architect of genius; from Antonio Manetti's *Life of Brunelleschi*.

When he [*Brunelleschi*] was away in this or that community or with this or that Prince, some of the buildings were spoiled by failing in one way or another to carry out his orders exactly, either because of ignorance or presumption. Among others (I will begin with the early Florentine ones), he was asked by the Guild and University of Porta Santa Maria, the patron who had the responsibility, to construct the portico of the Ospedale degli Innocenti. A plan alone without a wooden model sufficed for that portico. And so he did. Inasmuch as he was asked about the space over the portico and one space only at either side of the portico between two fluted pilasters of *macigno*, he presented a drawing precisely scaled in small *braccia*. That plan in its original form is still in the Udienza de' Consoli of the aforementioned Guild. In it are many various and fine considerations and the reasons are understood by few. He explained it orally to the master builders, the stonecutters, certain citizens, the leaders of the Guild, and to the workers assigned to the undertaking, since he had to be absent for a time. On his return from that place the loggia was built the way it is today, which gave Filippo [*Brunelleschi*] much displeasure, since they had diverged from his plans in many things. They had built it that way because of the arrogance of one of the *operai*, who did not want to appear to have less authority than Filippo. They did it thinking that Filippo would praise it, and that in the event that he did not, of being able to defend what they had done. Since Filippo placed the blame on one of them in particular, the one who had erred the most prepared to defend himself. There are many prominent, very evident defects at variance with the plan Filippo left, which can be noted by anyone who looks for them. One is in the frieze over the loggia arcade; another is in the architrave; another in the two windows and in the small pilasters that were to rise from the [*lower*] cornice that functions as the sill for the windows up to the [*upper*] cornice; this [*upper*] cornice should be where the eaves of the roof are now. There is also a variation from Filippo's proportions in an addition – besides the error of the addition itself – built on the south side, and appearing on the outside façade of the loggia. Then there is an architrave that turns [*a corner*] downward and continues to the dado of the building. These lapses are, in short, nothing less than the presumption of the person who had it built in that manner on his own authority. The aforementioned person when defending himself was convinced of everything by Filippo. He did not know what to say and for the sake of courtesy I will not give his name. However, to spoil the works of such men [*as Filippo*] and to take things from them is very presumptuous. Experience proved in the end that nothing was subtracted from Filippo's work without removing beauty, increasing the cost, and in large measure weakening the buildings and damaging their usefulness.

[47] The children of slaves in the Innocenti; from Iris Origo's 'The Domestic Enemy'.

Of 7,534 children registered in the ninety years covered by the books of the Spedale degli Innocenti and that of San Gallo (1395 to 1485), 1,096 (i.e., fourteen per cent) are specifically mentioned as having slave mothers, while this may also have been true of others whose parentage is not specified. And at Lucca, at the beginning of the fifteenth century, no less than one third of the foundlings (55 out of 165) were the children of slaves.

The records in the hospital books – kept with meticulous care by the treasurers, with a very Tuscan mixture of shrewd realism, careful cheeseparing and rough kindliness – tell the little that is known about the foundlings: the date of their arrival and the origin of their parents (generally the mother's name, but very rarely the father's) and sometimes describe the rags in which they were wrapped. Here is a typical entry:

On the 6th of December, 1451, there were brought to us two female children, born in one body [*twins*] at one o'clock at night. They were baptized at once; we caused them to be baptized and gave them the names of Sandra Innocente and Nicolosa Innocente. They came from the house of Agostino

Capponi, born of Polonia his slave; they were brought by Monna Dorotea, the midwife . . . wrapped in two linen rags, without being swaddled. They arrived half dead: if they had been two dogs, they would have been better cared for.

And a few days later: 'Sandra died on January 30th in the hospital. God give her his blessing.' Sometimes a note or identifying sign was pinned to the child's garments, so that it could be found again.

Saturday, 29 May 1469. At one o'clock at night a little girl was put into the font with a scroll to identify her, with a piece cut out in the middle of it in the shape of an almond, in which these words were written: 'This child is called Margherita and has been baptized. Keep this note, put it in your files.' [*In another hand*]: 'So that the said child may be found when her mother wishes to do her some good. I have discovered that the child is called Elisabetta and her mother Margherita; she is a slave, though free, and the father who is a priest is called Ser Andrea, and he has taken this child from her mother and sent her to the hospital, and has made the slave give suck to the child of a fellow-townsman, telling her that her own child has been put out to nurse; and he does not wish her to know that she [*the child*] has come to the hospital.'

This particular story has, for once, a happy ending: 'On the 7th of June I gave her back to her mother.'

Often these notes of warning or pleading – scrawled in illiterate, shaky hands on scraps of coarse paper – are still preserved in the register, beside the treasurer's entry. Here is yet another:

18 December 1473. At about two o'clock a little girl was put in the font, brought by two men who said nothing. She was wrapped in two pieces of new greyish woollen cloth and was well swaddled, and had a note which said: 'Dearest Father in Christ, this is because I send you the child. I would like you to keep her hidden and to send me a note in your own hand, and do not show the child to anyone who does not come to you with that note in your own hand. And if any person or slave asks for her, say she is dead. And I pray you call her Smeralda.'

Perhaps the most touching of these entries is that recording the gift of 5½ *denari* (pence) left to the hospital by an anonymous slave-woman: 'For the love of God, in charity, so that she may find her child again.'

[48] A euology of the Grand Duke Pietro Leopoldo; from *Travels through Italy, in a series of letters . . . by President Charles Dupaty.*

(Charles Mercier Dupaty (1746–1788) was a brilliant and progressive French magistrate whose political bias is clearly implied in this pre-revolutionary account based on his journey of 1785.)

The finest gallery in the world is at Florence; but I will not now speak to you of paintings, statues and images; I have seen Leopold and his people.

Leopold loves his people, and has suppressed all such imposts as were not necessary: he has disbanded almost all his troops, retaining only sufficient to preserve the art of military discipline.

He has destroyed the fortifications of Pisa, the maintenance of which was very expensive; he has overthrown the stones which devoured mankind.

He found that his court concealed from him his people: he has no longer any court. He has established manufactures. He has every where opened superb roads, and at his own expence. He has founded hospitals. – You would imagine the hospitals in Tuscany were palaces of the grand duke. I have visited them, and found in them all, cleanliness, good order, and the most humane and attentive care. I have seen sick old men, who seemed as if waited on by their children. I have seen sick children, who seemed as if nursed by their mothers. I could not, without shedding tears, behold this luxury of compassion and humanity. In the inscriptions on the front of these hospitals, they have bestowed on Leopold the title of *Father of the Poor*. The hospitals themselves give him this title. These are monuments which stand in no need of inscriptions. The grand duke comes frequently to visit his poor and sick; he does not neglect the good he has done; he possesses not only the sudden feelings of humanity, he has a humane soul. He never makes his appear-

ance in this abode of anguish and sorrow without causing tears of
joy; he never leaves it without being followed with benedictions
which are the gratitude of a happy people: and these songs of
thanksgiving are sent up from an hospital!

You may be presented to the grand duke without having four
hundred years nobility, without descending from those who
disputed the crown with his ancestors. His palace, like the
temples, is open to all his subjects without exception. Three days
only in the week are more particularly consecrated to a certain
class of men; neither to the great nor the rich, neither to painters,
poets, nor musicians; but to the wretched.

In other countries, commerce and industry, like the lands, are
become the patrimony of a small number of individuals; with
Leopold, every thing you can do, you may do it: you have a
living, if you possess any peculiar talent; and there is no exclusive
privilege but genius.

[49] The Hospital of San Giovanni di Dio as inspected in
the 1780s; from John Howard's *The State of the Prisons in
England and Wales with preliminary observations and an account of
some foreign prisons and hospitals.*

(After a brief period of imprisonment in France, John Howard
(1726–1790) devoted the rest of his life to the reform of British
and continental prisons and hospitals, travelling widely and
publishing large illustrated volumes on the subject.)

The great *Hospital* of S. *Maria Nova* was crowded, and too close
. . . the *Hospital* which I most frequently visited, was S. *Giovan di
Dio*. The ascent into the sick ward is by a flight of thirty stone
steps. This ward was lofty and clean; and was a hundred and
twenty-three feet long, and thirty-three and a half wide. There
were in it thirty-three beds, three feet four inches wide, placed on
varnished boards, on iron bedsteads. This is very conducive to
cleanliness, and secures patients from vermin. – At one end there
are five rooms with single beds for sick priests. Three of them
were occupied. Neither the sides nor floors of this, and the other
hospitals of Italy, were *wood*, that being more retentive of scents
or infection than tarras or brick. – The great attention of this
order of friars to the sick, in every country where they have
hospitals, does them honour.

[50] A difficult patient in the Ospedale di Santa Maria Nuova; from Luca Landucci's *Diario Fiorentino*.

[*28 March 1487*] The following case happened: A man was hung on the gallows here in Florence, and was taken down for dead, but was later found not to be so. He was carried to Santa Maria Nuova, and remained there till the 11th of April. And those in charge at Santa Maria Nuova finding him of a bad nature, and hearing him talk of taking vengeance, etc., the 'Eight' decided to have him hung a second time, and their sentence was carried out.

[51] A British humanist in the 1540s enthuses over the up-to-date facilities at the hospital of Santa Maria Nuova; from William Thomas's *Historie of Italie* . . .

But amongest all other thei have divers goodlie hospitalles, for relieve of the sicke and poore, and one verie faire, so well ordred, that it receiveth a great number of men and women, but into severall houses: where they are applied with good phisicke, and their beddes, their shetes, and everie other thyng so cleane, that manie tymes righte honest men and women be not ashamed to seke their health there. For that hospitall alone maie dispende yerelie above .20000. crownes: by reason whereof they have excellente phisicions, good poticaries, dilygente ministers, and everie other thyng necessarie.

[52] Dr Samuel Sharp finds something to admire in the bug-resistant beds at Santa Maria Nuova; from Samuel Sharp's *Letters from Italy . . . in the years 1765, and 1766*.

(Though a professional physician, Samuel Sharp (c.1700–1778) is chiefly remembered for his highly critical *Letters from Italy, describing the Customs and Manners of that Country, in the years 1765, and 1766*, which provoked Dr Johnson's friend, Giuseppe Baretti, to write the defensive *Account of the Manners and Customs of Italy with observations on the mistakes of some travellers with regard to that country.*)

I am much pleased with the contrivance used in the great hospital here, to avoid bugs; it is no other than a plain bedstead of iron, made so simple, that there is not a crevice where a bug can conceal itself. I remember, that there have been attempts of this kind made in *England*, but they have proved ineffectual, because they fastened ticking to the frame, with oilet-holes, and cording, which afforded some harbour to these animals. In this hospital they only lay across the frame about four or five boards, a little longer than the width of the frame, and about a foot broad, upon which they lay the bedding; these are moveable, and if necessary, may be brushed when the bed is made, as easily, and in as short a time, as a man brushes his hat. In the hospitals at *London*, bugs are frequently a greater evil to the patient, than the malady for which he seeks an hospital; and, could I have interest enough with the governors, to bring about an imitation of this frame, I should be exceedingly rejoiced in the comfort it will afford to so many thousands of miserable wretches, that are tormented sometimes even to death, by these nauseous vermin.

Palazzo Corsini

[53] A visit to the Palazzo Corsini in 1848; from Sophia Hawthorne's *Notes in England and Italy.*

(Sophia Hawthorne, *née* Peabody, married the novelist Nathaniel Hawthorne in 1842. Following the publication of *The Scarlet Letter* and other novels between 1850 and 1853, Nathaniel was appointed American consul in Liverpool and the couple began the seven-year residence in Europe on which Sophia based her interesting *Notes.*)

July 23d. – To-day Louisa and Annie Powers accompanied us to the Guadagni and Corsini galleries. . . . The Corsini, on the Lung' Arno . . . is the richest private collection in Florence. We found the saloons covered with carpets – an unprecedented circumstance in galleries. There were beautiful pictures, and quite a crowd of 'Sweet Charleses' (as Mr H. calls Carlo Dolce), and I do not like his works, with one or two exceptions. His famous Poesie I do not fancy at all. Everything feminine is too sweet, except the Madonna in the Grand Duke's chamber in the Pitti, but some of his saints are fine, though too metallic. It was worth while to come here, if only to see Raphael's cartoon in pencil of his portrait of Julius II. It has all the immense power of will and thought of the oil-painting, and so far verifies Mr Powers' assertion, that color is not needful to expression. This drawing is of the size of life, and finished with the utmost nicety and truth. It is a wonder and a beauty and a lesson to observe how the greatest masters carefully and faithfully and patiently elaborated their work, never disdaining an exhaustive perfection in each item. What a vast labor is here, and not a line is omitted or hurried! It would seem as if Raphael had an eternity to work in, for he was never in haste; yet what an enormous amount he accomplished – dying too in early manhood! Michel Angelo, to be sure, did not show patience always, though he has left careful drawings. His genius seemed an Atè, lashing him with her brand often. Yet there sit the sublime prophets and sibyls in infinite calm; and the lovely form of Eve is the ideal of woman, delicate and new from the hand of the Creator, as if she peacefully dawned upon his mind, as he sat musing on primal beauty.

There was a small copy of his Last Judgement, in brilliant color, as it originally blazed on the walls of the Sistine Chapel, before some of the figures were draped by order of the pseudo-modest Pope, who insisted upon the resurrection of jackets and breeches. The hues of this copy are a revelation to me of the dazzling splendor of all those Sistine frescoes, in their first freshness. How stupid and short-sighted to smoke and spoil such divine productions with candles and incense-vapours . . .

In one of the saloons we saw a vase of marvellous beauty of design and execution – bronze, about two feet high. I exclaimed that it must be by Benvenuto Cellini, and the custode said it was so. It represents, in bas-relief, the triumph of Bacchus.

Ada tried to draw it on the spot, but in the midst the custode told her she must not do it, for it was forbidden. I suppose the Prince Corsini is afraid that some artist will attempt to imitate it, and then he would not have the only one in the world. But why should he? He cannot prevent my remembering it, however, so distinctly that I can sketch it here at home. The figures are of enchanting grace – and the baby Bacchus on the panther and the whole procession as perfect as possible.

Palazzo Medici

[54] A letter from Benozzo Gozzoli to Piero de' Medici about work in progress on the chapel frescoes in the Palazzo Medici in July 1459; from *Carteggio inedito d'artisti* . . . edited by Giovanni Gaye.

(Benozzo Gozzoli (1420–1497) worked first with the Ghiberti and then with Fra Angelico, travelling widely between Florence and Rome. His major work was the series of twenty-five frescoes in the Campo Santo at Pisa which was done some years after he had completed the 'Journey of the Magi' referred to here.)

This morning I received a letter from your Magnificence through Roberto Martegli and I understand that the seraphims I have done do not seem appropriate to you. I have done one in a corner among certain clouds owing to which one only sees bits of the wing and he is so well-hidden and covered by the clouds that far from deforming anything he rather gives beauty. And this is by the side of the column. I have done another on the other side of the altar also hidden in the same way. Roberto Martegli has seen them and said there is nothing to make a fuss about. Nonetheless I will do whatever you command me to do; two clouds will make them vanish. I would have come to speak with you myself but I began to apply the blue this morning and the job cannot be abandoned. The heat is great and from one moment to the next the glue might stop working. I reckon that by the week after next I should have finished this section [*puntata*]. I think you will want to see it before I take down the scaffolding. And I understand that you have ordered Roberto Martegli to give me what I need. I had him give me two florins and they will be enough for now.

[55] Galeazzo Maria Sforza informs his father, the Duke of Milan, how he was received by Cosimo il Vecchio in the newly decorated chapel in the Palazzo Medici; from a letter in the Archivio di Stato di Milano translated by Rab Hatfield in *The Three Kings and the Medici*.

(The fifteen-year-old Galeazzo was sent to Florence to escort
Pope Pius II to Mantua where an anti-Turkish council was to be
held. Contemporaries observed that Sforza's Florentine reception was more lavish than the Pope's.)

I took leave of the *Signoria* and, accompanied by a great
multitude of gentlemen and people, all of whom were on holiday
by public decree as if it were Christmas or Easter, I finally
arrived at the house of the magnificent Cosimo, where there
awaited me a house so noteworthy in its ceilings, the height of its
walls, the fineness of the doors and windows, the numbers of
rooms and reception halls, the decorations of the studies, the
number and quality of the books there, the pleasantness and
purity of the gardens; and likewise the tapestries with which it is
decorated, the chests of incomparable workmanship and inestimable value, masterly works of sculpture and pictures of infinite
kinds – and even of the most exquisite silver. It is the most
beautiful house I have ever seen; nor do I think that any person
could be found who, in speaking of this house, would not want to
discourse worthily about it and describe each of its parts; and for
this would be necessary not this inexperienced tongue of mine,
not just one day, not even a month – but many, and also the
eloquence of many great speakers. I went to visit the magnificent
Cosimo, whom I found in a chapel of his which was no less finely
decorated than the rest of the house. He embraced me most
gently and tenderly; and, nearly weeping with happiness and
affection, he said that at his age nothing could have happened to
him that pleased him more; for, since it was his desire above all
else to see Your Excellency, seeing me in this way made it seem
almost as if he were face to face with Yourself. And I, in the best
manner I knew how, made my reply – only in generalities,
however, and I did not speak of anything else. Afterwards,
having returned to my room and stayed there a while, I returned
to him a second time. He was still in the same chapel, indeed he
could not have gone out during the time I was away from him. I
found him there with two of his little ones, who were made to
deliver two speeches, one in prose, the other in verse, in a most
worthy manner – and almost unbelievable coming from the
mouths of boys at the age I imagine them to be (for both are most
tender in years); both the speeches were in praise of Your
Excellency, of the Most Illustrious Lord your father, and to

express their pleasure at my coming. Again I returned to my room, not having replied in other than generalities this time either; and I paid a visit to the ladies; and after a while it was time for dinner.

[56] Lorenzo the Magnificent; from Francesco Guicciardini's *History of Florence*.

(Born into an aristocratic Florentine family in 1483, Francesco Guicciardini became first a practising lawyer and then a diplomat. He meanwhile wrote histories of Florence and of Italy, dying in retirement in 1540.)

A day or two before his death, a thunderbolt had fallen at night on the lantern of the dome of Santa Liperata and brought down several large blocks of stone which fell toward the Medici house. Some also thought it a portent that Maestro Piero Leone da Spoleto, reputed the first doctor in Italy, who had treated Lorenzo, threw himself in despair down a well and drowned, although some said that he had been thrown in.

Lorenzo de' Medici was forty-three when he died, and he had been in power for twenty-three years, as he was twenty when his father Piero died in 1469. Although he was then so young and practically under the guardianship of Messer Tommaso Soderini and other elder statesmen, nonetheless in a short time he acquired such a standing and so great a reputation that he governed the city on his own. His authority grew daily, and subsequently became immense as a result of the events of 1478, and then after his return from Naples, so that until his death he ruled and disposed of the city as completely at his own whim as if he had been its absolute overlord. Because his greatness was extraordinary and Florence had never had a citizen like him, and because his fame was universal both during his lifetime and after his death, I do not think it will be irrelevant, but rather most useful to give a detailed description of his manners and character, which I have known not at first hand – because I was a child when he died – but from people and sources which are authentic and worthy of belief, and of such a kind that, if I am not mistaken, what I shall write will be the simple truth.

Lorenzo possessed many outstanding qualities. He also had

Vasari's posthumous portrait of Lorenzo de' Medici –
'The Magnificent'

certain vices – some natural, others induced by necessity. He had
such great authority that one may say that the city was not free in
his time, even though it was rich in all those glories and good
fortunes which a city may enjoy when free in name but in fact
ruled as a tyrant by one of its citizens. The things he did –
although some of them can be criticized – were nevertheless full
of greatness, so much so that they arouse our admiration far more

when we consider them than when we hear them enumerated, for they are lacking, through no fault of his but because of the nature of the times, in feats of arms and in military art and discipline which confer such fame on the ancients. We shall not read in his case of the brilliant defence of a city, the memorable taking of a stronghold, a stratagem in battle or a victory over the enemy. The story of his deeds does not shine with the glitter of arms. But we shall find in him all the signs and indications of virtues that are apparent and of value in civic life. No one even of his enemies and critics denies that he had a brilliant and outstanding mind; and the proof is that for twenty-three years he ruled the city and constantly increased her power and glory, and he would be a fool who denied it. This is all the more remarkable since Florence is a city accustomed to the greatest freedom of speech, full of the most volatile and restless spirits, and at the same time a small state incapable of supporting all its citizens from its own resources, so that it is necessary if the needs of one section are satisfied that the rest should suffer exclusion. A further proof is to be seen in the friendship and great credit which he enjoyed with many of the princes of Italy and outside Italy: with Innocent, with King Ferdinand, with Duke Galeazzo [*Visconti of Milan*], with King Louis of France and even the Grand Turk and the Sultan, from whom in the last years of his life he received a present of a giraffe, a lion and some geldings. All this arose simply from his ability to treat with these princes with great brilliance and skill. Furthermore, those who heard him can bear witness to his acumen and wit when speaking in public or in private, through which on many occasions and in many places, and especially at the Diet of Cremona, he achieved a considerable reputation. And there is proof too in the letters he dictated, so full of genius that they leave nothing to be desired; and they seemed all the finer as they were accompanied by great eloquence and a most elegant style. . . .

He desired glory and success more than any man. One may criticize him for carrying this passion even into things of small importance, so that even in poetry, in games and other pursuits he would not permit any to imitate or compete with him, and was angry with those who did so. Even in greater things his ambition was excessive, for he wished to rival and compete with all the princes of Italy in everything, which displeased Lodovico Sforza a great deal. Nevertheless, on the whole this ambition was

praiseworthy and made him famous everywhere even outside
Italy, for he strove to ensure that all the arts and talents should
flourish more brilliantly in Florence than in any other city in
Italy. . . . Thus the study of the humanities flourished in
Florence under Messer Agnolo Poliziano, Greek studies under
Messer Demetrio [*Calcondila*] and later under Lascaris, philosophy and arts had Marsilio Ficino, Maestro Giorgio Benigno,
Count Pico della Mirandola and other eminent men. He also
equally favored poetry in the vernacular, music, architecture,
painting, sculpture, and all the arts of the mind and hand, so that
the city abounded in all such ornaments of life. And they
flourished all the more because he was able, with his universal
taste, to appreciate them and favor their authors accordingly, so
that everyone competed in their works to please him. Another
factor was his infinite liberality, making abundant provision for
able men and providing all the necessary instruments for their
work. For example, to set up a Greek library he sent Lascaris, a
most learned man then teaching Greek in Florence, to search for
ancient and valuable books in Greece. . . .

He was by nature very arrogant, so that, besides not allowing
others to oppose him, he also wished them to understand him by
allusions, using in important affairs few and ambiguous words.
In ordinary conversation he was pleasant and witty; in his
domestic life rather plain and decent than sumptuous – except in
the magnificent feasts which he gave in honour of noble
foreigners who came to Florence. He was libidinous, amorous
and faithful in his loves, which would last for a number of years.
In the opinion of many he was so weakened by his amorous
excesses that he died relatively young. His last love, which lasted
for many years, was for Bartolomea de' Nasi, wife of Donato
Benci. Though she was not beautiful, she was gracious and
charming, and he was so obsessed with her that one winter when
she was in the country he would leave Florence at the fifth or
sixth hour of the night on horseback with several companions to
go and see her, and would start back again so early that he was in
Florence again by morning. . . . It seems absurd that a man of
such greatness, reputation and prudence should be so infatuated
in his fortieth year with a woman who was neither young nor
beautiful that he could do things which would have been
unworthy in a boy.

[57] The Medici's final abandonment of the family palazzo in the mid-seventeenth century; from John Chetwode Eustace's *A Classical Tour through Italy*.

(John Chetwode Eustace (1762(?)–1815) was a Douai-trained Catholic priest, a classical scholar, and a traveller. His book was based on a journey of 1802 supplemented by several subsequent excursions. Published in 1813, in two volumes, it was an immediate success, reaching seven editions by 1841.)

When we enter it the recollection of all the virtues and the honours of the first Medici inspire veneration; as we advance we seem to see the heroes and the sages of the fifteenth and sixteenth centuries rising successively before us, and claiming the homage due to their exertions in the cause of science and literature. . . . It must appear surprising, that a sovereign of this family should have sold a palace so intimately connected with the history of its fortunes, and not only the *incunabula gentis*, but a monument of the most honourable period of its existence. But Ferdinand II. lived at a time when the Medicean princes, then a degenerate race, had lost in the effeminacy and pride of sovereignty, even the memory of the virtues that made their ancestors great, and were probably indifferent or perhaps averse to trophies and monuments that only reproached them with their vices and their indolence.

The *Riccardi* family, the present proprietors of the Medicean palace, are not unworthy of such a residence. It still remains the repository of the arts and of the wisdom of antiquity; and its gallery and library open to public inspection, continue to announce the spirit, the judgement, and the liberality of its inhabitants.

[58] Luca Giordano and the frescoes in Palazzo Medici-Riccardi admired in the late eighteenth century; from *Travels through Italy, in a series of letters . . . by President Dupaty*.

The palace Ricardi merits to be seen: it was the residence of the first Medici.

In this palace the Liberty of Florence expired, and the fine Arts were born . . .

The gallery of the palace Ricardi is admirable. The pencil of Jordano, as fertile and brilliant as that of Ovid, assisted by the finest imaginations of the age he lived in, by philosophers and poets, painted and peopled the ceiling. It may be said to be a poem the subject of which is the destiny of man.

The first subject is the birth of man. Destiny, Time, the Fatal Sisters, and Nature are in expectation; Destiny makes a sign to Time, who repeats the signal to the Fatal Sisters; they at the same moment turn their spindle, and an infant is seen in the arms of Nature. Prometheus approaches the child, and shakes over him his torch: this is the spark of life. Already the infant crawls at the feet of Nature, he gets up, he walks, and tries to leave her. In vain does Nature strive to retain him, in vain does she shed tears; he is quickly at a considerable distance, and soon loses himself. After the youth has wandered some time, two paths open before him; the one, beset with flints, thorns, and every thing which can render it rugged: the other, on the contrary, level, and enamelled with flowers. On the side of each of these two roads is seen a company of men and women. Those, beside the first, have a mild, but serious air, without either dress or ornament, except a few leaves of laurel in their hair. They remain upon the edge of the road, from whence, without endeavouring to seduce the traveller, they accost, and seem merely to say to him: *Young man, behold the road of happiness.* These are the talents and the virtues. The company by the side of the level road, infinitely more numerous than the other, present the most striking figures. Their countenances are animated; they laugh, they sing, and play a thousand wanton tricks. How luxurious are their dresses! They have flowers in their hair, on their foreheads, and in their hands. From their manner of smiling, you would imagine them to be the Loves and Graces; yet, on looking at them behind, a light ribbon which binds their heads, discovers that these charming faces are but masks, and through some openings in those masks you get a glimpse of hideous countenances. This troop press forward to meet the traveller; they smile at him, they caress, they flatter him, they take him by the hand: *Charming stranger*, say they, *this is the road of pleasure, then follow us.* He follows them . . . the unfortunate man is entangled in the snares of vice and vicious habits.

Ingenious allegory! Never did Truth assume a more splendid or more transparent veil!

Palazzo Pitti

[59] An inaccurate but interesting early account of the Palazzo Pitti and the Fortezza di Belvedere; from Fynes Moryson's *An Itinerary* . . ., describing Florence in 1594.

The Duke hath two Pallaces within the City, whereof one is called Pallazzo di Pitti, seated in this part of the City, which a Gentleman of Florence by name Lucca della Casa de Pitti, began to build, but falling into poverty, and not able to finish it, was forced to sel the same to Cosmo de Medicis, being Great Duke of Florence, and shortly after convicted of treason, was beheaded. This is the most stately Pallace in the Citie, in the Garden whereof, called Belveder, are many most sweete among pleasant Groves, together with a pleasant Cave and Fountaine. They say, that one Mule did bring all the matter to this building, in memorie whereof, these verses are written upon the picture of the said Mule:

Lecticam, lapides, & marmora, ligna, Columnas
Vexit, conduxit, traxit, & ista tulit.

The Litter, these stones, marbles, pillers, wood,
Did carry, leade, draw, beare, this Mule so good.

The outward side of the Pallace is of Free-stone engraven, and the Ornaments within are Regall. Betweene the two Chambers, wherein the Duke and the Dutchesse lie apart, is a very fair Gallery, and in the Chamber of the Dutchesse, is a second bed most like her owne for the Duke when he pleaseth to lie there, and there is a Table wrought with silver and pretious stones, valued at 3000 Crownes. In the dining roome are many faire statuaes, and the figure of thirty Cardinals chosen at one time by Pope Leo the tenth, being of the house of Medici. In the very Court are two great loadstones. The strong Fort called Saint Meniato, lies over this Pallace, and indeede over all the Citie, which was built by Alexander de Medicis, nephew to Pope Clement the seventh, and had lately been kept by a Garison of two thousand Spaniards, as likewise another Fort on the other side of Arno, built in the time of the free State, was likewise kept by a Garison of 100 Spaniards: For the Dukes of Medici advanced to their Dukedome by the Emperor Charles the fifth, did at first admit these Garisons of Spaniards under an Italian Captaine, either to shew their confidence in Spaine, or to fortifie themselves against the Citizens, whose libertie they had invaded; but Duke Ferdinand then living (the Families of Citizens being now extinct or suppressed, who had lived in the free state, and could not indure subjection) being now confirmed in his Dukedome had lately effected, that these Spaniards should yeeld the Fortes to him, and depart the Countrey.

[60] The Pitti, in the time of Ferdinand I, considered the most magnificent palace in the world; from *The Life and Letters of Sir Henry Wotton*, edited by Logan Pearsall Smith.

(After an education at Winchester and Oxford, Henry Wotton (1568–1639) travelled extensively and, as was necessary in the Elizabethan period, somewhat surreptitiously. This provided the basis for his career as spy and diplomat. He also became a scholar and a poet, however, and after three ambassadorships in Venice published the excellent *Elements of Architecture* (1624) and became Provost of Eton College.)

Being desirous, albeit I dare promise little fruit or pleasure to others by any use of my pen, yet at least to record unto myself some such observations as I picked up abroad in the time of my former travels and employments, I stand obliged in grateful memory, to say somewhat of a prince long since at rest, namely, Ferdinando Grand Duke of Tuscany, which was the ancient Hetruria; whose Palace of Piti at Florence [*when*] I came often to review, and still methought with fresh admiration; being incomparably (as far as I can yet speak by experience, or report) for solid architecture, the most magnificent and regular pile within the Christian world. It pleased him by means of the Cavalier Vinta, his principal secretary of estate, to take some notice of my person, though no intruder by nature, and (God knows) of little ability.

[61] A visit to the Palazzo Pitti and the Boboli Gardens in the mid-seventeenth century; from Richard Lassels's *Voyage of Italy* (1670).

This long *Corridor* [*the Vasari corridor from the Uffizi*] led us to the *new Pallace,* called the *Palazzo di Piti,* because it was begun to be built by *Luca Piti,* after the design of *Brunellischi:* but the expences growing too great for Piti's purse, it was bought by the Mother of great *Cosmus* the II, and afterwards carryed on by her to that perfection we now see it in, and which makes it one of the prime pallaces of *Europe.* The design of it (for it is not yet all quite built) is to be a perfect Roman H, with double roomes on all sides. As you ascend up to it, by an easy ascent from the Street, it presents you with a fair broad side of building, in which I counted two and twenty great windows all in a row, and all alike, and all of them cheekt up on either Side by Fine Stone Pillars. The fashion of the building in this Pallace, as in most of the best Pallaces of *Florence,* is that which they call in Architecture, *la maniera rustica*; where great freestones are made advanceing a little one over the other. Entering into the Pallace, we saw the fair Court; and in the end of it, the *Grotta* or Fountain with a larg basin, in which they keep fish for present use. This Court is squar, and open onely on one side towards the garden, but hedged in with a high terrass of stone, whose top is level with the ground of the Garden. Beyond this *terrass* and Court, lies a fine green spot of ground level with the first story of the pallace, and half compassed about with a demicircle of *laurel trees* high and thick. Under these trees of the demicircle, rise up stone seats, six rowes high, like the seats in an Amphitheater; and capable of two thousand men, who may all fit here with ease, and behold the sports of Cavalry which are often exhibited upon this fair green spot of ground by the nobility: the *Great Duke* and the Court beholding all this from the windows of the pallace, while the rest of the *Nobility* and *Ladies* are seated conveniently in the *Amphitheater* under the Trees. The rest of this garden is curiously set forth with thickets of bayes, close shady walkes, fine high open walkes overlooking both the Town and Country, great Ponds of water, a World of statues of Marble and Stone, a rare round basin of water, with Fountains, and much wetting sport, the place for Birds and Beasts; the curious *Ice-house* and cool Cellar under it, where the melting Ice dropping down upon the Barrels of Wine, refresh it so exceedingly, that in all my life time I never drunk so coole as I did at the Tap in this Cellar.

But to returne againe to the pallace, from whence this garden hath led me; from the Garden we ascended into the Chambers of the *Great Dukes* appartiment, and found them most sumptuous, both for contrivance and furniture. Some of them are painted over head by *Pietro di Cortona* the prime painter now living: others expect his returne againe from *Rome*, and scorne to be painted by any hand but his: in another Chamber we were shown the History of *Saleucus*, giving to his onely son *Antiochus* (languishing and pineing away with the love of his Mother in Law) his owne beloved wife *Stratonica*; shewing by this strange and unick example, that *paternal love* is greater then *Conjugal*. All this is rarely painted upon the wall over the hangings. In another chamber (the *Great Dukes* Chamber of Audience) I saw a Sute of Hangings valewed at a hundred and fifty thousand crownes: The Ground of them is Cloth of Gold, upon which are embrodered a world of *birds*, *beasts*, *flowers*, *trees*, *rivers*, *landskips* in silk and silver; and in such a rich manner, that I take this to be one of the fairest sutes of hangings in *Europe*. In another chamber here, I saw a rare collection of pictures, all originals, and of the best hands in the World, *Titians*, *Raphaels*, *Michael Angelos*, *Andrea del Sartos*, and many others. The best of them is that of *Raphael* and painted by his owne hand. This is the best collection of pictures that ever I saw, and it belongs to *Prince Leopold* the *Great Dukes* Brother, and a great *Virtuoso*. In the *Great Dutchesses* Chamber I saw half a dozen of excellent peeces of *Raphael* and others.

[62] A novel method of extracting a tip; from Johann Keysler's *Travels* . . .

(Johann Georg Keysler (1693–1743) was a German antiquarian and travelling tutor, whose *De Dea Nehelennia numine veterum Walachorum topico* earned him Fellowship of the Royal Society, and whose *Neueste Reisen* was translated into several languages.)

On the right of the entrance of this palace [*the Pitti*] lies a large magnet, which Spon makes to weigh five thousand pounds, but it has since been damaged by fire. The Swiss guards here, upon seeing any foreigners approaching, immediately run to rub their

A fountain in the Boboli Gardens

halbards on this load-stone, and afterwards hold them up with a
range of keys hanging to them by magnetism. This artifice for
getting a little money is excessively mean; but that the guards
should in plain terms here, and likewise at the Palazzo Vecchio,
teize strangers for a few pence, seems very little to comport with
the dignity and munifence of their master.

[63] The Earl of Cork meditates on the history of Palazzo
Pitti and, paraphrasing Bishop Berkeley, prophesies
American imperialism; from *Letters from Italy, in the years
1754 and 1755, by the late Right Honourable John Earl of Corke and
Orrery.*

(John Boyle, fifth Earl of Orrery (1707–1762) was the friend of
Swift, Pope and Johnson. As well as the posthumously published
Letters from Italy he is responsible for the *Remarks on Swift* and the
Translations of Letters of Pliny the Younger, both published in 1751.)

Luca Pitti verified his boast, but ruined his fortune. He built his
palace, and he erected a most magnificent front on the outside,
magnificent, but heavy; truly *Tuscan*, durable as the world
itself. . . . *Cosimo* I. whose riches and grandeur were boundless,
bought the palace *Pitti*, which, from his time till the total
extinction of his family, has been receiving additional ornaments
of every kind that can be named. Behind the palace is a large
garden, called *Boboli*, laid out in what is now deemed the old-
fashioned taste. I mean statues, fountains, long strait alleys, and
clipt hedges, or at least what were clipt hedges, the garden being
at present in a desolate, and almost a ruinous state. Heretofore
crowds of people have enlivened *Boboli:* of late it is totally
deserted. An amphitheatre of evergreens, formed and fitted
exactly to the garden-front of the palace, has a charming effect,
especially at this dead time of the year: they rise naturally,
gradually, and in variety of pleasing shades, one above another.
They are absolutely beyond the power of description. On the top
of one part of the garden is the great fort [*Belvedere*] which
defends the town. In another part a gentle ascent leads to a
banqueting-house, which commands a view of the whole city.
The banqueting-house is the plainest building imaginable. Such
an edifice would not be permitted to hold scythes or shovels, in

the gardens of *Stow, Chiswick*, or *Claremont*. I often walk amidst the novelty of this old taste. Now and then I light on some of my own countrymen, but seldom or never meet a *Florentine*. They are too lazy and too tender to walk in cold weather, and too polite, or rather of too *chichisbéan* [*see page 311*] a turn, to appear publicly without ladies. . . . The whole house is royal and splendid. One room, the bed-chamber of the late princess *Anna de Medici*, electress palatine, only daughter of *Cosmo* III. has chairs, tables, stools, and screens of solid silver; not so handsome, perhaps, as rich, singular, and extraordinary.

I confess, when I gaze on such profusion of wealth, so judiciously collected, and so carefully placed, now lying in empty rooms, and spread over desolated palaces, the sight strikes me rather with melancholy than pleasure. The dutchy of *Tuscany* and the city of *Florence* are of no more immediate consequence to me than the province of *Tangut* or the metropolis of *Huquang*, yet still I must be grieved to behold a state, that has once been glorious, once happy, once powerful, now mouldering away, panting its last, and sinking into nothing.

– – – *Fuit Ilium, et ingens*
  Gloria Teucrorum. – – –

Arts and sciences weep at the extinction of the house of *Medici*. The princes of that house were many of them learned; all of them encouragers of learning. '*Tuscany* was to *Italy*,' says monsieur *de Voltaire*, 'what *Athens* was to *Greece*.' What *Greece* is, *Tuscany* possibly may be, perhaps *Italy*, perhaps *Europe*. The ball of empire may hereafter roll westward, and may stop in *America*; a world, unknown when *Greece* was in its meridian glory; a world, that may save the tears of some future *Alexander*.

[64] An audience at Palazzo Pitti with the Grand Duke Leopold II; from Fenimore Cooper's *Gleanings in Europe*.

(James Fenimore Cooper (1789–1851), author of *The Last of the Mohicans*, was appointed US Consul in Lyons (1826–29) and then toured Switzerland and Italy.)

The time for quitting Florence having arrived, I wrote to ask an audience of leave of the royal family. The answer was favourable, the grand duke naming the following morning at the Pitti, and the grand duchess an hour a little later at the Poggio Imperiale, a palace just without the walls, and in the immediate vicinity of St. Illario.

Ten was the hour at which I presented myself at the Pitti, in an ordinary morning-dress, wearing shoes instead of boots. I was shown into an ante-chamber, where I was desired to take a seat. A servant soon after passed through the room with a salver, bearing a chocolate-cup and a bit of toast, a proof that his imperial highness had just been making a light breakfast. I was then told that the grand duke would receive me.

The door opened on a large room, shaped like a parallelogram, which had the appearance of a private library, or cabinet. There were tables, books, maps, drawings, and all the appliances of work. The library of the palace, however, is in another part of the edifice, and contains many thousand volumes, among which are some that are very precious, and their disposition is one of the most convenient, though not the most imposing as to show, of any library I know.

The grand duke was standing alone at the upper end of a long table that was covered by some drawings and plans of the *Maremme*, a part of his territories in reclaiming which he is said to be just now much occupied. As I entered, he advanced and gave me a very civil reception. I paid my compliments, and made an offering of a book which I had caused to be printed in Florence. This he accepted with great politeness; and then he told me, in the simplest manner, that 'his wife' was so ill, she could not see me that morning. I had a book for her imperial highness also, and he said it might be left at the Poggio Imperiale.

As soon as these little matters were disposed of, the grand duke walked to a small round table, in a corner, near which stood two chairs, and, requesting me to take one, he seated himself in the other, when he began a conversation that lasted near an hour. The prince was, as before, very curious on the subject of America, going over again some of the old topics. He spoke of Washington with great respect, and evidently felt no hostility to him on account of his political career. Indeed, I could not trace in the conversation of the prince the slightest evidence of a harsh feeling, distrust, or jealousy towards America; but, on the other hand, I thought he was disposed to view us kindly, – a thing so unusual among political men in Europe as to be worthy of mention. He left on my mind, at this interview, the same impression and integrity of feeling as at the other.

He observed that fewer Americans travelled now than formerly, he believed. So far from this, I told him, the number had greatly increased within the last few years. 'I used to see a good many,' he answered, 'but now I see but few.' I was obliged to tell him, what is the truth, – that most of those who came to Europe knew little of courts, that they did not give themselves time to see more than the commoner sights, and that they were but indifferent courtiers. He spoke highly of our ships, several of which he had seen at Leghorn, and on board of one or two of which he had actually been.

I found him better informed than usual on the subject of our history; though, of course, many of his notions had the usual European vagueness. He seemed aware, for instance, of the great difficulty with which we had to contend in the revolution, for the want of the commonest munitions of war, such as arms and powder. He related an anecdote of Washington connected with this subject, with a feeling and spirit that showed his sympathies were on the right side of that great question, on whichever side his policy might have been.

We had some conversation on the subject of the discovery of America, and I took the occasion to compliment him on there having been a Florentine concerned in that great enterprise [*Amerigo Vespucci*]; but he did not seem disposed to rob Columbus of any glory on account of his own countryman, though he admitted that the circumstances in a degree connected his own town with the event.

At length he rose, and I took my leave of him, after thanking him for the facilities that had been afforded me in Tuscany. When we separated, he went quietly to his maps; and as I turned at the door to make a parting salute, I found his eyes on the paper, as if he expected no such ceremony.

[65] Early nineteenth-century balls at Palazzo Pitti, hosted by Leopold II; from *What I Remember* by Thomas Adolphus Trollope.

(Thomas Adolphus Trollope (1810–1892) was the eldest son of a failed barrister and Frances Trollope, the novelist and author of the controversial *Domestic Manners of the Americans*. After America and Oxford he settled in Florence in the Villino Trollope in Piazza Independenza. He published many excellent books on Italian history and culture, but his reputation is overshadowed by that of his younger brother Anthony.)

No court dress was required save on the first day of the year . . . and no invitations were issued to foreigners save to a newcomer, it being understood that all who had been there once were welcome ever after. The Pitti balls were divided into two by a very handsome and abundant supper at which the guests used to behave abominably. The English would seize the plates of *bonbons* and empty the contents into their coat pockets. The ladies would do the same with their pocket handkerchiefs. But the Duke's liege subjects carried on their depredations on a far bolder scale. I have seen large portions of fish, sauce, and all, packed up in newspaper and deposited in a pocket. I have seen fowls and ham share the same fate, without any newspaper at all. I have seen jelly carefully wrapped in an Italian countess's laced *mouchoir*! I think the servants must have had orders not to allow entire bottles of wine to be carried away, for I never saw that attempted and can imagine no other reason why. The Grand Duke at these Pitti balls used to show himself and take part in them as little as might be. The Grand Duchess also would occasionally walk through the rooms; but her object, and indeed that of the Duke, seemed to be to attract as little attention as possible. His manner was about as bad and as unprincely as can well be conceived. His clothes never fitted him and he always appeared to be struggling painfully with the consciousness that he had nothing to say.

When strangers would venture some word of compliment on the prosperity and contentment of the Tuscans, his reply invariably was '*Sono tranquilli*' (they are quiet).

[69] The courtyard of Palazzo Pitti in the summer of 1944;
from Frederick Hartt's *Florentine Art under Fire.*

On August 11 the German forces defending the north bank of the
Arno in the centre of Florence withdrew to the periphery of the
city, leaving the major part of the town in the hands of the
Partisans but subject to sporadic shellfire. Only a few Allied
officers and their enlisted assistants were permitted into the
center of the city for the all-important purpose of bringing some
quantities, however small, of food, water, and medicine to the
stricken population. For nine days the inhabitants had been shut
up in their houses cut off from all public services by the blowing
up of the water mains, the gas and the light, always the last
graceful gesture of the Germans before leaving a city. . . .

After the complicated passes were completed and Franco and
I had lunched on rations under a pine tree, we started through
the crowded streets of Oltrarno for the Pitti Palace. From the
shade of Via Serragli with its overhanging eaves we drove
through crowds of liberated Florentines into the blazing sun of
Piazza Pitti and up the slope to the mountainous façade of the
palace. How many tourists from every country had once entered
that gate and gazed up through the courtyard of Ammanati at
the fountain playing against the sky, and to the cypresses and
oleanders of the Boboli gardens! Now the vast court was a
crawling mass of unfortunate humanity. The palace of the
Grand Dukes of Tuscany looked like the most crowded slum in
Naples. Mothers, babies, men, boys, with bundles of clothing
and mattresses and a few miserable belongings, lay under the
huge arches, swarmed through the courtyard and up the stairs,
screamed from the palace windows. Sheets and clothing hung in
quantities from every balcony. Here and there tables and even
little charcoal stoves were set up for the preparation of pathetic
meals. There was only one source of water in the palace, and
there were six thousand refugees who had come to find shelter in
these massive walls after the Germans had evacuated the whole
section of the city along the riverbanks. Even the royal
apartments had been put to use to accommodate this tide of
human misery, and the romantic walks of the Boboli Gardens
were used as a public toilet. It was months before the gardeners
got them clean again.

Palazzo Rucellai

[67] Criticism of Alberti's mid-fifteenth-century designs for the Palazzo and Loggia Rucellai; from Vasari's *Lives* . . .

For Cosimo Rucellai he made the design of the palace which he erected in the street called la Vigna, and that of the loggia opposite. In this he formed his arches over the narrow columns on the forward face, but as he wished to continue these and not make a single arch, he found he had too much space in every direction. Accordingly he was obliged to make brackets on the inside. When he came to the vaulting of the interior he found that to give it the sixth of a half-circle would result in cramped and awkward appearance, and so he decided to form small arches from one bracket to another. This lack of judgement and design proves that practice is necessary as well as theory, because the judgement can never be perfected unless knowledge is put into practice. It is said that he also made the design for the house and garden of these same Rucellai in the via della Scala . . .

[68] The festivities to celebrate the wedding of the 18-year-old son of Giovanni Rucellai with a sister of Lorenzo de' Medici in the Piazza Rucellai; from Giovanni Rucellai's *Zibaldone*, edited by Alessandro Perosa.

(Giovanni Rucellai (1403–1481) was a wealthy merchant and one of the leading patrons of architecture in mid-fifteenth-century Florence, commissioning Alberti to build his Palazzo, the façade of Santa Maria Novella and the Capella di San Sepolcro in San Pancrazio. The *Zibaldone* is a miscellany of memoirs and excerpts from his reading intended for his descendants. The manuscript once belonged to the nineteenth-century Anglo-Florentine, John Temple Leader.)

I hereby record that on the 8th of June 1466 we celebrated the marriage of my son Bernardo with his wife, Nannina, daughter of Piero di Cosimo de' Medici. She came to her husband accompanied by four knights, Manno Temperani, Carlo Pandolfini, Giovannozzo Pitti and Tommaso Soderini.

The party was held out of doors on a platform 1½ braccia [*just under a yard*] high and roughly 1600 braccia square, which filled the entire piazza across from our house and the loggia and the Via della Vigna [*Nuova*] right up to the walls of our house, constructed in the form of a triangle and hung with very beautiful cloths, tapestries, benches and supports and a ceiling above to keep off the sun made of turquoise cloths turned inside out adorned across the entire width with garlands of green foliage with roses in their midst and green festoons surrounding them with four escutcheons (half with the Medici arms and half with those of the Rucellai) and with many other adornments and above all a sideboard richly loaded with silver plate. The whole thing was generally considered to be the most beautiful and impressive display that had ever been prepared for a wedding feast and on the said platform people danced, celebrated and laid out tables to both lunch and dine. There were present at the said festivities fifty smart and richly dressed ladies and likewise thirty young men well turned out for the occasion. Between relations, friends and neighbours, about fifty of the most important citizens were invited to each meal so that at the first table when one includes women and unmarried girls, fifers and trumpeters, one hundred and seventy people sat down to dine, and at the second, third and fourth tables a multitude of people sat down to such a meal that five hundred were fed and for the repasts twenty confectioners [*distributing*] pine seeds and pumpkin cakes came outside onto the platform. The kitchen was established in the street behind our house, by closing it off from the Via della Vigna up to the corner where one turns to go to San Pancrazio, with boards. Here between cooks and scullions we had fifty people working. The expense was great . . .

Palazzo Strozzi

[69] A neighbour's-eye-view of the building of the Palazzo Strozzi during the late fifteenth century; from Luca Landucci's *Diario Fiorentino*.

(In May 1489 the Signoria granted exemption from taxes to those houses built within five years where building was not already in progress.)

10th July. They began to bring gravel to make the foundations of the *Palagio* of Filippo Strozzi, on the side of the *Canto de' Tornaquinci*, which was begun first on this side.

16th July. They began to dig the foundations on this side, and took about 10 *braccia* off the Piazza.

6th August. They began to fill in the foundations, at 10 in the morning [6 *a.m.*], here and there; and Filippo Strozzi was the first who began to throw down the gravel and chalk, on this side, together with certain medals.

20th August. They finished filling in the foundations on this side, in the *Piazza de' Tornaquinci*. And all this time they were demolishing the houses, a great number of overseers and workmen being employed, so that all the streets round were filled with heaps of stones and rubbish, and with mules and donkeys who were carrying away the rubbish and bringing gravel; making it difficult for anyone to pass along. We shopkeepers were continually annoyed by the dust and the crowds of people who collected to look on, and those who could not pass by with their beasts of burden.

21st July. They began to build the walls upon the aforesaid foundations.

And at this time all the following buildings were erected:

The *Osservanza di San Miniato de' Frati di San Francesco*; the sacristy of *Santo Spirito*; the house of Giulio Gondi; and the church of the *Frati di Sant' Agostino*, outside the *Porta a San Gallo*. And Lorenzo de' Medici began a palace at the *Poggio a Caiano*, on his property, where so much has been beautifully ordered, the *Cascine*, etc. Princely things! At Sarrezana a fortress was built; and many other houses were erected in Florence: in the street which goes to Santa Caterina, and towards the *Porta a Pinti*, and the *Via Nuova de' Servi*, at Cestello, and from the *Porta a Faenza* towards San Barnaba, and towards Sant' Ambrogio, and elsewhere. Men were crazy about building at this time, so that there was a scarcity of master-builders and of materials.

1490. 18th May. On the Palagio degli Strozzi they now placed the first cornice, below the *bozzi* (rough projecting stones), at the *Canto de' Tornaquinci*, always beginning at this corner before the others.

2nd June. They set up the crane for raising stones, always at the *Canto*.

11th June. They placed the first *bozzo* [*rough block of stone*] on the said *palagio*.

27th June. I, Luca Landucci, opened my new shop, here opposite the said *palagio* of the Strozzi, and I chose the sign of the *Stelle* [*Stars*]. The old shop at the other corner, which I left, belongs to the Rucellai, whilst this one belongs to the Popoleschi.

Palazzo Vecchio and
Piazza della Signoria

[70] The origins of the Palazzo Vecchio; from Nicolai Rubinstein's 'The Piazza della Signoria in Florence'.

The project to build a palace for the new government of Florence, the Priorate of the Guilds, is first recorded in 1285, three years after the Priorate was established, but the final decision to begin the building was not taken until 1298. During the intervening years, the Priors resided in rented houses which did not afford adequate protection at a time when the new popular regime was making determined efforts to suppress violence and lawlessness on the part of the Magnates. These efforts culminated in the Ordinances of Justice of 1293; yet as late as July 1294, the councils postponed a decision on the site of the new palace. These delays contrast with the large volume of legislation on constitutional and legal matters which took place during those years, and may, at least partly, be explained by the failure to resolve the question of the site of the palace. As early as 1290, it had been proposed in the general council of the Captain of the People that a decision on it be taken; in 1293, the Ordinances of Justice left it to the Priors to decide where they wanted to reside; over a year later, the council of One Hundred debated inconclusively 'super loco inveniendo, in quo . . . pallatium fieri debeat', and as late as December 1298, when the Priors in office until 14 February 1299 were given wide powers to start the building of the new palace, its site had not yet been settled, for they were put in charge of deciding, 'cum consilio sapientium virorum . . . in quo loco civitatis domini priores artium et vexillifer iustitie . . . residentiam facere debeant'.

There are no records of the deliberations which determined the Priors' final choice, but there can be little doubt that a major, if not the principal, reason for it was the availability, due to the demolition, about forty years earlier, of houses belonging to the Ghibelline Uberti, of an open space which could be used as a square. 'E colà dove puosono il detto palazzo', writes Giovanni Villani, 'furono anticamente le case degli Uberti . . . e di que' loro casolari feciono piazza'. Another reason was, probably, the vicinity of the existing communal palace, built under the previous popular regime of 1250 to 1260, in which the Podestà now resided.

This palace, the present Bargello, while bordering on the Piazza S. Apollinare, had no square of its own and faced, across the Via del Proconsolo, the Badia. Civic buildings in some Northern Italian towns, on the other hand, faced wide open

The courtyard of the Palazzo Vecchio

spaces, as did, by the time the Priors reached their decision, the site of the new communal palace in Siena. Examples such as these may well have influenced their choice, although, unlike the Sienese, they did not choose the market square, the Mercato Vecchio, for the site of the new Florentine palace.

[71] Cellini falls foul of Eleanor of Toledo in the Palazzo Vecchio; from *The Life of Benvenuto Cellini*, by Cellini.

(Benvenuto Cellini (1500–1571) was an extremely talented goldsmith and sculptor and an equally talented autobiographer. His account of his extraordinary life, often considered far-fetched, is in fact found to be surprisingly truthful where verifiable. After employment in Rome under Clement VII and Paul III, and in France under Francis I, he returned to his native Florence where he cast the 'Perseus' for Cosimo I.)

In these days he [*Cosimo I*] was building those new rooms towards the [*Via dei*] Leoni; so that, when His Excellency wished to retire apart more privately, he had fitted up for him a certain small chamber in these newly built apartments, and he directed me that I should come to him by way of his Wardrobe, whereby I passed very privately across the gallery of the Great Hall, and by way of certain small closets I used to go to the said small chamber most privately: of which (privilege) in the space of a few days the Duchess deprived me, causing all those conveniences for me to be closed up; in such a way that every evening when I arrived at the Palace I had to wait a long time for the reason that the Duchess for her private convenience remained in those ante-chambers, through which I had to pass; and since she was ailing I never arrived at any time when I did not incommode her. Now for this and for another cause she conceived for me so much dislike, that for no reason could she bear to see me; but in spite of all this my great discomfort and infinite trouble, I continued patiently to go thither. The Duke had however given express commands upon the point, so that directly I rapped upon those doors they were opened to me, and without saying anything to me I was allowed to enter anywhere; in such a way that it happened sometimes that, entering quietly thus unexpectedly by way of those private apartments, I found the Duchess employed upon her own private affairs; who immediately burst out upon me with so much angry fury, that I was terrified, and she kept always saying to me; 'When will you ever finish repairing those little figures? For I am now excessively annoyed at this coming and going of yours.' At which I gently answered: 'My lady! My sole patroness! I wish for nothing else but to serve you faithfully and with the utmost obedience. But since these commissions which the Duke has ordered of me will last for many months, will Your Most Illustrious Excellency tell me if you do not wish me to come here any more. I will not come for any reason whatsoever, let who will summon me. And although the Duke should summon me I will say that I am ill, and in no sort of way will I ever come here.' To these words of mine she replied: 'I do not tell you not to come here, and I do not tell you not to obey the Duke. But it appears plainly to me that these works of yours will never have an end.' Whether the Duke received some information about it, or that it fell out in some other way, His Excellency began again; as soon as it drew near to 24 of the clock he used to send to summon me; and the person who came to summon me said to me: 'I warn you not to fail to come, for the Duke is waiting for you:' and thus I continued under the same difficulties for several evenings. And upon one evening amongst the others, on entering according to my custom, the Duke, who must have been talking with the Duchess, perhaps upon private matters, turned upon me with the greatest fury in the world; and when I, somewhat terrified, wished to withdraw quickly, all of a sudden he said: 'Enter, Benvenuto! and go on with your work, and in a little while I will come and join you.' . . . Another evening, when I had finished those four small bronze figures, which are inserted into the base [*of the Perseus*] – which are *Jove, Mercury, Minerva* and *Danae with her little Perseus seated at her feet* – having had them brought into the said chamber where I worked in the evening, I set them in a row a little higher than the point of vision, in such a way that they made a most beautiful effect. The Duke having heard of this, came thither somewhat sooner than was his custom. And since that individual who informed His Most Illustrious Excellency must have reckoned them much higher than what they were (for he told him that they were better than antiques and such similar things), my Duke came, along with the Duchess, chatting cheerily about my work; and I rising immediately went to meet them. . . . Then they both sat down opposite the said statuettes, and for more than two hours they talked of nothing else but these beautiful little figures; in such a way that there came to the Duchess so immoderate a desire that she thereupon said to me: 'I do not want these beautiful little figures to go and be lost upon that base down in the Piazza, where they will run the risk of being injured. Rather do I wish you to arrange them for me in one of my apartments, where they will be preserved with that reverence which their very rare merits deserve.' To these words I raised opposition with many elaborate arguments, and when I saw that she was resolved that I should not place them in the base where they now are, I waited until the following day. And I went into the Palace at 22 of the clock, and finding that the Duke and Duchess were out riding, having already prepared my base, I had the little figures brought down and immediately soldered them in as they were intended to be. Oh! When the Duchess heard of it her anger grew so violent, that if it had not been for the Duke who skilfully assisted me, I should have caused her much harm. . .

[72] The government of Florence under Francis of Lorraine who, in 1745, had also become Emperor of Germany; from *Letters from Italy, in the years 1754 and 1755, by the late Right Honourable John Earl of Corke and Orrery.*

The present government of *Florence* is under the name of the emperor. The immediate exercise of the government is under count *Richecourt*, who lives in the *Old Palace* [*Palazzo Vecchio*] and has all the authority he can desire, and as the *Florentines* think, much more than he deserves. He is of a chearful aspect, and of a most princely personage; yet something sinister and obscure may be perceived in his countenance. He seems little inclined to the *English*; less indeed than is consistent with politeness. He is severe, just, and regular in his administration; rather inexorable than indulgent; a man of business; of a clear, comprehensive understanding, proud, and as the *Florentines* affirm, lucrative and tyrannical. Great allowances must be made for their prejudices against him. He is a *Lorrainese*; the shadow, not the substance of a sovereign; and he succeeds a man of a much milder, and more obsequious disposition, the prince *de Craon*, who resigned the reins of power unwillingly, and did not long survive the resignation.

The present frame of government is supported by a regency, which consists of a *Triumvirate*. Count *Richecourt* has no other title than 'the first of the regency.'

[73] The Commune's lions produce surviving offspring in the Piazza della Signoria, outside what are now the Uffizi; from Giovanni Villani's *Croniche Fiorentine*.

(What remains of San Pier Scheraggio, once the second largest church in Florence, is to be seen beyond the ticket office in the entrance hall of the Uffizi. Florence's lions continued to be maintained in this area for centuries, the Grand Dukes keeping up the tradition no less enthusiastically. Villani's new scepticism about at least one medieval myth – that lion cubs were born dead and raised to life by the parent's roar – is worth noting.)

In Florence that same year 1331 on the 25th of July – St Jame's Day – the Commune's lion and lioness, who were kept in a cage outside the church of San Pietro Scheraggio, had two cubs which lived and grew big. These were born alive – not dead as they say in the bestiaries; I can vouch for that, since I and a number of other townspeople saw them go and suck milk from the lioness as soon as they had been born. People were amazed that lions should be born and survive on this side of the Mediterranean, and as far as anyone can recall it has not happened before. It is true that two were born in Venice, but they died shortly after. This, then, was seen by many as a sign of good and prosperous times for the city of Florence.

[74] The demands of the Ciompi in 1378; from *Cronache e memorie del tumulto dei Ciompi* (author anonymous) in Gene Brucker's *The Society of Renaissance Florence*.

[July 21, 1378] When the *popolo* and the guildsmen had seized the palace [*of the podestà*], they sent a message to the Signoria . . . that they wished to make certain demands by means of petitions, which were just and reasonable . . . They said that, for the peace and repose of the city, they wanted certain things which they had decided among themselves . . . and they begged the priors to have them read, and then to deliberate on them, and to present them to their colleges. . . .

The first chapter [*of the petition*] stated that the Lana guild would no longer have a [*police*] official of the guild. Another was that the combers, carders, trimmers, washers, and other cloth workers would have their own [*guild*] consuls, and would no longer be subject to the Lana guild. Another chapter [*stated that*] the Commune's funded debt would no longer pay interest, but the capital would be restored [*to the shareholders*] within twelve years. . . . Another chapter was that all outlaws and those who had been condemned by the Commune . . . except rebels and traitors would be pardoned. Moreover, all penalties involving a loss of limb would be cancelled, and those who were condemned would pay a money fine. . . . Furthermore, for two years none of the poor people could be prosecuted for debts of 50 florins or less. For a period of six months, no forced loans were to be levied. . . . And within that six months' period, a schedule for levying direct taxes [*estimo*] was to be compiled. . . .

The *popolo* entered the palace and [*the podestà*] departed, without any harm being done to him. They ascended the bell tower and placed there the emblem of the blacksmiths' guild, that is, the tongs. Then the banners of the other guilds, both great and small, were unfurled from the windows of the [*palace of*] the podestà, and also the standard of justice, but there was no flag of the Lana guild. Those inside the palace threw out and burned . . . every document which they found. And they remained there, all that day and night, in honour of God. Both rich and poor were there, each one to protect the standard of his guild.

The next morning the *popolo* brought the standard of justice from the palace and they marched, all armed, to the Piazza della Signoria, shouting: 'Long live the *popolo minuto!*' . . . Then they began to cry 'that the Signoria should leave, and if they didn't wish to depart, they would be taken to their homes.' Into the piazza came a certain Michele di Lando, a wool-comber, who was the son of Monna Simona, who sold provisions to the prisoners in the Stinche . . . and he was seized and the standard of justice placed in his hands. . . . Then the *popolo* ordered the priors to abandon the palace. It was well furnished with supplies necessary [*for defense*] but they were frightened men and they left [*the palace*], which was the best course. Then the *popolo* entered, taking with them the standard of justice . . . and they entered all the rooms and they found many ropes which [*the authorities*] had bought to hang the poor people. . . . Several young men climbed the bell tower and rang the bells to signal the victory which they had won in seizing the palace, in God's honour. Then they decided to do everything necessary to fortify themselves and to liberate the *popolo minuto*. Then they acclaimed the wool-comber, Michele di Lando, as *signore* and standard-bearer of justice, and he was *signore* for two days. . . . Then [*the popolo*] decided to call other priors who would be good comrades and who would fill up the office of those priors who had been expelled. And so by acclamation, they named eight priors and the Twelve and the [*Sixteen*] standard-bearers. . . .

When they wished to convene a council, these priors called together the colleges and the consuls of the guilds. . . . This council enacted a decree that everyone who had been proscribed as a Ghibelline since 1357 was to be restored to Guelf status. . . . And this was done to give a part to more people, and so that each would be content, and each would have a share of the offices, and so that all of the citizens would be united. Thus poor men would have their due, for they have always borne the expenses [*of government*], and only the rich have profited.

. . . And they deliberated to expand the lower guilds, and where there had been fourteen, there would now be seventeen, and thus they would be stronger, and this was done. The first new guild comprised those who worked in the woolen industry: factors, brokers in wool and in thread, workers who were employed in the dye shops and the stretching sheds, menders, sorters, shearers, beaters, combers, and weavers. These were all banded together, some nine thousand men. . . . The second guild was made up of dyers, washers, carders, and makers of combs. . . . In the third guild were menders, trimmers, stretch-ers, washers, shirtmakers, tailors, stocking-makers, and makers of flags. . . . So all together, the lower guilds increased by some thirteen thousand men.

The lord priors and the colleges decided to burn the old Communal scrutiny lists, and this was done. Then a new scrutiny was held. The Offices were divided as follows: the [*seven*] greater guilds had three priors; the fourteen [*lower*] guilds had another three, and the three new guilds had three priors. And so a new scrutiny was completed, which satisfied many who had never before had any share of the offices, and had always borne the expenses.

[75] Exotic animals in the Piazza della Signoria given as diplomatic gifts; from Luca Landucci's *Diario Fiorentino*.

11th November [*1487*]. Certain animals arrived here, which were supposed to have been sent by the sultan; afterwards we heard, however, that they came from some good friends of Florence, who hoped to be duly rewarded. The animals were as follows: a very tall giraffe, beautiful and graceful; her picture can be seen painted in many parts of Florence, as she lived here for many years. Also a large lion, a goat, and some very strange wethers.

12th November. There was an attendant who looked after the lions, and with whom they were quite tame, so that he could go into their cages and touch them, especially one of them; and just lately, a boy of about fourteen, son of one of the Giuntini, a Florentine citizen, wished to enter the lions' cage with this tamer. But after he had been inside a little while, this lion threw himself upon him, seizing him by the back of the head; and it was only with difficulty, by shouting at the beast, that the tamer got him away. But the lion had so torn and mauled the boy, that he died in a few days.

18th November. The aforesaid ambassador of the sultan presented to the *Signoria* the giraffe, lion, and other beasts; and he sat in the midst of the *Signoria*, on the *ringhiera*, he speaking and they thanking him by means of an interpreter. A great crowd had collected in the Piazza that morning to see this. The *ringhiera* was decorated with *spalliere* [*cloth hangings*] and carpets, and all the principal citizens had taken their places upon it. This ambassador remained here several months, and was maintained at our cost and presented with many gifts.

[76] The execution of Savonarola in the Piazza della Signoria, May 1498; from Luca Landucci's *Diario Fiorentino*.

19th May. The Pope's envoy and the General of San Marco arrived in Florence, in order to examine Fra Girolamo [*Savonarola*].

20th May (Sunday). This envoy had him put to the rack, and before he was drawn up he asked him whether the things that he had confessed were true; and the *Frate* replied that they were not, and that he was sent by God. And then they put him on the rack, and he confessed that he was a sinner, the same as he had said before.

22nd May. It was decided that he should be put to death, and that he should be burnt alive. In the evening a scaffold was made, which covered the whole *ringhiera* of the *Palagio de' Signori*, and then a scaffolding which began at the *ringhiera* next to the 'lion' and reached into the middle of the Piazza, towards the *Tetto de' Pisani*; and here was erected a solid piece of wood many *braccia* high, and round this a large circular platform. On the aforesaid piece of wood was placed a horizontal one in the shape of a cross; but people noticing it, said; 'They are going to crucify him'; and when these murmurs were heard, orders were given to saw off part of the wood, so that it should not look like a cross.

22nd May (Wednesday morning). The sacrifice of the three *Frati* was made. They took them out of the *Palagio* and brought them on to the *ringhiera*, where were assembled the '*Eight*' and the *Collegi*, the papal envoy, the General of the Dominicans, and many canons, priests and monks of divers Orders, and the Bishop of the *Pagagliotti* who was deputed to degrade the three *Frati*; and here on the *ringhiera* the said ceremony was to be performed. They were robed in all their vestments, which were taken off one by one, with the appropriate words for the degradation, it being constantly affirmed that Fra Girolamo was a heretic and schismatic, and on this account condemned to be burnt; then their faces and hands were shaved, as is customary in this ceremony.

When this was completed, they left the *Frati* in the hands of the 'Eight', who immediately made the decision that they should be hung and burnt; and they were led straight on to the platform at the foot of the cross. The first to be executed was Fra Silvestro, who was hung to the post and one arm of the cross, and there not being much drop, he suffered for some time, repeating 'Jesu' many times whilst he was hanging, for the rope did not draw tight nor run well. The second was Fra Domenico of Pescia, who also kept saying 'Jesu'; and the third was the *Frate* called a heretic, who did not speak aloud, but to himself, and so he was hung. This all happened without a word from one of them,

The execution of Savonarola in the Piazzo della Signoria,detail
from an early sixteenth-century painting

which was considered extraordinary, especially by good and
thoughtful people, who were much disappointed, as everyone
had been expecting some signs, and desired the glory of God, the
beginning of righteous life, the renovation of the Church, and the
conversion of unbelievers; hence they were not without bitter-
ness and not one of them made an excuse. Many, in fact, fell from

their faith. When all three were hung, Fra Girolamo being in the middle, facing the *Palagio*, the scaffold was separated from the *ringhiera*, and a fire was made on the circular platform round the cross, upon which gunpowder was put and set alight, so that the said fire burst out with a noise of rockets and cracking. In a few hours they were burnt, their legs and arms gradually dropping off; part of their bodies remaining hanging to the chains, a quantity of stones were thrown to make them fall, as there was a fear of the people getting hold of them; and then the hangman and those whose business it was, hacked down the post and burnt it on the ground, bringing a lot of brushwood, and stirring the fire up over the dead bodies, so that the very last piece was consumed. Then they fetched carts, and accompanied by the mace-bearers, carried the last bit of dust to the Arno, by the Ponte Vecchio, in order that no remains should be found. Nevertheless, a few good men had so much faith that they gathered some of the floating ashes together, in fear and secrecy, because it was as much as one's life was worth to say a word, so anxious were the authorities to destroy every relic.

26th May. Certain women were found kneeling in the Piazza on the spot where the *Frati* had been burnt, out of veneration.

27th May. The papal envoy gave notice that anyone who had writings of the *Frate* was to bring them to him in San Piero Scheraggio, to be burnt, on pain of excommunication, and also the red crosses. Many were brought to him; and afterwards everyone mocked about it, because no heresy was found in anything of his.

[77] An eye-witness account of the installation of the 'David' outside the Palazzo Vecchio in 1504; from Luca Landucci's *Diario Fiorentino*.

14th May. The marble giant was taken out of the *Opera* [*del Duomo*]; it was brought out at 24 in the evening [*8 p.m.*], and they had to break down the wall above the door so that it could come through. During the night stones were thrown at the giant to injure it, therefore it was necessary to keep watch over it. It went very slowly, being bound in an erect position, and suspended so that it did not touch the ground with its feet. There were immensely strong beams, constructed with great skill; and

it took four days to reach the Piazza, arriving there on the 18th at
12 in the morning [*8 a.m.*]. It was moved along by more than 40
men. Beneath it there were 14 greased beams, which were
changed from hand to hand; and they laboured till the 8th July,
1504, to place it on the *ringhiera*, where the 'Judith' had been,
which was now removed and placed inside the *Palagio* [*Palazzo
Vecchio*] in the court. The said giant had been made by
Michelangelo Buonarrotti.

[78] A wild-beast hunt in the Piazza della Signoria in
1514; from Luca Landucci's *Diario Fiorentino*.

25th June. There was a hunt in the *Piazza de' Signori*: two lions,
and bears, leopards, bulls, buffaloes, stags, and many other wild
animals of various kinds, and horses; the lions were brought in
after the rest, and chiefly the one that came first did nothing, on
account of the great tumult of the crowd; except that certain big
dogs approaching him, he seized one with his paw and dropped
it dead on the ground, and a second one the same, without taking
any notice of the other wild beasts; when he was not molested, he
stood quite still, and then went away further on. They had made
a tortoise and a porcupine, inside of which were men who made
them move along on wheels all over the Piazza, and kept
thrusting at the animals with their lances. This hunt was thought
so much of, that the number of wooden platforms and enclosures
made in the Piazza was a thing never before seen, the cost of
bringing the timber and of erecting these stands being very great;
it seemed incredible that any city in the world could have such a
mass of timber. One carpenter paid 40 gold florins for the
permission to put up a platform against one of these houses, and
there were people who paid three or four *grossoni* [*grossone = about
⅓ of a florin*] for a place on the stands. All the stands and enclosures
were crowded, as also the windows and the roofs, such a
concourse of people never having been known, for numbers of
strangers had come from different parts. Four cardinals had
come from Rome disguised, and many Romans accompanied by
a quantity of horsemen. At the end of the evening it was found
that many men had been injured and about three killed in
fighting with wild beasts; one had been killed by a buffalo. They
had made a beautiful large fountain in the middle of the Piazza,

which threw water up in four jets, and round this fountain was a wood of verdure, with certain dens very convenient for the animals to hide in, and low troughs full of water round the fountain, for them to be able to drink. Everything had been very well arranged, except that someone without the fear of God did an abominable thing in this Piazza, in the presence of 40 thousand women and girls, putting a mare into the enclosure together with the horses; which much displeased decent and well-behaved people and I believe that it displeased even the ill-behaved people. Finally the lions made no more attacks, becoming cowed by the immense tumult of people. I remember another time when the same sort of hunt was made, more than 60 years ago, two lions also being brought in; and in the first attack one of them threw himself upon a horse, and caught hold of him in the soft part of his body, and the powerful horse, being terrified, dragged him from the *Mercatantia* to the middle of the Piazza; the lion got nothing but the mouthful of skin that was torn off; and this fact caused such a tumult, that the said lion was frightened and went and sat in a corner, and neither he nor the second one would make another attack. Which shows that there cannot be a display amidst the tumult of people. That earlier hunt had been held on the occasion of the Duke of Milan coming to Florence.

[79] An eight-sided temple built by Antonio da Sangallo the Elder as part of the celebrations to welcome the Medici Pope Leo X to Florence in 1515; from Luca Landucci's *Diario Fiorentino*.

The fifth [*of the specially created 'sights'*] was in the Piazza de' Signori, at the corner by the Lion [*the Marzocco at the north-west corner of the* ringhiera *around the Palazzo Vecchio*], where the design was so beautiful that one could not wish to better it. There was a sort of quadrangle, with four triumphal arches, under which one could pass crosswise in two directions, and at each corner there were two high and wide bases, on each of which stood a column, making eight columns, each more than 16 braccia [*about 30 feet*] high with its architrave, and the requisite cornices. The whole looked like marble, more perfectly arranged than one can imagine. It would be difficult for any city to make even this one edifice; it was so pleasing to the eye, that it was a pity to see it taken down, with all those wonderful figures by good masters.

[80] San Giovanni 1581: the Festa degli Omaggi in front of the Palazzo Vecchio; from Michel de Montaigne's *Journal du Voyage en Italie*.

The Saturday, is San Giovanni itself, Florence's principal holiday and the most famous, so much so that on that day even the virgins appear in public though I still didn't see any great beauties. In the morning in the piazza of the palazzo [*Vecchio*] the Grand Duke appeared on a platform which stretched the entire length of the wall of the palazzo under a baldaquin, and was adorned with very costly tapestries, having on his left the Papal Nuncio and much further away, the Ferrarese ambassador. Before him passed all his territories and castles as they were called by a herald. Thus Siena presented itself as a young man dressed in black and white velvet, carrying a great silver vase and the figure of the Sienese she-wolf. In this way he made his offering to the Grand Duke and a little speech. When this one had finished there came forward as they were called certain badly dressed boys on terrible-looking horses and mules, this one carrying a silver cup, another a torn and ruined flag. These came past in large numbers, and went on their way without making a speech, and without respect or ceremony, more as if they were joking than anything else; and these represented the castles and other places dependent on the State of Siena. For form's sake they repeat this every year.

There also passed by a cart and large wooden pyramid with a variety of putti ranged around it, some dressed in one way and some in another, as angels or saints, and at the top, which was as high as the tallest houses, was a man dressed as San Giovanni, bound to a piece of iron. This cart was followed by the officials, especially those of the mint.

Behind all this came another cart on which stood certain youths carrying three prizes for the various races, having at their side the Barbary horses which were to race that day and the boys who were to ride them, each with the livery of their masters, who are the leading citizens. The horses are small and beautiful. [*Later on*] the palace of the Grand Duke was open and full of

The Festa degli Omaggi in the Piazza della Signoria in the mid-
eighteenth century; by Giuseppe Zocchi

peasants to whom everything was available. The great hall [*Sala dei Cinquecento*] was full of different kinds of dancing, some here, some there. I believe that this sort of people thus get a glimpse of their lost liberty which is refreshed at this principal festival of the city.

[81] The casting of the 'Perseus' – the success of which endeavour Cosimo I had doubted; from *The Life of Benvenuto Cellini* by Cellini.
(*The 'Perseus' is now in the Loggia dei Lanzi.*)

In spite of all this I promised myself for certain that when I had finished the work of *Perseus* that I had begun, all my tribulations ought to be converted into highest pleasure and glorious well-

being. And so having recovered my energy, with all my forces
both of body and of purse, – although only a few coins remained
to me, – I began to endeavour to procure several loads of pine-
wood, which I got from the pine groves of the Seristori near
Monte Lupo. And whilst I was waiting for them I clad my [*wax*]
Perseus in those clays that I had prepared several months
previously, in order that they might be in their proper condition.
And when I had made his clay tunic [*tonaca di terra*] – for they call
it *tonaca* in the profession – and had very thoroughly supplied and
girdled it round with great care with iron supports, I began with
a slow fire to withdraw the wax, which issued through the many
vents that I had made: for the more one makes so much the better
do the moulds fill. And when I had finished removing the wax I
made a funnel around my *Perseus*; that is to say, around the said
mould, of bricks interlacing one above the other, and I left many
spaces, through which the fire could the better emerge. Then I
began to arrange the wood cautiously, and I kept up the fire two
days and two nights continuously; to such purpose that when all
the wax had been extracted, and the said mould was afterwards
well baked, I immediately began to dig the ditch wherein to bury
my mould, with all those skilful methods that this fine art directs
us. When I had finished digging the said ditch, I then took my
mould and with the assistance of windlasses and strong ropes I set
it carefully upright: and having suspended it a *braccio* above the
level of my furnace, holding it very carefully upright, in such a
fashion that it hung exactly in the middle of the ditch, I caused it
to descend very gently as far as the bottom of the furnace; and I
set it down with all the care that it is possible to imagine in the
world. And when I had completed this excellent job I began to
prop it up with the selfsame clay that I had dug out of it; and
hand over hand as I piled up the earth, I put into it air-holes
which were tubes of baked clay such as they use for water and
other similar purposes. When I saw that it was thoroughly firm,
as well as that method of filling it in, together with the placing of
those conduit pipes properly in their places and that those
workmen of mine had well understood my plan, the which was
very diverse from that of all the other masters in such a
profession; being assured that I could put my confidence in
them, I turned to my furnace, which I had made them fill with
many lumps of copper and other pieces of bronze. And having
piled the one upon the top of the other after the fashion that our

profession indicates to us, that is to say raised up, so as to make a way for the flames of the fire, whereby the said metal derives its heat quicker, and by it melts and becomes reduced to liquid [*riduciesi in bagnio*], I then cheerily told them to set light to the said furnace. And laying on those pieces of pine wood, which from the greasiness of that resin which the pine tree exudes, and from the fact that my little furnace was so well built, it acted so well that I was obliged to run about now upon one side and now upon the other with so much fatigue as was insupportable to me: but nevertheless I kept it up. And it chanced to me besides that the workshop took fire, and we were afraid lest the roof should fall upon us. From the other side towards the kitchen garden the heaven projected upon me so much water and wind, that it cooled my furnace. Combatting thus for several hours with these perverse chances, employing so much more effort than my strong vigour of constitution could possibly sustain; in such a way there sprang upon me a sudden fever, the greatest that can possibly be imagined in the world, by reason of which I was forced to go and throw myself into my bed. . . . [*Cellini lies exhausted and feverish in bed, leaving the work to his assistants, until one comes crying that the work is spoiled*] . . . Directly I heard the words of that wretch, I uttered a cry so loud that it might have been heard from the firmament of fire: and raising myself from the bed I seized my clothes and began to dress myself. And to the maid-servants, and my boy, and every one who approached to assist me, to all I gave kicks or blows; and I lamented saying: 'You traitors, and envious ones! This is a betrayal made on purpose. But I swear by God that I will understand it thoroughly, and that before I die I will leave such a proof of myself to the world that more than one of you will remain in astonishment.' Having finished dressing myself I went in an angry spirit towards my workshop, where I saw all those people whom I had left with so much courage: all stood astonished and terrified. I began by saying: 'Up! Listen to me! And since you have not either known how, nor wanted to obey me after the fashion that I instructed you, obey me now that I am with you in the presence of my own work, and do not let any one contradict me, for such cases as these have need of help and not of advice.' To these words of mine there replied a certain Alessandro Lastricati, and he said: 'See here! Benvenuto! you want to set about an undertaking, which the Profession does not allow of; nor can it be done by any means whatsoever.' At these

words I turned round with such fury, resolved on mischief, so
that he and all the others all with one voice said: 'Up! Give us
your orders, for we will all help you as much as you can order us,
as long as we can endure it with our lives:' and I think that they
uttered these kindly words supposing that I must after a very
little time fall down dead. I went immediately to look at the
furnace and saw the metal congealed; a thing which they call
'being made into a cake' [*l'essersi fatto un migliaccio*]. I told two
labourers to go opposite into the house of Capretta, the butcher,
for a load of young oak boughs, that had been dried for more
than a year, the which wood Mª Ginevra, the wife of the said
Capretta, had offered me: and when the first armfuls had come I
began to fill the grate. And because oak of that kind makes a
fiercer fire than any other sort of wood (wherefore they employ
alder and pine wood for founding artillery, because it makes a
gentle fire); oh! when the cake began to feel that tremendous fire
it began to clear, and it became luminous. On the other hand I
was looking after the channels: and I had sent others (workmen)
up on to the roof to keep off the flame, which on account of the
greater force of that fire had kindled more violently; and on the
side of the kitchen garden I caused to be erected certain boards
and some carpets and coarse cloths, which sheltered me from the
water. After that I had provided a remedy for all these great
disasters, with a very loud voice I kept shouting, now to this man,
and now to that: 'Bring this here!' and 'Take that away!' in such
a way that, when they saw the said cake begin to liquefy, all that
troop obeyed me with such good will that each one did the work
of three. Then I made them take half a pig of pewter [*pane di
stagnio*], which weighed about sixty pounds, and I threw it in
upon the cake within the furnace, which, together with the other
ingredients and the wood, by stirring it up, now with irons, and
now with bars, in a short space of time became liquid. Now
seeing that I had restored the dead to life, against the belief of all
those ignorant people, there returned to me so much vigour that
I did not perceive that I had any more fever, or any more fear of
death. All of a sudden I heard a loud noise with a very great flash
of flame, which seemed exactly as if a bolt had been discharged
there in our presence; by the which unaccustomed appalling
fright every one was terrified, and I more than the others. When
that great noise and flash had passed, we began to look one
another in the face again; and when we saw that the cover of the

The 'Perseus' by Benvenuto Cellini

furnace had burst, and had been lifted in such a way that the bronze was overflowing, immediately I made them open the mouths of my mould, and at the same time I made them drive in the two plugs. And when I saw that the metal did not run with that rapidity that it was accustomed to do, having recognized that the cause was perhaps that the alloy had been consumed by virtue of that terrible heat, I made them take all my plates and bowls and platters of pewter, which were in number about two hundred, and one by one I set them in front of my channels, and part I made them throw into the furnace; in such a way that when every one saw that my bronze had very thoroughly liquefied, and that my mould kept filling, they all assisted and obeyed me cheerfully and with joy; and, now here, now there, I kept giving orders, kept helping, and kept saying: 'Oh God! Who with Thy immense Power hast raised Thyself from the dead, and hast ascended glorious into Heaven; in the same way that in a moment my mould has filled itself. For the which reason I kneel to you and thank God with all my heart.' Then I turned to a plate of salad that was there on a low bench, and with a great appetite I ate and drank together with all that troop. Afterwards I went to bed healthy and joyful, for it was 2 hours before daybreak; and as if I had never had any ailment in the world, so peacefully did I repose.

[82] Preferring Bandinelli to Michelangelo in the Piazza della Signoria – mid-seventeenth century; from *Il Mercurio Italico* by John Raymond.

(John Raymond (born c. 1630) wrote what was in effect the first English guidebook to Italy following a tour made in the company of his cousin Alexander Chapman, and of his uncle and travelling tutor, Dr John Bargrave, who no doubt helped in its composition.)

Betwixt this horse [*Giambologna's equestrian statue of Cosimo I*] and the *Palazzo vecchio*, is a Fountaine, which all *Italy* cannot shew the like besides, round about the Laver is the family of Neptune in brasse, with his Colosse of Marble in the midst, bore up by foure horses; The whole not possible to be equald, much less excel'd by humaine art.

In this same *Piazza*, is a Porch [*the Loggia dei Lanzi*] archt and adorn'd with some statues, amongst which that of *Judith*, in brasse with that of the Rape of the *Sabines*, three Persons in severall Postures cut all out of one stone are most remarkable.

Just against it is the Palazzo Vecchio, at the entrance stands two Colosses, the one of David, the other of *Hercules* trampling on *Cacus*, the first of *Michael Angelo*, which in my judgement comes short of the other, though he is the more famous statuary.

[83] The Grand-ducal zoo in the early eighteenth century; from Johann Keysler's *Travels* . . .

Lions, tygers, panthers, bears, buffaloes, and such wild beasts, are kept in another part of the city, not far from St Mark's square, called Seraglio de' Lioni, every one of these having, before its den, a long piece of ground to walk in for air. Some years ago a tygress whelped here, but eat [*sic*] up her young ones as soon as she had brought them forth. The close for hunting these wild beasts is very well contrived, and at the conclusion of the sport they are driven into their dens again, by means of a large hollow machine resembling a dragon; for, by placing two or three men, with lighted torches in the belly of it, the fire seems to blaze through its open mouth and eyes, which so terrifies these creatures, that they are glad to run to any place of shelter whither they are driven.

[84] A sensitive mid-nineteenth-century appreciation of the sculpture in the Piazza; from Hippolyte Taine's *Italy*.

But when the eye passes from the Palazzo-Vecchio and turns to neighboring monuments there appears on all sides a joyous aspect and a love of beauty. The Loggia de'Lanzi on the right presents antique statues, bold, original figures of the sixteenth century – a 'Rape of the Sabines' by John of Bologna, a 'Judith' by Donatello, and the 'Perseus' of Cellini. The latter is a Grecian ephebos, a sort of nude Mercury of great simplicity of expression. The renaissance statuary certainly revives or continues the antique statuary, not the earliest, that of Phidias, who is calm and wholly divine, but the later, that of Lysippus who aims at the human. This Perseus is brother to the Discobulus and has had his actual anatomical model: his knees are a little heavy, and the veins of the arms are too prominent; the blood spouting from Medusa's neck forms a gross, full jet, the exact imitation of a decapitation. But what wonderful fidelity to nature! The woman is really dead; her limbs and joints have suddenly become relaxed; the arm hangs languidly, the body is contorted and the leg drawn up in agony. Underneath, on the pedestal, amidst garlands of flowers and goats' heads, in shell-shaped niches of the purest and most elegant taste, stand four exquisite bronze statuettes with all the living nudity of the antique.

I try to translate to myself this term *living*, which I find constantly on my lips, contemplating renaissance figures. It just came into my mind on looking at the fountain of Ammanati from the other side of the palace, consisting of nude Tritons and graceful Nereids, with heads too small, and grand elongated forms in action, like the figures of Rosso and Primaticcio. Art, of course, degenerates and becomes mannered, exaggerating the prancing and the display of the limbs, and altering proportions in order to render the body more spirited and elegant. And yet these figures belong to the same family as the others, and are living, like them; that is to say they freely and unconsciously enjoy physical existence, content in spreading out and in lifting up their legs, in falling backward and in a parade of themselves like splendid animals. The bestial Tritons are thoroughly jovial; there could not be more honest nudity and greater effrontery without baseness. They rear up, clutch each other, and force out their muscles; you feel that this satisfies them, that that fine young fellow is content to take a spirited attitude and to hold a cornucopia; that this nymph, undraped and passive, does not transcend in thought her condition of superb animality. There are no metaphysical symbols here, no pensive expressions. The sculptor suffers his heads to retain the simple, calm physiognomies of a primitive organization; the body and its pose are everything to him. He keeps within the limits of his art; its domain consists of the members of the body, and he cannot after all do more than accentuate torsos, thighs and necks; through this involuntary harmony of his thought and of his resources he animates his bronze and, for lack of this harmony, we no longer know how to do as much.

[85] The statues in the Piazza della Signoria – early twentieth century; from *Aaron's Rod* by D.H. Lawrence.

(David Herbert Lawrence (1885–1930) and his future wife Frieda von Richthofen, travelled through Europe and beyond, before and after the First World War, visiting Sicily, Sardinia, Australia, America and Mexico, and settling in Italy again when the tuberculosis which eventually killed him prevented further travelling.)

Michelangelo's 'David', now in the Galleria dell'Accademia

. . . in another minute he was passing between massive buildings, out into the Piazza della Signoria. There he stood still and looked round him in real surprise and real joy. The flat, empty square with its stone paving was all wet. The great buildings rose dark. The dark, sheer front of the Palazzo Vecchio went up like a cliff, to the battlements, and the slim tower soared dark and hawklike, crested, high above. And at the foot of the cliff stood the great naked David, white and stripped in the wet, white against the dark, warm-dark cliff of the building – and near, the heavy naked men of Bandinelli.

The first thing he had seen, as he turned into the square, was the back of one of these Bandinelli statues: a great naked man of marble, with a heavy back and strong naked flanks over which the water was trickling. And then to come immediately upon the David, so much whiter, glistening skin-white in the wet, standing a little forward, and shrinking.

He may be ugly, too naturalistic, too big, and anything else you like. But the David in the Piazza della Signoria, there under the dark great Palace, in the position Michelangelo chose for him, there, standing forward stripped and exposed and eternally half-shrinking, half-wishing to expose himself, he is the genius of Florence. The adolescent, the white, self-conscious, physical adolescent: enormous, in keeping with the stark, grim, enormous palace, which is dark and bare as he is white and bare. And behind, the big, lumpy Bandinelli men are in keeping too. They may be ugly – but they are there in their place, and they have their own lumpy reality. And this morning in the rain, standing unbroken, with the water trickling down their flanks and along the inner side of their great thighs, they were real enough, representing the undaunted physical nature of the heavier Florentines.

Aaron looked and looked at the three great naked men. David so much whiter, and standing forward, self-conscious: then at the great splendid front of the Palazzo Vecchio: and at the fountain splashing water upon its wet, wet figures; and the stone-flagged space of the grim square. And he felt that here he was in one of the world's living centres, here, in the Piazza della Signoria. The sense of having arrived – of having reached a perfect centre of the human world: this he had.

And so, satisfied, he turned round to look at the bronze Perseus which rose just above him. Benvenuto Cellini's dark hero looked female, with his plump hips and his waist, female and rather insignificant: graceful, and rather vulgar. The clownish Bandinellis were somehow more to the point. Then all the statuary in the Loggia! But that is a mistake. It looks too much like the yard of monumental mason.

Ponti (bridges)

[86] The building of the Ponte alla Carraia; from Giovanni Villani's *Croniche Fiorentine*.

In [*1218*] the foundations of the bastions of the ponte alla Carraia were begun . . . In 1220 . . . the building of the bridge was completed, and it was called the new bridge because in that time Florence had but two bridges, the Ponte Vecchio and this new one.

[87] How the Ponte alla Carraia collapsed and many people were thereby killed; from Giovanni Villani's *Croniche Fiorentine*.

On the first day of May, 1304, just as in the good old times of the tranquil and good estate of Florence, it had been the custom for companies and bands of pleasure-makers to go through the city rejoicing and making merry, so now again they assembled and met in divers parts of the city; and one district vied with the other which could invent and do the best. Among others, as of old was the custom, they of Borgo San Friano were wont to devise the newest and most varied pastimes; and they sent forth a proclamation that whosoever desired news of the other world should come on the 1st day of May upon the Carraia Bridge, and beside the Arno; and they erected upon the Arno a stage upon boats and vessels, and thereupon they made the similitude and figure of hell, with fires and other pains and sufferings, with men disguised as demons, horrible to behold, and others which had the appearance of naked souls, which seemed to be persons, and they were putting them to the said divers torments, with loud cries, and shrieks, and tumult, which seemed hateful and fearful to hear and to see; and by reason of this new pastime there came many citizens to look on, and the Carraia Bridge, which then was of wood from pile to pile, was so burdened with people that it gave way in many places, and fell with the people which were upon it, wherefore many were killed and drowned, and many were maimed; so that the pastime from sport became earnest, and, as the proclamation had said, many by death went to learn news of the other world, with great lamentation and sorrow to all the city, for each one believed he must have lost his son or his brother there; and this was a sign of future ill, which in a short time should come to our city through the exceeding wickedness of the citizens, as hereafter we shall make mention.

[88] The Ponte alle Grazie, formerly the Rubaconte; from Giovanni Villani's *Croniche Fiorentine*.

The year of Christ 1237, Messer Rubaconte da Mandello of Milan being Podestà of Florence, and he laid the first stone with his own hand, and threw the first trowelful of mortar, and from the name of the said Podestà the bridge was named Rubaconte. And during his Government all the roads in Florence were paved; for before there was little paving save in certain particular places, master streets being paved with bricks; and through this convenience and work the city of Florence became more clean and more beautiful and more healthy.

[89] The 1269 flood and how it carried away the Ponte Santa Trinita and the Ponte alla Carraia; from Giovanni Villani's *Croniche Fiorentine*.

In the said year 1269, on the night of the first of October, there was so great a flood of rain and waters from heaven, raining down continually for two nights and one day, that all the rivers of Italy increased more than had ever been known before; and the river of Arno overflowed its borders so beyond measure that a great part of the city of Florence became a lake, and this was by reason of much wood which the rivers brought down, which was caught and lay across at the foot of the Santa Trinita Bridge in such wise, that the water of the river was so stopped up that it spread through the city, whence many persons were drowned and many houses ruined. At last so great was the force of the river that it tore down the said bridge of Santa Trinita, and again by the disgorging thereof the rush of the water and of the timber struck and destroyed the Carraia Bridge; and when they were destroyed and cast down the height of the river, which had been kept up by the said retention and damming of the river, went

The Ponte Vecchio seen under Ammannati's
Ponte Santa Trinita

down, and the fulness of the water ceased which had spread
through the city.

[90] Ordering a piece of jewellery on the Ponte Vecchio in
1819; from Lady Morgan's *Italy*.

(The daughter of an actor, Lady Sydney Morgan, *née* Owenson
(1783–1859) made her name as a novelist and then went on to
write two of the most successful travel books of the nineteenth
century: *France* (1817) and *Italy* (1821). In Florence she and her
husband stayed at the Palazzo Corsini.)

At the *Tocco* (as one o'clock *p.m.* is termed in Florence,) [*the petty trader or shopkeeper*] shuts up his shop, which is not always his domicile, and retires to dine and dose for as long a time as appetite or weariness may induce. I remember giving a commission to one of the many goldsmiths who inhabit the *ponte vecchio*, and occupy the same sort of wooden bulks that roofed the ingenious *orefici* of former ages, which, by the manner and tardiness of its execution, illustrates the facts alluded to. Having explained most circumstantially the nature of the ornament I bespoke, sketched it with my pencil, and cut it out with my scissors, I left him with the full conviction that my order was understood, and would be well executed – a conviction impressed by the manner in which it was received; for while I stood before him, in all the eagerness of detail suited to the importance of the subject, he was squatted in an easy chair in a fine breathing heat after his siesta! – his thumbs twirling, his eyes closing and his answers laconically confined to '*Sara fatto!*' (It shall be done!) repeated every second. Calling on the following day to see how '*sara fatto*' was going on; to my inquiries the only answer I could obtain was, '*Veramente non mi ricordo niente, Signora mia,*' ('Truly I remember nothing of all this, my lady.') To stimulate his memory for the future, I wrote down the order in the best Italian I could muster; and the day was fixed for the delivery of the article, with a promise of punctuality, which all the saints were called on to witness; but that day, and many a following one passed, and the answer to all inquiries was, '*Sara fatto,*' and '*Pazienza, Signora cara mia!*' My *patience* and residence at Florence had nearly however expired together, when, a day or two before our departure, '*sara fatto*' entered my room with the long-expected *bandeau* glittering between his finger and thumb; and with a look of the most obvious triumph distending his apoplectic face, he exclaimed, '*Mirate, Signora! che gran bella cosa!! Questa è cosa per far stupire!! veramente è degna di nostro divino Benvenuto Cellini!!!*' ('See, Madam, what a beautiful thing! – a marvellous work! and worthy of our divine Benvenuto Cellini.') His self-approbation had now banished the languor of his habitual indolence; and the naïveté and hyperbole with which he applauded his own work, resembled the very manner, in the self-same dialect, with which '*Nostro divino Benvenuto*' charms his readers, and leads them back to the frank simplicity of the sixteenth century.

[91] The entry of Hitler into Florence in spring 1938; from *The Life and Death of Radclyffe Hall* by Lady Una Troubridge.

It was during the spring of 1938 when Mussolini brought him to Florence and such preparations were made for his reception as the Florentines are never likely to forget. From house to house across the narrow streets and across the façades of the ancient palaces were hung great swathes of evergreens studded with brightly-coloured fruits such as were beloved of Mantegna and Crivelli. Every house in the city, including our own, was supplied with silken flags, hand-painted and fringed, which displayed the devices of the city-guilds of Tuscany: dragons and tortoises, Lambs of God and geese mounted on velvet-covered halberds, hung beneath every window and formed a continuous archway across the Ponte Vecchio and the Por Santa Maria. And through this pageant of medieval beauty, standing beside him in a modern car driven at walking pace, through streets lined with angry Florentines who refused to applaud, in a silence no coercion could exorcise, the Duce drove with his honoured guest, Adolf Hitler. An unimpressive-looking little man with a nervous smile, he seemed sheepishly anxious to propitiate the Duce, who appeared to treat him rather cavalierly.

[92] Ugo Procacci's eye-witness account of the blowing up of the Florentine bridges in August 1944; from Frederick Hartt's *Florentine Art under Fire*.

Monday morning, I walked along the corridor which unites Palazzo Pitti to the Uffizi to see what was happening around the bridges. One had to go cautiously knowing that the Germans would certainly have fired upon whoever was found in the evacuated zone. I arrived at the arch of Via de' Bardi and looked toward Borgo San Jacopo. Two Germans were battering down the door of a house; as the door resisted, they stepped backward and quickly threw a hand grenade. The entrances to the houses ahead, nearer to Ponte Vecchio, appeared all broken open. In that moment I guessed everything which was to happen – in addition to the bridges, they were mining even the houses; they were going to blow up the ancient quarter of the city. I had to move back from the window because one of the German soldiers glanced in my direction. A lump closed my throat; there was nothing to hope for now. I looked at the bare walls of the corridor; I would never see them again. I returned toward Palazzo Pitti; I had tears in my eyes and my closed throat almost kept me from breathing. . . .

That evening I went out with my wife into the courtyard among the crowd of refugees. Suddenly, a little before nine, there was a formidable explosion; everything seemed to crumble and for a moment we thought it was the end. It seemed that the earth was trembling and that the great palace would be conquered from one moment to the next; at the same time from every side glass and pieces of window rained on the crowd, and the air became unbreathable. Terror seized the crowd; a few began to cry 'The bridges, the bridges!' This brought back a little calm. Most of the people fled immediately to the ground-floor rooms and to the shelters; the more courageous applied themselves to helping the wounded. My wife and I tried to run to our children who were left in the palace. A second explosion caught us while we were in a narrow corridor between two courtyards. We were beaten to the wall along with the other people.

In the apartment the children were calm; after a few minutes my brother arrived. From the height of the Boboli Gardens, where he was at the moment of the first explosion, he had seen a streak of smoke gliding above the Via Guicciardini to only a few score yards from the palace. Now there was nothing left to hope for. My thoughts rested on one thing only: Ponte Santa Trinita – if at least that were saved! This idea became almost a nightmare; it did not leave me, and often, shaking myself as from a state of unconsciousness, I found myself repeating, 'Ponte Santa Trinita, Ponte Santa Trinita, Ponte Santa Trinita.' For a few hours there were no more explosions. With my brother I went to the high rooms of the Palace toward the Arno; everything was shattered. I looked from the windows hoping to see something, but darkness enveloped all Florence. Toward midnight the explosions began again, loud but not terrifying like the first two, and they continued until dawn. In the early light I looked from a window onto the Piazza. There was no one, but in a moment from behind the wing of the palace toward Piazza San Felice came two Partisans. I opened the window and cried 'Where are the Germans?' 'There are none here any more, but they are still across the Arno!' came the answer. 'And the bridges?' 'All blown up except Ponte Vecchio.' 'Viva l'Italia!' cried one of the Partisans. 'Viva l'Italia!' I answered. But Italy no longer had the Ponte Santa Trinita! . . .

It was not possible to leave the palace by the front entrances; all the doors had been barred. I ran therefore into the Boboli Gardens, up, up, all the way to the Kaffeehaus. I climbed the stairs in haste. 'Don't look out!' cried a woman, 'The Germans are firing!' I looked out nonetheless and in the still feeble light of the early morning I saw the massacre of my Florence. The ruins of Oltrarno were there at a few paces. That marvelous panorama which for generations had been admired by the whole world showed a tremendous gash in a tragic foreground along the Arno around Ponte Vecchio, and the dust and smoke were still rising from the rubble. . . .

I had hardly returned to the palace when suddenly came the rumour, 'The Allies are here!' The crowd rushed to one side, I along with the others. On the grand staircase of the palace you could not pass. While I was trying to get through, suddenly on the landing of the staircase appeared an English soldier and an English officer, embraced on every side by the crowd. Everyone shouted enthusiasm and applauded; for a moment I forgot everything. A sort of delirium seized me; the abjection of more than twenty years, the agony of the last months were over. I was a free man again. With the others I began to applaud and shout frantically, and after the greatest of sorrows I experienced in that moment the greatest joy.

[93] The 1966 flood and the Ponte Vecchio; from Francis Steegmuller's 'A Letter from Florence'.

The only Florentines to be warned as a group were the jewellers with shops lining the Ponte Vecchio and the streets adjoining it. These merchants employed a private night watchman. At about one in the morning, he telephoned to the homes of those whom he could reach, and a number came, unlocked their shops, and filled their suitcases with what they could, the bridge trembling beneath them. Others, in the absence of any official warning, thought that their watchman was exaggerating, and went back to sleep. The jewellers who did come had to leave quickly; the water was already close, and, in addition to the trembling, there were frightening sharp reports, as though the bridge were cracking. The wife of one of the jewellers had said that when she and her husband arrived they found a number of noctambulous Florentines – some of them apparently hoodlums, some in cars with headlights pointed towards the scene – gathered at the end of the bridge, watching, as though hoping to see it break and collapse. The arrival of the jewellers with their suitcases was greeted with jeers. Two policemen were also standing there watching, and when the jeweller's wife angrily asked why they weren't out spreading the alarm, their answer was 'We have no orders.' The water continued to rise and about half the jewellery shops on the Ponte Vecchio are now gaping open – gutted by the tremendous force of a torrent that passed right through them. The worst damaged are those on the east side of the bridge; they took the full brunt of the current.

The flood damage to Florence has frequently been spoken of as 'worse than the war.' Apart from the physical differences of the two catastrophes, there can, of course, be no real comparison between deliberate destruction planned and executed by man against his fellows and a totally unlooked-for accident of nature. Even in the latter case, however, people are disposed to fix blame, at least for negligence. The knowledge that one small group of citizens was warned has done nothing to diminish the outcries of other Florentines, and charges are being loudly made in advance that the official investigations now under way will provide nothing but whitewash. But out of the mass of lamentations, accusations, and so-called 'evidence' that inevitably accumulates in the wake of such a disaster, a few details seem to be incontrovertible. First, the position of Florence is obviously a highly vulnerable one. At the bottom of a bowl of hills, it is watered by a river that during periods of rain and melting snow has always been swollen by tributaries from the deforested mountains among which it flows before reaching the city. One of these mountain tributaries, the Sieve, is particularly dangerous and has given rise to a Florentine proverb: *'Arno non cresce se Sieve non mesce'* – 'The Arno doesn't rise unless the Sieve rushes into it.' The only way to be sure of avoiding Florentine floods, someone has said, would be to move Florence.

Santissima Annunziata

[94] Michelozzo's tabernacle in Santissima Annunziata which contains the miracle-working painting of the Annunciation (said to have been finished by an angel); from the life of Michelozzo Michelozzi in Vasari's *Lives* . . .

Piero de' Medici next proposed to make the chapel of the Annunciation in the church of the Servites entirely in marble, and desired Michelozzo, who was by this time an old man, to give his opinion, both because he greatly admired his talents and also because he knew what a faithful friend and servant he had been to his father, Cosimo. When Michelozzo had complied, the charge of the work was entrusted to Pagno di Lapo Partigiani [*Portigiani*], sculptor of Fiesole, who had many things to take into consideration, as it was necessary to include a great deal in a small space. Four marble columns of about 9 braccia, double fluted and of Corinthian work, the bases and capitals being variously carved and the members doubled, support the chapel. Above the columns are laid architraves, a frieze and cornices, also double and carved, full of varied fancies and containing the device and arms of the Medici and foliage. Between these and the other cornices made for another row of windows there is a large inscription carved in beautiful marble. Below it, by the ceiling of the chapel and between the four columns, there is a marble slab richly carved with enamels worked in fire and mosaics with various fancies, of the colour of gold and precious stones. The pavement is full of porphyry and serpentine, mixed with other rare stones, well joined and tastefully arranged. The chapel is enclosed by a bronze grille [*by Maso di Bartolomeo*] with chandeliers above, all fixed to a marble framework, which makes a very fine finish to the bronze and chandeliers. The front exit from the chapel is also of bronze and excellently disposed. Piero left instructions that thirty silver lamps should be put about the chapel to light it, and this was done, but as they were destroyed in the siege the duke many years ago gave orders that they should be replaced. This has now been done for the most part and the work goes on. However, lamps have always been kept lighted there, as Piero directed, although they were not of silver. To these ornaments Pagno added a large copper lily which rises from a vase, which is placed at an angle of the cornice, and is made of painted wood, the part holding the lamps being overlaid with gold. However, the cornice alone does not bear this great weight, as the whole is sustained by two branches of the lily made of iron and painted green. These are fastened with lead into the marble angle of the cornice, holding the others, which are of copper, suspended in the air. This work was indeed carried out with judgment and invention, for which reason it deserves much admiration as a beautiful and ingenious production.

[95] John Evelyn admires Andrea del Sarto's Madonna del Sacco and describes the restoration of del Sarto's fresco of the funeral of San Filippo Benizzi in the forecourt of Santissima Annunziata, a few years before his visit; from Evelyn's *Diary*.

(Like many of his contemporaries, John Evelyn (1620–1706) avoided the Civil Wars by travelling on the Continent in the 1640s. As well as the famous *Diary*, he also wrote books on engraving and forestry, and edited others on painting, gardening and architecture.)

We could not forbeare in this Passage to revisite the same & other Curiosities which we had both seene & omitted at our first being at *Florence* [*i.e. on the way down to Rome and Naples*]. We went therefore to see that famous Piece of *Andrea del Sarto* in the Annunciata: The storie is that this Painter in a time of dirth borrow'd a sack of Corne of the Religious of that Convent, & being demanded to repay it, wrought it out in this Picture, which represents *Joseph* sitting on a Sack of Corn & reading to the B: *Virgin*, a piece infinitly valued: There fell downe in the Cloister [*dei Voti*] an old mans face painted in the wall in fresco, greatly esteemed, & brake all into crumbs: The *Duke* sent his best Painters to make another instead of it, but none of them would presume to touch a pencil, where *Andrea* had wrought, like another *Apelles*; but one of them [*Domenico Passignano*] was so industrious & patient, that picking up the fragments he laied & fastned them so artificialy together, as the injury it had received was hardly discernable: *Del Sarto* lies buried in the same place [*actually at the foot of the statue of St Peter to the left of Alberti's great arch within the church*].

[96] Albert Camus meditates among the tombs of Santissima Annunziata; from *Reflections on Florence*, edited by Simone Bargellini and Alice Scott.

(Albert Camus was born in Algeria in 1913. Despite persistent tuberculosis, he produced plays, journalism, and in 1942 the novel, *L'Étranger*, for which he is perhaps best known.)

The most repulsive materialism is not what we think it is, but that which wants to make us accept dead ideas for living realities, and to deform with sterile myths, that insistent, lucid attention we have attributed to that part of us which must perish forever.

I remember how in Florence, in the cloister of the dead in Santissima Annunziata, I was transported by a feeling I believed to be dismay, but which was really only anger. I was reading the inscriptions on the tombstones and votive offerings. One had been a tender father and faithful husband; another, both the best of husbands and a shrewd businessman. A young woman, paragon of all virtues, spoke French 'like a native'. Then there was a young girl who was the future hope of her parents, 'but joy in this world is fleeting'. And yet I was not struck by any of this. According to the inscriptions, they were all resigned to the idea of death, and without any perplexities, seeing that they had accepted other duties. That day, some children had invaded the cloisters and played leapfrog on the tombstones that were intended to perpetuate their virtues. Night fell; I sat on the ground against a column. A priest passing by smiled at me. The muffled playing of an organ came from inside the church and the warm tone of parts of the general tune emerged in between the shouting of children. Alone, leaning against the column, I felt like someone gripped at the nape of the neck shouting his faith as the last word. Everything inside me rebelled against such resignation. 'It is necessary', read the inscription. But it is not and my rebellion was right. That same joy that proceeded indifferent and enraptured like a pilgrim wandering in the world; it was necessary to follow it step by step. But for all the rest, I did not want it. I said no to it with all my strength.

The tombstones taught me that it was useless and that life goes with 'sunrise and sunset'. But still today I cannot see what uselessness my rebellion removes, and can see perfectly well instead what it adds.

Santa Croce

[97] An unsuccessful hunt in the Piazza Santa Croce to celebrate the baptism of the first son of the Grand Duke Francesco I; from Bastiano Arditi's *Diario di Firenze* . . .

(The anti-Medicean tailor, Bastiano Arditi, was born in 1504. He started his fascinating diary at the age of seventy and continued it for five and a half years until the winter of 1579–80 when he probably died.)

And on Sunday 29 [*September*] the son of Duke Francesco was baptised in San Giovanni. . . The following Tuesday, the first of October; they held a hunt in the Piazza Santa Croce with an infinite variety of animals, including bulls, deer, lions and other sorts, and they constructed platforms around the piazza, eight braccia high, to accommodate all the visitors who had come to see the baptism, with a gutter-like ditch to keep the lions at bay. It was an inane hunt, which no one enjoyed and no one praised.

[98] The celebration of carnival in the Piazza Santa Croce in 1819; from Antoine Laurent Castellan's *Letters on Italy*.

(The painter and author Antoine Laurent Castellan was born in Montpellier in 1772 and died in Paris in 1838. As well as the *Lettres sur l'Italie*, he published works on Greece, Turkish customs and painting techniques.)

The square of Santa Croce . . . is the great rendezvous of the masks. Its length, and the beauty of the palaces which surround it, fit it for the theatre of the festivals which are given in it, and which were formerly more frequent. Here were tiltings, and tourneys, and races, and lastly games at foot-ball. We have descriptions of many of these festivals; and, amongst others, of a magnificent masquerade given by Cosmo I. in the carnival of 1565: the carnival of 1615 has been engraved by Callot, and many others have exercised the graver of La Bella. The taste for these amusements was so great that during the reign of Ferdinand II. and in the space of five months, six fêtes of different kinds were given, each more magnificent than the preceding.

The square of Santa Croce is surrounded with a boundary of chains, which leave sufficient space for the passage of carriages before the houses. On certain occasions amphitheatres are raised, round which also carriages can drive. The square was thus laid out in 1738 for the last festival of the *Calzio* or foot-ball, which has been engraved by Gioseppe Zocchi. This print gives a good idea of the masquerades of Florence. Besides the harlequins and punchinellos, which the French have in such numbers, the other characters are very various and well kept up.

All ranks, without exception, are turned into ridicule. A carriage filled with porters has a judge dressed in a long robe and large wig, for a coachman. A physician is mounted on a lean ass, with panniers and cages filled with cats, and carrying a long staff, from which some large dead rats are suspended, while a scroll on the top of it bears the words *Remedi da topi*, 'antidotes against rats:' to these may be added doctors with asses' heads, &c. The spectators themselves form a spectacle; the windows of the houses, and the balconies of the palaces, are all ornamented with rich tapestry, and graced with brilliant company. The people cover the tiles of the houses, and on these aerial theatres engage in games, from which Italian confidence and address take away all danger, and which afford a very diverting appearance.

The spectacle which we ourselves saw was very agreeable. The carriages, which throng the road, give great brilliancy to the scene; they are filled with masks who answer the joy and acclamations of the multitude by throwing them cakes and *confetti*, and by sprinkling showers of perfumed water from little syringes towards the spectators who line the windows and the balconies: some of the carriages contain musicians, and others are in the shape of triumphal cars, ornamented with different symbols.

[99] A 1594 visit to Santa Croce and two tall stories about Michelangelo inspired by his tomb; from Fynes Moryson's *An Itinerary* . . .

Upon the wals of the Church S. Croce, is a monument of Arno overflowing, with this inscription in the Italian tongue: In the yeere 1333. the water of Arno overflowed to this height, and in the yeere 1557. to this, yet higher. In this Church is the sepulcher of Michaele Angelo Bonoritio, a most famous Engraver, Painter, and Builder, whose bones were brought from Rome, at the instance of Duke Cosmo, in the yeere 1570, and laid here. It is most certaine that he was most skilfull in those Arts, and of him the Italians greatly boast, and with all tell much of his fantasticke humours: namely, that when he painted the Popes Chappell, (whereof I spake in discribing the Popes Pallace) that he first obtained the Popes promise, that no man should come in, till the worke were finished; and understanding that the Pope had broken this promise, comming in himselfe with some Cardinals at the backe doore of the vestery, that he being then to paint the last Judgement, did so lively figure the Pope and the Cardinall (that tempted him) amongst the Divels, as every man might easily know them. But that is abhominable, which the Romans of the better sort seriously tell of him, that he being to paint a crucifix for the Pope, when he came to expresse the lively actions of the passion, hired a Porter to be fastned upon a Crosse, and at that very time stabbed him with a penknife, and while he was dying, made a rare peece of worke for the Art, but infamous for the murther: and that hereupon he was banished Rome, and went to the Court of the Duke of Urbino, where he was entertained with much honour. And they report also that when he was recalled to Rome with pardon of that fault, the Dutchesse of Urbino being bold upon her former acquaintance, should entreat him at his leasure to paint all the Saints for her: and that he to shew that so great a taske should not be imposed upon a workman of his sort, should satisfie this request, or rather put it off with a rude & uncivill jest, sending her the picture of a mans privy part, most artificially painted, and praying her to take in good part the Father of all the Saints, till he could at leasure send their pictures.

[100] Stendhal enthuses over Volterrano and Bronzino in Santa Croce in 1811; from *The Private Diaries of Stendhal*, edited and translated by Robert Sage.

(Marie-Henri Beyle (1783–1841) first used the pseudonym M. de Stendhal when he published *Rome, Naples et Florence en 1817*.

After entering Italy in 1800 with Napoleon's reserve army, Beyle never lost his enthusiasm for that country.)

My admiration for St Cecilia, the Madonna della Sediola and the Madonna in the Luxembourg has never gone as far as rapture.

I found this sensation yesterday in front of the four sibyls painted by Vol[t]errano in the chapel of the Niccolini.

The ceiling of the same chapel is very effective, but my eyesight is not good enough to judge ceilings. It merely appeared to me to be very effective. As for the four sibyls, anything I could say would be inadequate. It's majestic, it's living, it appears to be nature in relief; one of them possesses that grace which, combined with the majestic, makes me fall in love at once.

I believed I'd never find anything as beautiful as these sibyls, when my servant stopped me, almost by force, to look at a painting of *Limbo*. I was almost moved to tears. They start to my eyes as I write this. I've never seen anything so beautiful. What I require is either expression or beautiful female figures. All the figures are charming and sharply outlined, nothing is confused. Painting has never given me such pleasure. I was dead tired, my feet swollen and pinched in new boots – a little sensation which would prevent God from being admired in the midst of His glory, but I overlooked it in front of the picture of *Limbo*. *Mon Dieu*, how beautiful it is!

September 27. – I was all aflutter for two hours. I'd been told that this picture was by *Guerchino;* I worshipped this painter from the bottom of my heart. Not at all; I was told two hours later that it was by Agnolo Bronzino, a name unknown to me. This discovery annoyed me a great deal. I was also told that the colouring was pale. At that, I thought of my eyes.

My eyesight is tender, nervous, apt to become agitated, sensing the slightest nuances, but shocked at the dark and harsh tones of the Carrachis, for example. The pale manner of Guido Reni is almost in harmony, not with my manner in judging the arts, but with my eyesight.

My whole admiration may be the result of the physical structure of my eyes. At any rate, I'm going back to Santa Croce. . . .

I realize that my critical reflections tend only to substitute my taste for that of others. If someone were to say to me, 'What proof have you that your taste is worth more than that of President Dupaty?' I'd answer, 'None.' I can guarantee but one thing, and that is that I write what I think. There are perhaps eight or ten people in Europe who think as I do. I love these people without knowing them. . . .

[101] Byron meditates on the tombs of four great Florentines in Santa Croce; from *Childe Harold's Pilgrimage* by Lord Byron.

In Santa Croce's holy precincts lie
   Ashes which make it holier, dust which is
   Even in itself an immortality,
   Though there were nothing save the past, and this,
   The particle of those sublimities
   Which have relapsed to chaos:– here repose
   Angelo's – Alfieri's bones – and his,
   The starry Galileo, with his woes;
Here Machiavelli's earth returned to whence it rose.

These are four minds, which, like the elements,
   Might furnish forth creation: – Italy!
   Time, which hath wronged thee with ten thousand rents
   Of thine imperial garment, shall deny
   And hath denied, to every other sky,
   Spirits which soar from ruin:– thy Decay
   Is still impregnate with divinity,
   Which gilds it with revivifying ray;
Such as the great of yore, Canova is to-day.

[102] An Englishwoman, Susan Horner, visits Santa Croce and admires its Gothic painting; from Susan Horner's 1847/8 manuscript diary in the British Institute of Florence.

(Ann Susan Horner (1816–1900) continued the Anglo-Florentine interests established by her father Leonard, who had translated Villari's *History of Savonarola*. Together with her sister Joanna she published in 1873 the most detailed guidebook of its day, *Walks in Florence* in two volumes.)

Sta Croce is very large and very ancient, having been built in the 13th century. Round it lie buried, Michael Angelo, Galileo, Macchiavelli, and Leonardo Aretino [*Bruni*]. At the end of the church in the transept and sacristy are very beautiful frescos by Taddeo Gaddi, of the life of the Virgin, and Mary Magdalene. It is most interesting to observe the progress of art, and though none of the pupils of Giotto, whose works I have seen, possess his power and force, there is always an advance to a closer representation of nature, life and action. There is much grace and beauty too in these frescos; none, however, made the astonishing progress of Masaccio, who stepped at once from an age when men were slowly groping their way in an awakening twilight, to the full light. One figure in the fresco of Taddeo Gaddi struck me much. It is that of Mary sitting at the feet of our Saviour when Martha is busy with her household cares. There is no effort at grace of action, too little perhaps, but the expression of the head, the way in which she sits, is so completely that of one absorbed in listening, is very true. The choir contains frescos by Angiolo Gaddi, the son and pupil of Taddeo, of the legend of the Cross, but as the friars were just beginning service, we could not remain there. One was preaching, and his manner was most energetic; I could not help admiring the effect of his large audience, *out of pews*, some standing, some sitting, grouped in a half circle below, and all most attentive to what he said. The pulpit is of marble richly carved in alto-relief by Benedetto da Majano; we went into the sacristy, and were much pleased with frescos by Taddeo Gaddi, and by a curious crucifix of enormous size, painted by Margheritone of Arezzo [?] (a very early master) for Farinata degli Uberti; It is painful in expression. There are two other crucifixes, one by Cimabue, singularly green in colour, perhaps to give it the effect of death, the other by Giotto, darker in colour, and with a red mark in the face, proceeding probably from some injury.

[103] Ruskin gets the most out of the worn tomb slab of an ancestor of Galileo in Santa Croce; from *Mornings in Florence* by John Ruskin.

But first, look at the two sepulchral slabs by which you are standing. That farther of the two from the west end is one of the most beautiful pieces of fourteenth century sculpture in this world: and it contains simple elements of excellence, by your understanding of which you may test your power of understanding the more difficult ones you will have to deal with presently.

It represents an old man, in the high deeply-folded cap worn by scholars and gentlemen in Florence from 1300 to 1500, lying dead, with a book on his breast, over which his hands are folded. . . .

Mr Murray tells you that the effigies 'in low relief' (alas, yes, low enough now – worn mostly into flat stones, with a trace only of the deeper lines left, but originally in very bold relief,) with which the floor of Santa Croce is inlaid, of which this by which you stand is characteristic, are 'interesting from the costume,' but that, 'except in the case of John Ketterick, Bishop of St David's, few of the other names have any interest beyond the walls of Florence.' As, however, you are at present within the walls of Florence, you may perhaps condescend to take some interest in this ancestor or relation of the Galileo whom Florence indeed left to be externally interesting, and would not allow within her walls. . . .

It is the crowning virtue of all great art that, however little is left of it by the injuries of time, that little will be lovely. As long as you can see anything, you can see – almost all; – so much the hand of the master will suggest of his soul.

And here you are well quit, for once, of restoration. No one cares for this sculpture; and if Florence would only thus put all her old sculpture and painting under her feet, and simply use them for gravestones and oilcloth, she would be more merciful to them than she is now. Here, at least, what little is left is true.

And, if you look long, you will find it is not so little. That worn face is still a perfect portrait of the old man, though like one struck out at a venture, with a few rough touches of a master's chisel. And that falling drapery of his capes, in its few lines, faultless, and subtle beyond description.

And now, here is a simple but most useful test of your capacity for understanding Florentine sculpture or painting. If you can see that the lines of that cap are both right, and lovely; that the choice of the folds is exquisite in its ornamental relations of line; and that the softness and ease of them is complete, – though only sketched with a few dark touches, – then you can understand Giotto's drawing, and Botticelli's; – Donatello's carving, and Luca's. But if you see nothing in *this* sculpture, you will see nothing in theirs, *of* theirs. Where they choose to imitate flesh, or silk, or to play any vulgar modern trick with marble – (and they often do) whatever, in a word, is French, or American, or Cockney, in their work, you can see; but what is Florentine, and for ever great –unless you can see also the beauty of this old man in his citizen's cap, – you will see never.

There is more in this sculpture, however, than its simple portraiture and noble drapery. The old man lies on a piece of embroidered carpet; and, protected by the higher relief, many of the finer lines of this are almost uninjured; in particular, its exquisitely wrought fringe and tassels are nearly perfect. And if you will kneel down and look long at the tassels of the cushion under the head, and the way they fill the angles of the stone, you will – or may – know, from this example alone, what noble decorative sculpture is, and was, and must be, from the days of earliest Greece to those of latest Italy.

'Exquisitely sculptured fringe!' and you have just been abusing sculptors who play tricks with marble! Yes, and you cannot find a better example, in all the museums of Europe, of the work of a man who does *not* play tricks with it – than this tomb. Try to understand the difference: it is a point of quite cardinal importance to all your future study of sculpture.

I *told* you, observe, that the old Galileo was lying on a piece of embroidered carpet. I don't think, if I had not told you, that you would have found it out for yourself. It is not so like a carpet as all that comes to.

But had it been a modern trick-sculpture, the moment you came to the tomb you would have said, 'Dear me! how wonderfully that carpet is done, – it doesn't look like stone in the least, – one longs to take it up and beat it, to get the dust off.'

[104] Miss Lavish and Lucy Honeychurch find Santa Croce without using their Baedeker; from E.M. Forster's *A Room with a View.*

'Bless us! Bless us and save us! We've lost the way. '

Certainly they had seemed a long time in reaching Santa Croce, the tower of which had been plainly visible from the landing window. But Miss Lavish had said so much about knowing her Florence by heart, that Lucy had followed her with no misgivings.

'Lost! lost! My dear Miss Lucy, during our political diatribes we have taken a wrong turning. How those horrid Conservatives would jeer at us! What are we to do? Two lone females in an unknown town. Now, this is what *I* call an adventure.'

Lucy, who wanted to see Santa Croce, suggested, as a possible solution, that they should ask the way there.

'Oh, but that is the word of a craven! And no, you are not, not, *not* to look at your Baedeker. Give it to me; I shan't let you carry it. We will simply drift.'

Accordingly they drifted through a series of those gray-brown streets, neither commodious nor picturesque, in which the eastern quarter of the city abounds. Lucy soon lost interest in the discontent of Lady Louisa, and became discontented herself. For one ravishing moment Italy appeared. She stood in the Square of the Annunziata and saw in the living terra cotta those divine babies whom no cheap reproduction can ever stale. There they stood, with their shining limbs bursting from the garments of charity, and their strong white arms extended against circlets of heaven. Lucy thought she had never seen anything more beautiful; but Miss Lavish, with a shriek of dismay, dragged her forward, declaring that they were out of their path now by at least a mile.

The hour was approaching at which the continental breakfast begins, or rather ceases, to tell, and the ladies bought some hot chestnut paste out of a little shop, because it looked so typical. It tasted partly of the paper in which it was wrapped, partly of hair oil, partly of the great unknown. But it gave them strength to drift into another Piazza, large and dusty, on the farther side of which rose a black-and-white façade of surpassing ugliness. Miss Lavish spoke to it dramatically. It was Santa Croce. The adventure was over.

'Stop a minute; let those two people go on, or I shall have to speak to them. I do detest conventional intercourse. Nasty! they are going into the church, too. Oh, the Britisher abroad!'

'We sat opposite them at dinner last night. They have given us their rooms. They were so very kind.'

'Look at their figures!' laughed Miss Lavish. 'They walk through my Italy like a pair of cows. It's very naughty of me, but I would like to set an examination paper at Dover, and turn back every tourist who couldn't pass it.'

'What would you ask us?'

Miss Lavish laid her hand pleasantly on Lucy's arm, as if to suggest that she, at all events, would get full marks. In this exalted mood they reached the steps of the great church, and were about to enter it when Miss Lavish stopped, squeaked, flung up her arms, and cried:

'There goes my local-colour box! I must have a word with him!'

And in a moment she was away over the Piazza, her military cloak flapping in the wind; nor did she slacken speed till she caught up an old man with white whiskers, and nipped him playfully upon the arm.

Lucy waited for nearly ten minutes. Then she began to get tired. The beggars worried her, the dust blew in her eyes, and she remembered that a young girl ought not to loiter in public places. She descended slowly into the Piazza with the intention of rejoining Miss Lavish, who was really almost too original. But at the moment Miss Lavish and her local-colour box moved also, and disappeared down a side street, both gesticulating largely.

Tears of indignation came to Lucy's eyes – partly because she had taken her Baedeker. How could she find her way home? How could she find her way about in Santa Croce? Her first morning was ruined, and she might never be in Florence again. A few minutes ago she had been all high spirits, talking as a woman of culture, and half persuading herself that she was full of originality. Now she entered the church depressed and humiliated, not even able to remember whether it was built by the Franciscans or the Dominicans.

Of course, it must be a wonderful building. But how like a barn! And how very cold! Of course, it contained frescoes by Giotto, in the presence of whose tactile values she was capable of feeling what was proper. But who was to tell her which they were? She walked about disdainfully, unwilling to be enthusiastic over monuments of uncertain authorship or date. There was no one even to tell her which, of all the sepulchral slabs that paved the nave and transepts, was the one that was really beautiful, the one that had been most praised by Mr Ruskin.

Then the pernicious charm of Italy worked on her, and, instead of acquiring information, she began to be happy. She puzzled out the Italian notices – the notices that forbade people to introduce dogs into the church – the notice that prayed people, in the interest of health and out of respect to the sacred edifice in which they found themselves, not to spit. She watched the tourists; their noses were as red as their Baedekers, so cold was Santa Croce. She beheld the horrible fate that overtook three Papists – two he-babies and a she-baby – who began their career by sousing each other with the Holy Water, and then proceeded to the Machiavelli memorial, dripping but hallowed. Advancing toward it very slowly and from immense distances, they touched the stone with their fingers, with their handkerchiefs, with their heads, and then retreated. What could this mean? They did it again and again. Then Lucy realized that they had mistaken Machiavelli for some saint, hoping to acquire virtue. Punishment followed quickly. The smallest he-baby stumbled over one of the sepulchral slabs so much admired by Mr Ruskin, and entangled his feet in the features of a recumbent bishop. Protestant as she was, Lucy darted forward. She was too late. He fell heavily upon the prelate's upturned toes.

San Lorenzo

[105] Brunelleschi starts work on San Lorenzo and quarrels with Donatello; from Antonio Manetti's *Life of Brunelleschi*.

He [*Filippo Brunelleschi*] therefore unwillingly set himself to building the church with three aisles [*without side chapels*], since it seemed a poor thing to him. However, that [*namely, the lack of patrons*] was the reason. Those three aisles were constituted as follows: two chapels are in the transept and one in the [*crosssing*] arms on either side of the church; there are two side aisles, that is say the [*space*] from the columns to the wall, thus placing the body of the church in the middle so that it is a uniting of three aisles like Santa Croce and Santa Maria Novella. He ordered the sacristy and confirmed it by consultations with citizens and artisans of similar profession and started work inside. Patrons for the chapels were gradually assembled. The sacristy went forward before anything else and arrived at that state which aroused the marvel, for its new and beautiful style, of everyone in the city and of the strangers who chanced to see it. The many people constantly assembling there caused great annoyance to those working.

When the sacristy was finished, or while it was being built together with part of the transept, Giovanni de' Medici died. His sons, Cosimo and Lorenzo, two respectable and generous citizens, survived him and they took charge of it with the same good will, solicitude, and care, encouraging the citizens who had agreed to build the chapels. The old church was used for a long time after the church was begun in this form. The main chapel was in large part built in a different way from what it is now, since Cosimo had not yet decided to move the choir for the clergy there. When he later decided to do so, Filippo changed it to the form it has today. The small doors in the sacristy place the chapel in the center between them and open onto the basin and the well. The other door opens to the storage place for candles. As it had not yet been decided whether the doors should be made of wood or another material – as they are now – they remained unfinished. The walls were also left unfinished, with only the opening with a relieving arch above. Later when it was decided that they should be of bronze and contain figures, as they now are, they were commissioned to Donatello. While making them he was also entrusted to make the doors in *macigno* in his manner, along with all the decorations for them. That commission made him so proud and arrogant that, presuming on his authority as the sculptor of the bronze doors and without asking anyone's opinion and without consulting Filippo, he gave them their present form, even though he knew little of pictorial composition – as is evident from his pulpit in Santa Maria del Fiore and others, and from all like works involving pictorial composition. His works in the sacristy, individually and collectively, never had the blessing of Filippo. When Donatello saw and realized that, it became the motive of great indignation against Brunelleschi. Donato detracted as much as he could from Filippo's achievement and fame at the instigation of some inconsequential person. But Brunelleschi laughed at this talk and attached little importance to it. However, after a great deal of such talk caused by Donatello's persistence in his presumptuousness, Brunelleschi composed some sonnets in his own defense in order to make it clear that he was not responsible for anything on those walls containing the doors between the corner pilasters, from the [*altar*] chapel to the side walls. Certain of these [*sonnets*], which absolve him completely, are still to be found.

As far as the sacristy is concerned, it was furnished as it is today – with the things required for a sacristy – when death came to Filippo; the transept of the church had not yet been finished, nor was the crossing cupola executed. That cupola was built far from Filippo's concept both inside and outside, which is why it does not even please those who give the responsibility to Filippo.

[106] Vasari decides on his own iconography and respects Brunelleschi's intentions in painting an altarpiece for the Martelli chapel in San Lorenzo; from Vasari's *Lives* . . .

At this period Gismondo Martelli died in Florence, leaving instructions in his will that a picture of the Virgin and saints should be done for the family chapel in S. Lorenzo. Luigi and Pandolfo Martelli, with Cosimo Bartoli, my close friends, asked me to do this picture, and I consented, having obtained permission from Duke Cosimo, the patron and chief warden of the church, but on the condition of doing something I had thought of about St Sigismund, that being the testator's name. This being arranged, I remembered having learned that Filippo di Ser Brunelleschi, the architect of the church, had constructed the chapels so that each should have one large picture filling the whole space, and not a little one. Wishing to respect Brunelleschi's idea and thinking more of honour than of the slight gain to be made from a small picture with few figures, I did the martyrdom of St Sigismund, the king, ten braccia broad by thirteen high, when he, his wife and two children are thrown into a pit by another king or tyrant. I adapted the semicircular frame of the chapel as the space of the door of a large rustic palace opening on to a square courtyard, surrrounded by doric pilasters and columns. In the middle is an octagonal pit with steps up to it, which the servants mount to throw the two naked children in. In the surrounding loggias I painted spectators regarding the horrid scene. On the left I represented ruffians who have roughly seized the king's wife and are carrying her to the pit to her death. At the main doorway I made a group of soldiers who are binding St Sigismund. The saint is patiently prepared for his martyrdom and regards four angels in the air, who show him the palms and crowns of the martyrdom of himself and family, and this seems to afford him great consolation. I also endeavoured to represent the cruelty of the impious tyrant, who is standing in the courtyard to see his revenge and the death of St Sigismund. I exerted all my powers to give the figures the appropriate expressions and attitudes. I must leave others to decide how far I have succeeded, but I can claim to have done my best.

Meanwhile Duke Cosimo desired that the book of the Lives, now practically completed with all the speed I could muster, should be printed. So I gave it to Lorenzo Torrentino, the ducal printer, who set to work . . .

[107] The obsequies of the Emperor Ferdinand III in San Lorenzo in 1657; from Sir John Reresby's *Travels and Memoirs* . . .

(Sir John Reresby, baronet (1634–1689), 'left England in that unhappy time when honesty was reputed a crime, religion superstition, loyalty treason . . . and no gentleman assured of any thing he possessed' – that is, during Cromwell's Common-wealth from the post-Restoration perspective of a Royalist. He became an MP in 1675 and recorded the events of his time in his *Memoirs*.).

During my stay at Florence died the Emperor Ferdinand the Third, whose obsequies the Great Duke, as allied to the house of Austria, caused to be solemnized in this church; the manner whereof I have thought fit here to insert.

The whole church was hung round with black cloth, on which was pictured death, in various forms, intermixed with the imperial arms and crown. In the body of the choir, before the high altar, was erected a lofty arch, lighted with two hundred wax torches set round it; on the top of the arch stood the form of a magnificent tomb, to which you mounted by an ascent of twelve steps; before this, the bishop, assisted by the chief of the clergy, sung several masses, said many prayers for the dead, and used the same rites and ceremonies as if the body had effectually been there. The duke [*Ferdinando II*] and the cardinal his brother, were here present, heard the sermon or oration, in commenda-tion of the deceased, which is always pronounced by some secular person, and a gentleman, for the clergymen never perform it. This ceremony continued three hours, set off with the best voices and other music in Italy; amongst which I cannot omit taking notice of a trumpeter, who played an upper part in concert with violins and hautboys, so exactly both as to flats, sharps, and measure, that it was impossible for any instrument to have been more just and harmonious, as he governed it.

[108] The first coherent account in English of Michelangelo's New Sacristy in San Lorenzo; from Richard Lassels's manuscript *Voyage of Italy* (1664)

The Church of S. Lorenzo, which belongs to this Chappel above [*the Cappella dei Principi*], or rather to which Church this Chappel belongs. It is a very hansome Church designed by Brunelleschi himself a rare Architect. The things that grace this Church, are: The neat pillars which beare up the roof: the last *Judgement* of *Pontorno* [*sic*] painted over the Quire: the two brazen pulpits wrought into historyes by rare Donatello: the curious designed

The obsequies celebrated in San Lorenzo by the Grand Duke for the death of the Emperor Matthias; by J. Callot

picture (in a Chappel on the right hand) of S. Anne and our B. Lady, *in chiaro e osscuro* by *Fra Bartolomeo*, commonly called *Del Frate*: the new Sacristy made for to serve the new Chappel here, in which are depositated the bodyes of the Princes of this family of *Medices*, and in which are seen the four statues of *Michel Angelo*, representing the four parts of the day which compose *Time* who brings all men to their grave, to wit, the *Day*, the *Night*, the *Aurora* and the *Evening*. That of the *Night* is a rare statue and hugely cryed up by all sculptors. See allso here the tombe of *John* and *Peter Medices* sonns of Cosmus Pater Patriae, it is the worke of Andrea Varrochio, and set within the wall of the old Sacristy on the left hand. See allso the tombe, or tombestone rather, of Cosmus Pater Patriae who lyes buryed before the High Altar. See in fine, the tombe and statue of *Paulus Jovius* in the cloister of this Church, and the rare Library of Manuscripts called the *Bibliotheca Laurentiana*, the catalogue of whose books is printed at Amsterdame (in octavo an. 1642).

[109] Samuel Rogers is temporarily obsessed by Michelangelo's sculpture of Lorenzo, Duke of Urbino, in the New Sacristy; from *The Italian Journal of Samuel Rogers*.

(Samuel Rogers (1763–1855) was a wealthy but generous banker's son who became one of the most popular poets of his day (Byron considering him superior to Coleridge and Wordsworth), partly thanks to the illustrations Turner and Stothard contributed to his *Italy* in 1830.)

I am no longer my own master. I am become the slave of a demon. I sit gazing, day after day, on that terrible phantom, the Duke Lorenzo in M. Angelo's Chapel. All my better feelings would lead me to the Tribune & the lovely forms that inhabit there. I can dwell with delight on the membra formosa of the Wrestlers, the Fawn & the Apollo, on the sunshine of Titian & the soul of Raphael; but the statue loses none of its influence. He sits, a little inclining from you, his chin resting upon his left hand, his elbows on the arm of his chair. His look is calm & thoughtful, yet it seems to say a something that makes you shrink from it, a something beyond words. Like that of the Basilisk, it fascinates – & is intolerable! When you shift your place to the left his eye is upon You. . . .

The visage of Lorenzo under the shade of that scowling & helmet-like bonnet is scarcely visible. You can just discern the likeness of human features; but whether alive or dead, whether a face or a scull, that of mortal man or a Spirit from heaven or hell, you cannot say. His figure is gigantic & noble, not such as to shock belief, or remind you that it is but a statue. It is the most real & unreal thing in stone that ever came from the chissel.

[110] Vasari's version of the origins of the Cappella dei Principi; from the final page of his *Lives* . . .

I have certainly said more than enough, and will only add that, important as are the things that I have kept putting before Duke Cosimo, I have never been able to attain to, much less surpass, the magnificence of his conceptions. There is for example, a third sacristy which he wants to make near S. Lorenzo, like that of Michelagnolo, but with variegated marbles, to form a mausoleum for his children, his father, mother, the Duchess Leonora and himself. I have already made a model from his instructions, to his satisfaction, and when carried out it will form a magnificent and truly royal structure. Let this suffice for myself. At the age of fifty-five I have completed these labours, in the hope that I may live so long as God wills, to His honour and in the service of friends, so far as my strength allows for the increase of our noble arts.

[111] A typically enthusiastic seventeenth-century account of the unfinished Cappella dei Principi behind San Lorenzo; from Richard Lassels's manuscript *Voyage of Italy* (1664).

The *Chappel of S. Lorenzo* is absolutely the most trimm thing that eye ever beheld. All the inside of it is to be overcrusted with Jasper stones of several coulors and countryes; and, with other rich stones all above marble; and all so neatly polished and shining, that though the matter be stately, yet the art exceeds farre the materials. This Chappel is round, and round about are placed in the walls, the tombes of all the great Dukes of Florence in a most gallant manner, and of most exquisit polished stones: the statue of every Duke in brasse guilt standing over every tombe in the Ducal robes. The roof of it is be vaulted with an overcrusting of *Lapis Lazuli* (a blew pretious stone with vaines of gold in it) which will make it looke like heaven it self. Between the Tombes, are expressed in the walls, the armes or Scutchions of the several townes of the Great Dukes dominions, all enlayed or blazoned according to their several coulors in Heraldry, by several pretious stones which compose them. The townes are these: *Florence, Siena, Pisa, Livorno, Volterra, Arezzo, Pistoia, Cortona, Monte Pulciano* &c. In fine, this Chappel is so rich within, that it scornes all hangings, painting, guilding, mosaical worke, and such like helpers off of baire walls, because it can finde nothing richer and hansomer then its owne pretious bair walls. Its now above threescore yeares since it was begunn, and there are ordinarily threescore men at work every day; and yet theres but onely the Tombe of Ferdinand the second perfectly finished. The very cushing with the Crowne which lyeth upon his tombe cost threescore thousand crownes. Guesse at the rest by this. Inded these stately tombes make even death looke lovelily on it, and dead mens ashes grow prowd againe.

[112] The Cappella dei Principi compared with the Taj Mahal; from Joseph [Moyle] Sherer's *Scenes and Impressions in Egypt and in Italy.*

(Moyle Sherer (1789–1869) was a professional soldier who aspired with limited success to a literary career, publishing travel accounts, some fiction, and a biography of Wellington.)

Near the church of San Lorenzo is the celebrated chapel of the Medici, designed as a mausoleum for the princes of that family. It is octangular, and six sides have already their vast sarcophagi of granite; jasper, agate, lapis lazuli, profusely adorn this splendid mansion of the dead. Two statues of bronze, and regal crowns on cushions of red jasper, are among the finished wonders; but the chapel never has been, probably never will be, completed: bare bricks, scaffoldings, canvass curtains, and ladders, dust and workmen, speak of some effort to finish the splendid design; but the most sanguine *cicerone*, as he tells you that twenty years will be required to effect the object proposed, shakes his head with a doubt, which a corresponding shake from your head helps to confirm. My taste may be bad, but I think I have seen a monument of greater magnificence and a more chaste splendour than this ever would have been; although, to be sure, in it there are no huge sarcophagi or bronze statues – I mean the *Taaje Mahal* on the plains of Agra. I never saw, any where in Italy, mosaic-work of flower-patterns at all to be compared with the designs which fill that beauteous and costly dome.

[113] An Elizabethan view of the Biblioteca Laurenziana; from Sir Robert Dallington's *Survey of the Great Dukes State of Tuscany*.

(Sir Robert Dallington (1561–1637) became a schoolteacher after graduating from Cambridge. He then travelled in France and Italy, writing extremely original books about both on his return. In 1624, on the recommendation of the future Charles I, he was appointed Master of Charterhouse.)

In the Cloisters of the Church of *San Lorenzo* is a faire and beautifull Librarie, built and furnished with Bookes by the familie of *Medici*: the roofe is of Cedar very curiously wrought with knots and flowers, and right under each knot is the same wrought with no lesse Arte in the pavement. In this Library I told three thousand nine hundred bookes very fairely bound in Leather, after one sort, all bound to their seates, which were in number sixtie eight: and, which is the greatest grace and cost also, very many of the bookes were written with the Authours owne hands. There is also at the farther end of this Librarie one other of prohibited bookes, which I could not see.

[114] The Biblioteca Laurenziana two hundred years later; from Lady Morgan's *Italy*.

The Convent adjoining [*the Capella dei Principi*] and its fine old cloisters, with here and there an orange-tree laden with golden produce, springing from amidst masses of ruin and rubbish, is best worth visiting for its library, the far-famed Bibliotheca Mediceo-Laurenziana. This precious collection owes its commencement to the free times of Tuscany; the first donations were from the old merchant Cosimo, his brother Lorenzo, and his son Peter. Then came the splendid contributions of the Dictators and the Popes of the House of Medici, Lorenzo the Magnificent,

Leo the Tenth, and Clement the Seventh. The Grand Dukes seem to have done little; and the Austrian masters of Tuscany, who succeeded to the last of the Medici, particularly Leopold, were the first, after a long lapse of years, to increase its stores: the libraries of suppressed convents enabled the latter to do so with great effect. This library was raised after the designs of Michael Angelo, and there is an air of Gothic grandeur and gloom about it that well belongs to its destination: the windows, the cornices, the architraves, the very doors, are beautiful, and an exquisite simplicity and symmetry reigns over the whole, that soon effaces the gaudy impressions of the Medicean chapel, and restores the mind to those pure enjoyments, which no associations of moral degradation sully and embitter.

It is not for some time after having entered this library, and having passed and repassed along the old oaken seats carved by Battista del Cinque, and Ciapino, that one perceives, here and there, a ponderous tome, wrapped in vellum, clasped in brass, and chained in iron, on desks as curious as its own contents. Still this collection is multifarious, consisting of precious and rare MSS. in almost all known languages, illuminated with the most beautiful and curious miniatures. But more interesting than its Manuscripts of Virgil and Tacitus, its Pandects of Justinian, or its Councils of Florence, is the MS. of *Boccacio's* Decamerone and of *Benvenuto Cellini's* Life, to those who prize not books for the antiquity of the dust that lies on them, but for their bearings on the social history of man, and the progressive development of his nature.

On a table in the centre of this spacious hall stands a small crystal vase, covering the fore-finger of one, who had been destined to the flames of an *auto da fe* – of Galileo – a relic which some will kiss with as much devotion as the Majesty of Spain salutes the tooth of his patron, St Dominick. This was the finger that traced the luminous 'Dialogues on the System of the World.' The books of this collection are all locked up in their old presses, as they were in days when books, like gems, were preserved in caskets. Among the few pictures that decorate its walls, are three original portraits of great interest and value – one of Politian, one of Petrarch, and one of Laura, by their friend Martini, whose saints were all Lauras, as Raphael's *Madonnas* were all Fornarinas.

San Marco

[115] The rebuilding of the monastery of San Marco in the mid-fifteenth century; from Vasari's *Lives* . . .

The church of S. Giorgio being given to the friars of S. Domenico of Fiesole, they only remained there from mid-July to the end of January, because Cosimo de' Medici and his brother Lorenzo obtained for them from Pope Eugenius the church and convent of S. Marco, where the Silvestrine monks had originally been stationed, to whom S. Giorgio was given in exchange. The Dominicans being much inclined to religion and to the divine service and worship, ordained that the convent of S. Marco should be rebuilt on a larger and more magnificent scale from the design and model of Michelozzo, with all the conveniences which the friars could desire. It was begun in 1437, the first part constructed being the section which answers to the place above the old refectory, opposite the duke's stables, which Duke Lorenzo de' Medici had previously caused to be built. In this part twenty cells were constructed and roofed in, while the wooden furniture of the refectory was supplied and the whole finished in its present condition. From that point the work was not pursued for some time, as the friars were awaiting the result of a lawsuit brought against them by Maestro Stefano, general of the Silvestrines, who claimed the convent. When this was concluded in favour of the friars of S. Marco, the building was pursued. But as the principal chapel had been built by Ser Pino Bonaccorsi, there arose a dispute afterwards with a lady of the Caponsacchi, and through her with Mariotto Banchi, which afterwards led to endless litigation. Mariotto gave the chapel to Cosimo de' Medici after having deprived Agnolo della Casa of it, to whom the Silvestrines had either given or sold it, and Cosimo gave Mariotto 500 crowns for it. After Cosimo had in like manner bought from the company of the Holy Spirit the site where the choir now is, the chapel, the tribune and the choir were erected from designs by Michelozzo, and completed by 1439. After this the library was constructed, 80 braccia long and 18 broad both above and below, furnished with 64 cases of cypress wood full of the most beautiful books. The dormitory was the next thing to be finished, being made square, and then the cloister and all the other apartments of the convent, which is believed to be the best appointed, finest and most convenient in all Italy, thanks to the talents and industry of Michelozzo, who completed it in 1452. It is said that Cosimo expended 36,000 ducats upon it, and that while it was building he gave the friars 366 ducats a year for their living. Concerning the building and consecration of that temple there is an inscription on a marble slab over the door leading into the sacristy . . .

[116] The merits, and the consecration, of the new Dominican Convent of San Marco; from Giuliano Lapaccini's *Cronaca di San Marco*, translated by Creighton Gilbert in *Italian Art 1400–1500: Sources and Documents*.

(Fra Lapaccini was prior of San Marco in 1444 and from 1448–53. His account of the 'spontaneous' transfer of the rights to the main chapel disguises the extent to which Cosimo de' Medici had put pressure on Mariotto de' Banchi to hand it over following the similarly pressurized transfer of the Convent from the Silvestrines to the reformed Dominicans.)

And note that certain special distinctions are to be seen in the building, among which the highest place belongs to the library . . . the second distinction belongs to the reciprocity and dovetailing arrangement of the dwelling areas . . . and to this contribute the many walls in logical places, both for providing water for the use of the brothers and for collecting the rainwater.

The third distinction is to be found in the paintings. For the altar-piece of the high altar, the figures of the chapter house and of the first cloister, and of all the upper cells, and of the Crucified in the Refectory, are all painted by a certain brother of the order of preachers and of the convent of Fiesole who was held to be the finest master in the art of painting in Italy, who was called brother Giovanni di Pietro of Mugello [*Fra Angelico*] a man of complete modesty and religious life.

The fourth distinction is the garden. . . . The fifth distinction is the delightfulness of the dwelling areas both above and below; the convent always seems to smile upon all who enter.

. . . In the year of our lord 1442 in January, on the solemn feast of the Epiphany, though the convent was not completely built, the church was consecrated, by order of our sacred lord Pope Eugene IV, by a certain cardinal bishop of Saint Marcellus, named Nicholas, called Cardinal Capuano, to whose solemn mass came the aforesaid supreme pontiff with the whole college of cardinals and a great multitude of bishops and prelates of the church of God, and a whole crowd of people, and the high altar was consecrated by the said cardinal in honor of saints Mark the Evangelist and Cosmas and Damian, and there was also consecrated the altar of the chapel next to the choir, which is called of the Martini, painted throughout with the history of our Lady the Virgin Mary, and it was named in honor of the Assumption of the same lady, and so too the whole chapel is named, and it was consecrated by a bishop who is a member of our order. . . .

[117] The siege of San Marco in 1498, and the arrest and torture of Savonarola; from Luca Landucci's *Diario Fiorentino*.

The adversaries of the *Frate*, especially the *Compagnia de' Compagnacci*, rushing towards the convent, cried: *A' Frati, a' Frati, a San Marco!* and all the people and the children joined them and ran along with stones, making it impossible for many men and women who were in *San Marco* to come out. I chanced to be there; and if I had not managed to get out through the cloister, and go away towards the *Porta di San Gallo*, I might have been killed. Everyone was arming himself, in fact; and a proclamation from the *Palagio* offered 1000 ducats to anyone who should capture Fra Girolamo and deliver him up to the authorities. All Florence was in commotion, and none of the *Frate's* adherents dared to speak, or else they would have been killed. Before 22 in the evening [*6 p.m.*], some of the *Gonfaloni* came armed into the Piazza, and crying *Popolo!* nearly all of them being *Compagnacci*, and beginning to shout: *A casa Francesco Valori!* [*To Francesco Vallori's house!*]; *a sacco!* [sack it!], they ran there and set fire to the door, and pillaged everything. . . . Meanwhile there was fighting round *San Marco*, where the crowd increased all the time; and they brought three stone-throwing machines into the Via Larga and the Via del Cocomero, by which some people were wounded and killed. It was said that 15 or 20 persons were killed here and there, and about 100 wounded.

At about 6 in the night [*2 a.m.*] they set fire to the doors of the church and the cloister of *San Marco*, and penetrating into the church began to fight. Finally, whilst the *Frate* was in the chancel singing the office, two *Frati* came out and said: 'We will agree to give up the *Frate* to you, if you will take him to the *Palagio* in safety,' and this was promised; so at 7 [*3 a.m.*] the Frate himself and Fra Domenico and Fra Silvestro were given up to them, and they led them off to the *Palagio* with many insults on the way. It is said that they kicked him, saying: *Va lá, tristo!* [*Go along with you, bad man!*]; his hands and feet were put in irons, and they confined him closely like a great malefactor, heaping abuse and outrages upon him.

9th April. The same sort of thing went on; weapons were laid aside, but tongues continued to wag, and hell seemed open; people never tired of saying *ladro e traditore* [*Wretch and traitor*]. And no one dared to say a word for the *Frate*, or they would have been killed; the citizens were jeered at as *Piagnoni* and hypocrites.

10th April. At 9 in the evening [*5 p.m.*] the *Frate* was carried to the *Bargello* by two men on their crossed hands, because his feet and hands were in irons, and Fra Domenico also; and they seized them and put Fra Girolamo to the rack three times and Fra Domenico four times; and Fra Girolamo said; 'Take me down, and I will write you my whole life.' You may imagine that it was not without tears that right-minded men who had faith in him, heard that he had been tortured; he who had taught this prayer, *Fac bene bonis et rectis corde*. No, it was not without tears and grief, and urgent prayers to God.

[118] Mid-seventeenth-century enthusiasm for the work of Fra Bartolomeo in the church of San Marco; from Richard Lassels's *Voyage of Italy* (1670).

. . . going to the *Church of S. Mark* belonging to the *Dominicans*, I saw there the Tombe of S. *Antoninus* Archbishop once of this towne, and a *Fryar* of this order. The Tombe is under the Altar in a neat Chappel on the left hand, made by *Iohn* di *Bologna*. In this *Church* also I saw a rare picture of S. *Mark*, made by *Bartholomeo del Frate*, it stands full in your sight as you enter into the Church;

and a man must be blind not to see it, and dull not to like it. On the left hand, as you enter into the Church is the *Tombe* of *Picus Mirandula* commonly called the *Phoenix of Princes*, with this *Epitaph* written upon the side of the Wall,

Ioannes iacet hîc Mirandula, caetera norunt
Et Tagus & Ganges, forsan & Antipodes.

Neare this tombe is a fine *picture* upon an *Altar*, where two *Little Angels* are made playing upon *Musical* instruments. These *Angels* are held to be the rarest peeces that can be seen in painting. They are of the hand of *Bartholomeo del Frate*. In the *Convent* of these Fryars I saw often their still house, where they made, and sell, excellent extractions and cordiall waters. There is also a neat *Library* here filled with good books.

[119] Fra Angelico at San Marco; from Hippolyte Taine's *Italy*.

April 13. – What commotion and what travail in this fifteenth century! In the midst of this pagan tumultuous hive there stands a tranquil convent wherein sweetly and piously dreams a mystic of ancient days, Fra Angelico da Fiesole.

This convent remains almost intact; two square courts in it expose their files of small columns surmounted by arcades, with their litttle old tile roofs. In one of the rooms is a sort of memorial or genealogical tree, bearing the names of the principal monks who have died in the odor of sanctity. Among these is that of Savonarola, and mention is made of his having perished through false accusation. Two cells are still shown which he inhabited. Fra Angelico lived in the convent before him, and paintings by his hand decorate the chapter-hall, the corridors and the gray walls of the cells.

He had dwelt a stranger in the world, and maintained amidst fresh sensations and curiosities the innocent, ravished life in God which the 'Fioretti' describe. He lived in a state of primitive simplicity and obedience; it is said of him that 'one morning being invited to breakfast by Pope Nicholas V. his conscience forbade him to eat meat without the permission of his prior, never reflecting that the Pope's authority was superior.' He refused the dignities of his order, and concerned himself only with prayer and penitence. 'When any work was required of him he would answer with singular goodness of heart that they must go and ask the prior, and if the prior wished it he would not fail them.' He never desired to paint any but the saints, and it is narrated of him that 'he never took up his brushes without kneeling in prayer, and never painted a Christ on the cross without his eyes being filled with tears.' It was his custom not to retouch or recast any of his pictures, but to let them remain as they first left his hand, 'believing that they were as they were through the will of God.' We can well understand why such a man did not study anatomy or contemporary models. His art is primitive like his life. He began with missals and so continued on the walls; gold, vermilion, bright scarlet, brilliant greens, the illuminations of the middle ages display themselves on his canvases the same as on old parchments. He even sometimes applies them to the roofs; an infantile piety is eager to decorate its saint or idol and render it radiant to excess. When he abandons small figures and composes on a grand scale a scene of twenty personages, he falters; his figures are bodiless. Their affecting devotional expression is inadequate to animate them; they remain hieratic and stiff; all he comprehended was their spirit. That which he paints understandingly, and which he has everywhere repeated, are visions and the visions of blessed and innocent spirits. . . . There is displayed to the eye the magnificence of eternal day, and . . . every effort of the painter centres on expressing it. Glittering staircases of jasper and amethyst rise above each other up to the throne on which sit celestial beings. Golden aureoles gleam around their brows; red, azure and green robes, fringed, bordered and striped with gold, flash like glories. Gold runs in threads over baldachins, accumulates in embroideries on copes, radiates like stars on tunics and gleams from tiaras, while topazes, rubies and diamonds sparkle in flaming constellations on jewelled diadems. All is light ; it is the outburst of mystic illumination . . . Fra Angelico is the last of the mystic flowers. The society that surrounded him and of which he knew nothing, ended in taking an opposite direction, and, after a short respite of enthusiasm, proceeded to burn his successor, a Dominican like himself and the last of the Christians, Savonarola.

[120] A modern account of the frescoes of Fra Angelico; from Sir John Pope-Hennessy's *Fra Angelico*.

. . . by 1443 all the cells on the upper floor [*of the convent of San Marco*], to a total of forty-four, were fit for habitation. Structural work in one part of the building or another continued until 1452. Close contact must have been maintained between Angelico and Michelozzo during the years in which the convent was being built. The fruits of this are to be found in the convent frescoes, where the settings depend for their effect upon the same unerrring use of interval as do the cloister and library of Michelozzo. . . . The frescoes on the ground floor of the convent comprise a *Christ on the Cross adored by Saint Dominic* and five lunettes in the cloister. A fresco of the *Crucifixion* in the refectory was destroyed in 1554. On the first floor there are three frescoes in the corridor (*a Christ on the Cross adored by Saint Dominic*, an *Annunciation*, and a *Virgin and Child with Saints*) and forty-three frescoes in forty-five cells opening off it. All the frescoes on the ground floor are wholly or partly by Angelico. On the extent of his responsibility for the remaining frescoes a wide variety of view has been expressed, and at one time or another he has been charged with as many as forty-one and as few as six of the narrative scenes. The *Cronaca di San Marco* proves beyond all reasonable doubt that as early as 1457 (the terminal date for the completion of the chronicle) Angelico was credited with the entire fresco decoration of the convent as it then stood. But this view is sanctioned neither by examination of the frescoes nor by common sense, for the execution of so many frescoes in so short a time was beyond the capability of a single artist, and the frescoes themselves reveal the presence of three or four main hands. That the class of frescoes in the cells was ideated by Angelico and that Angelico himself supervised the decoration of the convent is not open to doubt, but the frescoes for which he was directly responsible are vastly outnumbered by the scenes in which assistants were charged with executing his cartoons, or which were conceived by his disciples within the framework of his style.

Santa Maria del Carmine

[121] The significance of Masaccio's frescoes in the Brancacci Chapel of Santa Maria del Carmine; from Bernard Berenson's *Italian Painters of the Renaissance*.

(Bernard Berenson (1865–1959) was a Lithuanian Jew who was educated at Harvard and became a world authority on Italian Renaissance drawing and painting. His beautiful Villa I Tatti on the hills outside Florence was left to Harvard as a post-doctoral research institute for Italian Renaissance Studies.)

In sculpture Donatello had already given body to the new ideals when Masaccio began his brief career, and in the education, the awakening, of the younger artist the example of the elder must have been of incalculable force. But a type gains vastly in significance by being presented in some action along with other individuals of the same type; and here Donatello was apt, rather than to draw his meed of profit, to incur loss by descending to the obvious – witness his bas-reliefs at Siena, Florence, and Padua. Masaccio was untouched by this taint. Types, in themselves of the manliest, he presents with a sense of the materially significant which makes us realize to the utmost their power and dignity; and the spiritual significance thus gained he uses to give the highest import to the event he is portraying; this import, in turn, gives a higher value to the types, and thus, whether we devote our attention to his types or to his action, Masaccio keeps us on a high plane of reality and significance. In later painting we shall easily find greater science, greater craft, and greater perfection of detail, but greater reality, greater significance, I venture to say, never. Dust-bitten and ruined though his Brancacci Chapel frescoes now are, I never see them without the strongest stimulation of my tactile consciousness. I feel that I could touch every figure, that it would yield a definite resistance to my touch, that I should have to expend thus much effort to displace it, that I could walk around it. In short, I scarcely could realize it more, and in real life I should scarcely realize it so well, the attention of each of us being too apt to concentrate itself upon some dynamic quality, before we have at all begun to realize the full material significance of the person before us. Then what strength to his young men, and what gravity and power to his old! How quickly a race like this would possess itself of the earth, and brook no rivals but the forces of nature! Whatever they do – simply because it is they – is impressive and important, and every movement, every gesture, is world-changing. Compared with his figures, those in the same chapel by his precursor, Masolino, are childish, and those by his follower, Filippino, unconvincing and without significance, because without tactile values. Even Michelangelo, where he comes in rivalry, has, for both reality and significance, to take a second place. Compare his 'Expulsion from Paradise' (in the Sistine Chapel) with the one here by Masaccio. Michelangelo's figures are more correct , but far less tangible and less powerful; and while he represents nothing but a man warding off a blow dealt by a sword, and a woman cringing with ignoble fear, Masaccio's Adam and Eve stride away from Eden heartbroken with shame and grief, hearing, perhaps, but not seeing, the angel hovering high overhead who directs their exiled footsteps.

Masaccio, then, like Giotto a century earlier – himself the Giotto of an artistically more propitious world – was, as an artist, a great master of the significant, and, as a painter, endowed to the highest degree with a sense of tactile values, and with skill in rendering them. In a career of but few years he gave to Florentine painting the direction it pursued to the end. In many ways he reminds us of the young Bellini. Who knows? Had he but lived as long, he might have laid the foundation for a painting not less delightful and far more profound than that of Venice. As it was, his frescoes at once became, and for as long as there were real artists among them remained, the training school of Florentine painters.

[122] How Michelangelo got his nose broken in the Brancacci Chapel and Henry VIII lost the chance to employ Benvenuto Cellini; from *The Life of Benvenuto Cellini* by Cellini.

At that time there came to Florence a sculptor who was named Piero Torrigiani. He came from England where he had resided many years, and since he was a great friend of my master's, he came every day to see him. And when he saw my drawings and my work, he said: 'I have come to Florence to engage as many young men as I can; for having a great work to execute for my king [*Henry VIII*] I want the aid of my Florentine fellow-citizens; and since your style of execution and your designs are more those of a sculptor than of a goldsmith, and as I have vast works in bronze to carry out, I will make you at one and the same time both skilful and wealthy.' This man was of the most handsome presence, and most bold-looking; he had more the air of a great soldier than of a sculptor, especially in his magnificent gestures and his sonorous voice, together with a trick of contracting his brows enough to terrify most men. And every day he talked of his bold doings among these beasts of Englishmen. In this connection he chanced to speak of Michelagniolo Buonarroti, which was caused by a drawing that I had made, a copy of a cartoon by that most divine Divine Michelagniolo. This cartoon was the first fine work wherin Michelagniolo displayed his marvellous talents, and he executed it in competition with one made by another artist, namely, Lionardo da Vinci, which were to adorn the Sala del Consiglio in the Palace of the Signoria. . . . These two cartoons stood, one in the Palace of the Medici, and the other in the Sala del Papa [*at the Convent of Santa Maria Novella*]. Whilst they continued in existence they formed a school of Art for the world. Although the divine Michelagniolo subsequently painted the Great Chapel [*Sistine*] for Pope Julio, he never by half reached this point; his talents never again arrived at the power of these early efforts. We return now to Piero Torrigiani, who with my drawing in his hand, spake thus: 'This Buonaaroti [*sic*] and I from boyhood used to go to study in Masaccio's chapel in the Church of the Carmine; and because Buonaaroti was accustomed to make fun of all those who were drawing there, one day when the said youth was annoying me among the rest, he aroused in me more anger than usual, and clenching my fist I gave him so violent a blow upon the nose, that I felt the bone and the cartilage of the nose break under the stroke, as if it had been a wafer; and thus marked by me he will remain as long as he lives.' These words begat in me so great a hatred, since I saw continually the works of the divine Michelagniolo, that, notwithstanding that I had conceived a desire to go with him to England, I could not bear even to see him.

Santa Maria Novella

[123] Cardinal Latino, nephew of the Pope and a Dominican, lays the foundation stone of Santa Maria Novella's
magnificent nave, and concludes peace between the Guelfs
and the Ghibellines in the Piazza; from Giovanni Villani's
Croniche Fiorentine.

And in like guise the Ghibelline refugees from Florence sent their
ambassadors to the said Pope, to pray and entreat him to put into
execution the treaty of peace which Pope Gregory IX. had
commanded between them and the Guelfs of Florence. For the
foregoing reasons the said Pope put forth and confirmed the said
treaty, and ordained a mediator and legate, and committed the
said questions to the Cardinal Frate Latino which represented
the Church in Romagna; a man of great authority and learning,
and highly considered by the Pope, who, by command of the
Pope, departed from Romagna, and came to Florence with 300
horsemen, in service of the Church, on the eighth day of the
month of October, in the year of Christ 1278 [*1279*] and by the
Florentines and the clergy was received with great honour and
with a procession, the carroccio coming out to meet him, with
many jousters; and afterwards the said legate on the day of S.
Luke the Evangelist in that same year and month, founded and
blest the first stone of the new church of Santa Maria Novella,
which pertained to the Order of Preaching Friars, whereof he
was a friar; and in that place of the friars he dealt with and
ordained generally the treaties of peace between all the Guelf
citizens, and between the Guelfs and Ghibellines. And the first
was between the Uberti and the Bondelmonti (and it was the
third peace between them), save only that the sons of M. Rinieri
Zingane de' Bondelmonte would not consent thereto, and were
excommunicated by the legate and banished by the commonwealth. But the peace was not set aside on their account; for
afterwards the legate very happily concluded it in the month of
February following, when the people of Florence were assembled
in parliament on the old piazza of the said church, which was all
covered with cloths and with great wooden scaffolds, whereon
were the said cardinal, and many bishops, and prelates, and
clergy, and monks, and the Podestà, and the Captain, and all the

Façade of the church of Santa Maria Novella embellished for the
obsequies of Luis I of Spain, 1724

counsellors, and the orders of Florence. And at that time a very
noble speech was made by the said legate with citation of great
and very fine authorities, as behoved the matter, seeing that he
was a very dexterous and beautiful preacher; and this done, he
caused the representatives ordained by the Guelfs and Ghibellines to kiss one another on the mouth, making peace with great
joy among all the citizens, and there were 150 on either side. And
in that place, and at that same time, he gave judgment as to the
terms and agreements and conditions which were to be observed,
both on one side and on the other, confirming the said peace with
solemn and authentic documents, and with all due sureties. And

from that time forward the Ghibellines and their families were to be allowed to return to Florence; and they did return, and they were free from all sentence of banishment and condemnation; and all the books of condemnation and banishment which were in the chamber were burnt; and the said Ghibellines recovered their goods and possessions, save that to some of the chief leaders, it was commanded for more security of the city that for a certain time they should be under bounds. . . . and the city of Florence abode thereafter long time in peaceful and good and tranquil state.

[124] Leon Battista Alberti designs the upper part of the façade and the portal of Santa Maria Novella at the request of Giovanni Rucellai in circa 1456; from Vasari's *Lives* . . .

It happened that when Giovanni di Paolo Rucellai wished to build the façade of S. Maria Novella in marble at his own cost, he consulted Leon Battista, his close friend, who not only gave him advice, but the design, so that he decided to execute the work as a memorial of himself. Accordingly it was begun and finished in 1477, to general satisfaction, the whole work giving pleasure, but especially the door, upon which Leon Battista clearly bestowed more than ordinary pains.

[125] Luca Landucci records the completion of Ghirlandaio's fresco cycle and the carved stalls behind the main altar of Santa Maria Novella in 1490; from his *Diario Fiorentino*.

22nd December. The chapel, that is, the *Capella Maggiore*, of *Santa Maria Novella* was opened. Domenico del Grillandaio [*sic*] had painted it, at the order of Giovanni Tornabuoni. And the choir of carved wood was also made round the chapel. The painting alone cost 1000 gold florins.

[126] For better or worse Cosimo I and Vasari modernize
Santa Maria Novella and plan to do the same for Santa
Croce; from Vasari's *Lives* . . .

The duke, so admirable in every way, not only delights in
building palaces, cities, fortresses, gates, loggias, squares, gardens, villas and other splendid and magnificent things, but also,
as befits a Catholic prince, in restoring churches, like King
Solomon. Thus recently he got me to remove the screen of S.
Maria Novella, which spoilt all its beauty, and to make a new
and handsome choir behind the high altar, removing the one
that took up a great part of the middle of the church. This makes
it indeed a handsome new church. As things lacking proportion
cannot be perfectly beautiful, he had directed a rich decorative
framework to be made round the columns of the side aisles to
form chapels with their altars, in one or two styles, to be
furnished with pictures, seven braccia by five, at the pleasure of
their owners. On one of these frameworks of my own design I did
for Alessandro Strozzi, bishop of Volterrra, my venerable and
beloved patron, a Christ on the Cross, as seen by St Anselm, with
the seven Virtues, without which we cannot mount the seven
steps to Jesus Christ, and other circumstances of the same vision.
In the same church, for Andrea Pasquali, the duke's physician, I
did a Resurrection in a similar framework, as God inspired me,
to please this good friend. Our great Duke has wished the same
thing to be done in the great church of S. Croce, Florence,
namely to remove the screen and put the choir behind the high
altar, drawing the altar slightly forward and setting over it a
handsome tabernacle for the Most Holy Sacrament, richly
gilded and decorated with scenes and figures, and further to
make fourteen chapels along the walls, just as in S. Maria
Novella, spending more on the decorations, as S. Croce is much
larger. The pictures, including two by Salviati and Bronzino, are
to represent all the chief mysteries of Our Saviour, from the
beginning of His Passion to the sending of the Holy Spirit upon
the Apostles. Having designed the chapels and the stone
ornamentation, I have in hand the picture of the Descent of the
Holy Spirit, for M. Agnolo Biffoli, general treasurer of the
Government and my good friend. . .

[127] The Strozzi and the Medici fight it out in a cinquecento chariot race on the eve of San Giovanni in the Piazza Santa Maria Novella; from Michel de Montaigne's *Journal du Voyage en Italie*.

On 23 [*June*] they held a chariot race in a large and beautiful piazza, longer than it is wide and surrounded on every side by beautiful houses. At each end of this place was set a square wooden obelisk between which is strung a long rope so that one could not cross the piazza and men were posted across the rope to support this effect. All the balconies were full of women and in a palazzo belonging to the Grand Duke were his wife and the court. The people were spread along the length of the piazza and on certain grandstands, as I was. Five empty chariots were in the race. They took up their positions, according to lot, next to one of the pyramids. According to some, the furthest away had the advantage by being able to turn more easily. They started at the sounding of the trumpets. The first to reach the pyramid from which the race began after completing three turns, is the victor. Until the third lap the Grand Duke's chariot held the lead, but then Strozzi's chariot that had always held second place speeded up, giving the horses free rein, and pressing close put in doubt the victory. I noticed that the silence broke when the people saw Strozzi coming up behind, and with shouts and applause showed him all the favour they could, given that they were under the eyes of the Prince. And when the ensuing dispute came to be judged by certain gentlemen, the Strozzi supporters referring the matter to the assembled crowd, the people let out another yell in favour of the Strozzi, who in the end won, contrary to reason in my opinion. The prize [*palio*] was worth a hundred scudi. I liked this spectacle more than any other I saw in Italy because of its similarity to the ancient races.

[128] A nineteenth-century description of the chariot race and the *corso*; from Fenimore Cooper's *Gleanings in Europe*.

The great Florentine fête was celebrated a short time since. One of the ceremonies is so peculiar, that it may amuse you to have a short account of it. There are several considerable squares in the town, but the largest is that of Santa Maria Novella. At the festival of St John, who is the patron saint of the city, an imitation of the ancient chariot-races is held in this square, which affords the most space. The games are called the *corsi dei cocchi*. There are two small obelisks on opposite extremities of the square, and the temporary circus is constructed by their means. A cord is stretched from one to the other; a sort of amphitheatre is formed by scaffoldings around the whole, the royal and diplomatic boxes being prepared near the goal. As there is much scenic painting, a good parade of guards both horse and foot, a well-dressed population, and a background of balconies garnished by tapestry and fine women, to say nothing of roofs and chimneys, the general effect is quite imposing.

The falling off is in the chariots. The ancient vehicle was small and had but two wheels; whereas these were large and clumsy, had four wheels, and unusually long and straggling perches, – an invention to keep them from upsetting. In other respects the form was preserved, and the charioteers were in costume.

Four chariots, to use the modern language, entered for the race. The start was pretty fair, and the distance twice round the obelisks. If you ask me for the effect, I shall tell you that, apart from the appliances – such as the court, the guards, the spectators and the dresses, and perhaps I might add the turns, – one may witness the same any fine evening in New York, between two drunken Irish cartmen who are on their way home. There was certainly a little skill manifested at the turns, and it was easy to see that betting should have been on the outside chariot; for those nearer to the obelisks were obliged to go considerably beyond them before they could come round, while the one farthest from the poles just cleared them. This outside chariot won the race, the charioteer having the sagacity not to make his push before the last turn.

After the chariot-races, we had the *corso dei barberi*, or a race between barbs. The horses were without riders, and the track was the longest street of the town. To this amusement every one who could went in a carriage, and the *corso* of vehicles was much the most interesting part of the exhibition. Two lines are made, and the coaches move in opposite directions through the same street, on a walk. Of course, everybody sees everybody, – and pretty often the somebodies, see nobodies, for the mania to make one on these occasions is so strong, that half the artisans are abroad in carriages, as well as their betters. The royal equipages moved in the line, the same as that of the milliner. When we were well tired of looking at each other, the grand duke went into a gallery prepared for him, and the race was run. The latter does not merit a syllable; but so strong is the rage for sporting, that I heard some Englishmen betting on the winner.

[129] Boccaccio and Santa Maria Novella; from Lady Morgan's *Italy*

On entering one of the most interesting of all Florentine Churches, the venerable Chiesa of Santa Maria Novella, the first association awakened by its Gothic aisles, is that which it excites as the site of *Boccacio*'s first scene, with his fair band of young novellists, his '*Brigata Novellatrice*.' Fancy soon decides on the high painted casement under which the seven pretty Pietists were seated in a circle; when, having 'said a Pater,' they began to lament the moral and mortal effects of that plague which was depopulating and destroying their native city. One sees too *Boccacio* gliding from the high altar in his '*abito lugubre,* ' in which he says he came to assist at the divine office, approaching the 'brigata,' overhearing their councils on the prudence of retiring to the safe and rural retreat of the Villa *de Sc[h]iffanoja*, and then timidly approaching and presenting himself to the little circle for whom his *Decamerone* was afterwards composed. Much of this venerable edifice remains as Boccacio left it, and as it was finished in 1350. Here are still to be seen unfaded the first attempt of Cimabue at a representation of the Madonna (a horrible monster!); some paintings of the Greek artists, who were then the first masters of the Florentine school; and a crucifix, one of Giotto's early works. The choir and several of the chapels are painted by Filipp[in]o Leppi and Ghirlandajo: they are singularly curious, as giving the portraits of several historical characters, in the representation of scriptural stories.

[130] Ghirlandaio's frescoes in the choir of Santa Maria Novella according to John Ruskin; from *Mornings in Florence*.

Today, as early as you please, and at all events before doing anything else, let us go to Giotto's own parish-church, Santa

Maria Novella. If, walking from the Strozzi Palace, you look on your right for the 'Way of the Beautiful Ladies,' it will take you quickly there.

Do not let anything in the way of acquaintance, sacristan, or chance sight, stop you in doing what I tell you. Walk straight up the church, into the apse of it; – (you may let your eyes rest, as you walk, on the glow of its glass, only mind the step half-way;) – and lift the curtain; and go in behind the grand marble altar, giving anybody who follows you anything they want, to hold their tongues, or go away.

You know, most probably, already, that the frescos on each side of you are Ghirlandajo's. You have been told they are very fine, and if you know anything of painting, you know the portraits in them are so. Nevertheless, somehow, you don't really enjoy these frescos, nor come often here, do you?

The reason of which is, that if you are a nice person, they are not nice enough for you; and if a vulgar person, not vulgar enough. But, if you are a nice person, I want you to look carefully, to-day, at the two lowest, next the windows, for a few minutes, that you may better feel the art you are really to study, by its contrast with these.

On your left hand is represented the birth of the Virgin. On your right, her meeting with Elizabeth.

You can't easily see better pieces – (nowhere more pompous pieces) – of flat goldsmith's work. Ghirlandajo was to the end of his life a mere goldsmith, with a gift of portraiture. And here he has done his best, and has put a long wall in wonderful perspective, and the whole city of Florence behind Elizabeth's house in the hill-country; and a splendid bas-relief, in the style of Luca della Robbia, in St Anne's bedroom; and he has carved all the pilasters, and embroidered all the dresses, and flourished and trumpeted into every corner; and it is all done, within just a point, as well as it can be done; and quite as well as Ghirlandajo could do it. But the point in which it *just* misses being as well as it can be done, is the vital point. And it is all simply – good for nothing.

Extricate yourself from the goldsmith's rubbish of it, and look full at the Salutation. You will say, perhaps, at first, 'What grand and graceful figures!' Are you sure they are graceful? Look again, and you will see their draperies hang from them exactly as they would from two clothespegs. Now, fine drapery, really well drawn, as it hangs from a clothes-peg, is always rather impressive, especially if it be disposed in large breadths and deep folds; but that is the only grace of their figures.

Secondly. Look at the Madonna, carefully. You will find she is not the least meek – only stupid, – as all the other women in the picture are.

'St Elizabeth, you think, is nice'? Yes. ' And she says, "Whence is this to me, that the mother of my Lord should come to me?" really with a great deal of serious feeling'? Yes, with a great deal. Well, you have looked enough at those two. Now – just for another minute – look at the birth of the Virgin. 'A most graceful group, (your Murray's Guide tells you,) in the attendant servants.' Extremely so. Also, the one holding the child is rather pretty. Also, the servant pouring out the water does it from a great height, without splashing, most cleverly. Also, the lady coming to ask for St Anne, and see the baby, walks majestically, and is very finely dressed. And as for that bas-relief in the style of Luca della Robbia, you might really almost think it *was* Luca! The very best plated goods, Master Ghirlandajo, no doubt – always on hand, at your shop.

[131] Henry James reacts against Ruskin in Santa Maria Novella; from *Italian Hours* by Henry James.

(James began *Roderick Hudson*, his first major novel, in a 'high, charming, shabby old room' overlooking the Piazza Santa Maria Novella on the corner of Via della Scala in the spring of 1874.)

Seeing one morning, in a shop-window, the series of *Mornings in Florence*, published a few years since by Mr Ruskin, I made haste to enter and purchase these amusing little books, some passages of which I remembered formerly to have read. . . . The wreck of Florence, says Mr Ruskin, 'is now too ghastly and heart-breaking to any human soul that remembers the days of old;' and these desperate words are an allusion to the fact that the little square in front of the cathedral, at the foot of Giotto's Tower, with the grand Baptistery on the other side, is now the resort of a number of hackney-coaches and omnibuses. This fact is un-doubtedly lamentable, and it would be a hundred times more

agreeable to see among people who have been made the heirs of
so priceless a work of art as the sublime campanile some such
feeling about it as would keep it free even from the danger of
defilement. But there is more than one way of taking such things,
and a quiet traveller, who has been walking about for a week
with his mind full of the sweetness and suggestiveness of a
hundred Florentine places, may feel at last, in looking into Mr
Ruskin's little tracts that, discord for discord, there is not much
to choose between the importunity of the author's personal ill-
humour and the incongruity of horse-pails and bundles of hay.
And one may say this without being at all a partisan of the
doctrine of the inevitableness of new desecrations. . . .

I am almost ashamed to say what I did with Mr Ruskin's little
books. I put them into my pocket and betook myself to Santa
Maria Novella. There I sat down, and after I had looked about
for a while at the beautiful church, I drew them forth one by one,
and read the greater part of them. Occupying oneself with light
literature in a great religious edifice is perhaps as bad a piece of
profanation as any of those rude dealings which Mr Ruskin justly
deplores; but a traveller has to make the most of odd moments,
and I was waiting for a friend in whose company I was to look at
Giotto's beautiful frescoes in the cloister of the church. My friend
was a long time coming, so that I had an hour with Mr Ruskin,
whom I called just now a light *littérateur* because in these little
Mornings in Florence he is for ever making his readers laugh. I
remembered, of course, where I was; and, in spite of my latent
hilarity, I felt that I had rarely got such a snubbing.

I had really been enjoying the good old city of Florence; but I
now learned from Mr Ruskin that this was a scandalous waste of
charity. I should have gone about with an imprecation on my
lips, I should have worn a face three yards long. I had taken great
pleasure in certain frescoes by Ghirlandaio, in the choir of that
very church; but it appeared from one of the little books that
these frescoes were as naught. I had much admired Santa Croce,
and I had thought the Duomo a very noble affair; but I now had
the positive assurance I knew nothing about it. After a while, if it
was only ill-humour that was needed for doing honour to the city
of the Medici, I felt I had risen to a proper level; only now it was
Mr Ruskin himself I had lost patience with, not the stupid
Brunelleschi, not the vulgar Ghirlandaio. Indeed, I lost patience
altogether, and asked myself by what right this informal votary

of form pretended to run riot through a quiet traveller's relish for the noblest of pleasures – his enjoyment of the loveliest of cities. The little books seemed invidious and insane, and it was only when I remembered that I had been under no obligation to buy them that I checked myself in repenting of having done so.

San Miniato

[132] The martyrdom of San Miniato and the building of his church; from Giovanni Villani's *Croniche Fiorentine*.

This blessed Miniato was first-born son to the king of Armenia, and having left his kingdom for the faith of Christ, to do penance and to be far away from his kingdom, he went over seas to gain pardon at Rome, and then betook himself to the said wood [*Arisbotto*], which was in those days wild and solitary, forasmuch as the city of Florence did not extend and was not settled beyond Arno, but was all on this side; save only there was one bridge across the Arno, not however where the bridges now are. And it is said by many that it was the ancient bridge of the Fiesolans which led from Girone to Candegghi, and this was the ancient and direct road and way from Rome to Fiesole, and to go into Lombardy and across the mountains. The said Emperor Decius [*of Rome*] caused the said blesed Miniato to be taken, as his story narrates. Great gifts and rewards were offered him as to a king's son, to the end he should deny Christ; and he, constant and firm in the faith, would have none of his gifts, but endured divers martyrdoms: in the end the said Decius caused him to be beheaded where now stands the church of Santa Candida alla Croce al Gorgo; and many faithful followers of Christ received martyrdom at that place. And when the head of the blessed Miniato had been cut off, by a miracle of Christ, with his hands he set it again upon his trunk, and on his feet passed over Arno, and went up to the hill where now stands his church, where at that time was a little oratory in the name of the blessed Peter the Apostle, where many bodies of holy martyrs were buried; and when S. Miniato was come to that place, he gave up his soul to Christ, and his body was there secretly buried by the Christians; the which place, by reason of the merits of the blessed S. Miniato, was devoutly venerated by the Florentines after that they were become Christians, and a little church was built there in his honour. But the great and noble church of marble which is there now in our times, we find to have been built later by the zeal of the venerable Father Alibrando, bishop and citizen of Florence, in the year of Christ 1013, begun on the 26th day of the month of

April by the commandment and authority of the catholic and holy Emperor Henry II. of Bavaria, and of his wife the holy Empress Gunegonda, which was reigning in those times; and they presented and endowed the said church with many rich possessions in Florence and in the country, for the good of their souls, and caused the said church to be repaired and rebuilt of marbles, as it is now; and they caused the body of the blessed Miniato to be translated to the altar which is beneath the vaulting of the said church, with much reverence and solemnity by the said bishop and the clergy of Florence, with all the people, both men and women, of the city of Florence; but afterwards the said church was completed by the commonwealth of Florence, and the stone steps were made which lead down by the hill; and the consuls of the art of the Calimala were put in charge of the said work of S. Miniato, and were to protect it.

[133] A group of trecento artists working at San Miniato discuss modern art and women's make-up; from Franco Sacchetti's *Trecentonovelle*.

In the city of Florence, which has always been full of original men, there was once a group of painters and craftsmen who, being at a place outside the city called San Miniato a Monte in order to do some work on the church there, when they had dined with the abbot and felt well fed and tipsy, starting arguing. And among other topics, one of these men by the name of Orcagna, who was master-builder at the noble oratory of Our Lady of Or' San Michele, proposed for discussion: 'Who, apart from Giotto, is the greatest artist of all time?' There were those who claimed that it was Cimabue, another Stefano, another Bernardo [*Daddi*] and another Buffalmacco, each proposing different names. Taddeo Gaddi, who was one of this gang, said: 'There have certainly been many skilled painters that have painted in a way that would now seem impossible for humans to achieve, but this art is decadent and declines daily.'

Then one of the group whose name was Maestro Alberto [*Orlandi*], who was a great master of marble sculpture and inlay, said: 'It seems to me that you are all gravely mistaken, for I will show you how human skill has never been so ingenious as it is today, and especially in the field of painting as also in the

Florence seen from the terrace of San Miniato; by an unknown
artist

sculpting of the human figure.'

All the other artists hearing this laughed as if he'd gone out of
his mind. But Alberto responded: 'Oh you may laugh! I will spell
it out for you if you wish . . .

'I believe that the greatest master who ever painted or
sculpted figures is our Lord God. But it seems that many see
serious defects in the figures he has created and these days they
correct them. Who are these modern painters and correctors?
They are the Florentine women. And was there ever a painter
that from black could make white, if not they? Often there is born
a young girl, or maybe more, like a pair of cockroaches; she rubs
a little here, plasters a little there, puts herself in the sun and
becomes whiter than a swan. And what craftsman is there,
whether painter or clothworker that can turn black to white?
Certainly none, since it is contrary to nature. You will see a
blonde pallid figure transformed by artificial colours into the
form of a rose. That which, either through defect or the effect of

age, seems shrivelled up, they make fresh and florid. Neither Giotto nor any other painter ever coloured better than these. But best of all she who has an ill-proportioned face with eyes which are too large will instead appear as sleek as a falcon, she who has a crooked nose will have it straightened, she who has an ass's jawbone will adjust it, she whose shoulders are too broad will narrow them down, when one is higher than the other she will pad out the lower one to the required height. And they do the same thing with their bosoms thus achieving without a chisel that which Policletus would have been incapable of even with one.'

[134] A rainy excursion to San Miniato in 1848; from Susan Horner's 1847/48 manuscript diary in the British Institute of Florence.

Though the day was cloudy we set out to walk to the little church of San Miniato, situated on a hill a little out of Florence; we had not gone far, before the rain began to fall in a steady pour, which continued all the way there and back; but we gallantly proceeded on our expedition. The hill is covered with olive-trees, and the hedges and bushes were all coming into leaf, and violets scented the air. A paved steep road with cypresses on each side, reminded me still more of the fir-tree road up to the Kreuzberg at Bonn. We looked back on a glorious view. Below us lay beautiful Florence, her cupola and campanile, and her many towers and many steeples rising above her rows of goodly houses, the Arno with its four bridges dividing the town, and then winding along the distant plain with wooded hills rising on either side. Behind Florence, or rather to the right, the hills sparkled with little white villas and the hill of Fiesole, the parent city, crowned with houses. Fiesole was the Etruscan city from whence Florence was a colony, planted on the Arno, for commercial purposes; while Fiesole too was the native city of the Beato Fra Angelico, whose works have so delighted us. San Miniato iself is a perfect gem. Here it was Michael Angelo planted his fortifications, when he undertook to defend Florence against the Pope and Emperor, who wanted to force Alexander de' Medici upon the people; he was successful for a time, but finally Alexander became the first duke of Florence. He so feared the enemy's artillery might injure this beautiful little church, that he had great sacks fastened round the steeple &c. The façade is all inlaid in rich patterns in black and white marble. It is in the form of an ancient basilica. The floor all round the nave is of black and white marble in strange devices of animals, the centre being composed of the signs of the Zodiac; thick columns which had once probably been painted support round arches, and the remains of frescos which had once covered the walls may be discovered, but alas! the whole is in bad preservation, the monastery having been dispersed, and service only being performed there three times in the year. The choir is raised, and it would be vain to attempt to describe the elaborate workmanship of the marble screen pulpit &c. Some of the columns are of serpentine. The mosaic work of one chapel was Opus Alexandrinum which is only used in ancient basilicas, of green porphyry and red, black and white marbles in beautiful patterns. The windows behind the altar are composed of a transparent marble instead of glass, which not being uniformly transparent, and where it is so giving a yellow light (like candles behind it), has an odd effect. Above is a colossal mosaic of Christ, St Miniato and St John, all glittering with gold and silver. This is very ancient, and there is something majestic in their rigid forms. In the sacristy are a fine series of frescos by Spinello of Arezzo who lived at the conclusion of the 14th century.

Santa Trinita

[135] The Guelfs subdivide into Blacks and Whites and fight in the Piazza Santa Trinita; from Giovanni Villani's *Croniche Fiorentine*.

For the which cause, the Guelf party, fearing lest the said parties should be turned to account by the Ghibellines, sent to the court to Pope Boniface, that he might use some remedy. For the which thing the said Pope sent for M. Vieri de' Cerchi, and when he came before him, he prayed him to make peace with M. Corso Donati and with his party, referring their differences to him; and he promised him to put him and his followers into great and good estate, and to grant him such spiritual favours as he might ask of him. M. Vieri, albeit he was in other things a sage knight, in this was but little sage, and was too obstinate and capricious, insomuch that he would grant nought of the Pope's request; saying that he was at war with no man; wherefore he returned to Florence, and the Pope was moved with indignation against him and against his party. It came to pass a little while after that certain both of one party and of the other were riding through the city armed and on their guard, and with the party of the young Cerchi was Baldinaccio of the Adimari, and Baschiera of the Tosinghi, and Naldo of the Gherardini, and Giovanni Giacotti Malispini, with their followers, more than thirty on horseback; and with the young Donati were certain of the Pazzi and of the Spini, and others of their company. On the evening of the first of May, in the year 1300, while they were watching a dance of ladies which was going forward on the piazza of Santa Trinità, one party began to scoff at the other, and to urge their horses one against the other, whence arose a great conflict and confusion, and many were wounded, and, as ill-luck would have it, Ricoverino, son of M. Ricovero of the Cerchi, had his nose cut off his face; and through the said scuffle that evening all the city was moved with apprehension and flew to arms. This was the beginning of the dissensions and divisions in the city of Florence and in the Guelf party, whence many ills and perils followed on . . . and like as the death of M. Bondelmonte the elder was the beginning of the Guelf and Ghibelline parties, so this was the beginning of the great ruin of the Guelf party and of our city.

[136] A fifteenth-century Florentine leaves money to provide dowries and enable four orphan girls to marrry in Santa Trinita each year; from the will of Bongianni Gianfigliazzi, translated by Rab Hatfield.

Likewise he does will that within one year from the day of the same testator's death, there be spent by his hereinafterwritten heirs and executors: one thousand two hundred florins of gold on immovable goods, located wherever and however it seems right to and pleases the Consuls of the Arte di Calimala, and wherever they adjudge them to be best and most useful; the yields of which possessions are to be distributed every year in perpetuity in support of the dowries of four poor girls, virgin and well raised, and brought up on good morals and of good reputation, who are to be given in wedlock; the which girls shall be chosen by the Consuls of the said guild who will be at the time, each year during the month of January (being unable to choose other than the orphan girls of the Innocenti, and in case the said orphanage should cease to be or should close, they shall choose as seems right to the said Consuls); there shall be paid among all of them one hundred sixty *lire* in all, that is , forty *lire* for each girl; and every remainder of the said yields, returns, and income shall be cashed each year for wax for an offering that shall be made every year in perpetuity by the Consuls and corps of the Arte di Calimala on the day of Saint Anthony in the church of Santa Trinita at the said high chapel; by the which Consuls and men of the said guild, and before the abbot of the said church, the aforesaid girls must be wed to their husbands; and the abbot of the said church, for the time it exists, shall replace and act *de facto* as the father of the same girls, and of each of the said girls; and at that moment the forty *lire* shall be paid for each, and at that time the forty *lire* shall be acknowledged by their aforesaid husbands for the dowry or portion of the dowry of the same girls, with the usual obligations and clauses; and to the which girls and their husbands it shall be brought back to mind by the same abbot how these alms were given to them through the bequest made to the said guild by Bongianni Gianfigliazzi, for the love of God and for the remedy of his soul and that of those near and dear to him, for whom they shall intercede before God that he pardon their every sin and give them everlasting life.

Santo Spirito

[137] The building of the new church of Santo Spirito gets off to a slow start just before the death of Brunelleschi; from Antonio Manetti's *Life of Brunelleschi*.

About this time one of the Masters of Sacred Theology of Santo Spirito, a monk named Master Francesco Zoppo, was preaching the Lenten sermons, and . . . spoke extemporaneously, as is done during the Easter season. He exhorted them about the Convent, their Studio, and finally the church, pointing out that as it was the principal church of the most important quarter of the city in which there were many prominent citizens (since Florence flourished during that period), it was time to consider renewing it in conformity with what was appropriate to the Quarter and the generosity of their hearts. As no one had given thought to it earlier, it began from that. Afterward they concluded that the honor it would confer on the preacher would be no less for them and for the whole city. And they decided, since they knew how to manage, that with the authority and commission of the Signoria, *operai* should be appointed. Thus, about the year 1428 five prominent citizens, all from the Quarter, decided at their first meeting that for the time being a *provveditore* should be appointed and together with him the organization of the Ufficio, the Notary, the location, and then the whole building should be studied. And they agreed easily (since the principal chapel of the old church belonged to the Frescobaldi and Stoldo was a capable and valiant man with affection for the church) that because of the many advantages he should be their *provveditore*. And they nominated him and he accepted willingly. And before any provision was made for expenditures Stoldo saw to everything, hoping to recover his outlay when the money was provided. In meeting and discussing the new office, since Filippo [*Brunelleschi*] was famous . . . the citizens had all their hopes in him because of his many experiments pertaining to similar things, and so they appointed him to bring them some good ideas, offering him advantage and honor in compensation, saying clearly to him: We might not be able to pay even if you make something similar to what we are hoping for. So Filippo made a plan with only the foundations of the building and with this explained to them

orally what the elevation would look like. Being pleased with it
they commissioned him to make, or have made, a scale model in
wood and ordered the *provveditore* that he be paid whatever he
said. And that is how it happened that he made and brought to
them a very beautiful model, and why, in considering carrying
out the new church whether it would be well to turn it rather one
way than another in the rebuilding, Filippo pressed them to
make the front of the church different from that of the old one
(and opposite to what it is today). He wanted the piazza of the
church to begin at [*the street known as*] the *fondaccio* and go toward
the church, and he wanted the front of the church to begin at the
far end, or actually to begin it at the river and make an
appropriate piazza and then build the front of the church about
where the piazza is today. He gave them many reasons, too long
to recount, why it would be better. Actually, had it been built in
that way the Quarter would not have lost any of its usefulness
and would have become more convenient for all the rest of the
city; and with the façade turned about in such a way those who
come to Florence from the Genoese coast would have seen the
façade when passing by the way, and it would not have removed
any convenience from the monks' dwelling, and nothing would
have been ruined, and all of the dwellings, cloisters, refectories,
and chapter houses would have been preserved no less than they
were in the way it was actually constructed. And furthermore it
would have faced the river. It did not appeal to the powerful men
of that time. Later they regretted that because of unimportant
motives it was not so built. When Filippo had made the model
and founded a part of [*the church*], he said at some point that,
insofar as the composition of the edifice was concerned, it seemed
to him that he had begun a church in accordance with his
intentions. Certainly he did not depart from his model. He began
it and founded some chapels and erected a part of it in his day in
accordance with this intention. It was a beautiful thing which,
with the projection of the material toward the exterior [*i.e., the
externally projecting semicircular chapels*], had no peer in Christen-
dom, not even with the errors made and consented to by others.

Sesto Fiorentino

[138] The Ginori factory in the 1870s; from *Italy Revisited* by Antonio Gallenga.

(Born and educated in Parma, Antonio Gallenga (1810–1895) was obliged to live much of his life in exile, in America, Canada and Britain, as a consequence of political activities in his youth. He eventually became Professor of Italian at University College, London, and *The Times* correspondent in Italy.)

There is no one in England unacquainted with the specimens of the china manufactory situated at Doccia, near Sesto, five miles from Florence, and which bears the name of the Marquis's family. It rose in 1735, at the same time with that of Sèvres, and it had been for several generations under the immediate management of each successive head of the house. The former Ginori, however, only carried on their trade as amateurs; they were proud to show that their private wealth could foster an industry which in other countries was dependent on royal patronage, and promoted it as a means of supplying employment to the impoverished population on their estates. But the present Marquis, aware of the struggle in which every aristocratic family must be involved if it aspire to keep afloat, has given the ancestral establishment the utmost development; he has raised the number of workmen from 52 to 550; he has enlarged his workshops to four times their size, and is now meditating the addition of a new house and furnaces in the neighbourhood to enable him to meet the demands which his success at the Exhibitions of London, Paris and Vienna, besides one held this summer in his own premises, is crowding upon him.

La Specola

[139] Belated tributes to Galileo in the Natural History Museum (now known as La Specola after the astronomical observatory in which Sir Humphrey Davy and Michael Faraday used Galileo's 'great burning glass' to explode the diamond); from Sophia Hawthorne's *Notes in England and Italy*.

On our return toward the Porta Romana, we went into the Museum of Natural History to see the Tribune of Galileo, a sort of temple erected to Galileo by the present Grand Duke Leopold – Galileo's heart being long ago thoroughly broken. In the centre of a circular apse stands his colossal statue, and around him in niches are busts of his pupils, and glass cases of his instruments; and one of his fingers, pointing upward, is preserved in a crystal vase. Another of his fingers is in the Laurentine Library. How little he dreamed, when he sat in prison, that even his fingers would become precious relics for posterity! But I wish he had kept firm, and not denied the truth he had discovered. That is an endless grief to me. The lunettes round the whole temple are painted in fresco, with incidents of his life, and the walls and floor are inlaid with precious marbles and precious gems, and the white marble pilasters are sculptured with his discoveries and inventions. The very telescopes are there with which he searched for and found stars. Galileo is not handsome, but has a tower of a head. Near the entrance, his Grand Grace has placed himself in marble, and several others of the ducal family keep him in countenance, and a very ugly countenance it is. He looks to have intellect, but a fearfully *cabeza dura*, and he has an unpardonable under-jaw.

Teatro della Pergola

[140] The Pergola and the state of Florentine theatre in 1766; from Dr Samuel Sharp's *Letters from Italy . . . in the years 1765, and 1766.*

There is but one theatre open at *Florence*, just at this juncture, and there is seldom more than one at a time, except in the season of the Carnival, when the rage of frequenting spectacles is such in *Italy*, that, in this small city, the people fill six or seven houses every night; but, in short, as if it were an act of devotion, every body makes a point of going; whereas in *France*, the madness of a carnival is, in a manner, unknown. There are, however, at *Florence*, but three considerable theatres, one very large, and two of about the dimensions of that in *Drury-lane*. The large one is dedicated to the serious Opera, the other two to comedy and burlettas. Upon a calculation, I find, that, though the extent of the house, now open, be equal to that of *Drury-lane*, it does not contain near the number of people, from the nature of its form, it having no galleries, but consisting merely of boxes and pit. The pit I apprehend to be twice as big as ours, but the boxes must be incommodiously crammed to receive seven hundred people; whereas, if I remember rightly, our two galleries alone will hold near a thousand. The comedy they exhibit here is very low indeed, by no means exceeding what is called, in *England*, a droll, and what would be very tiresome to an *Englishman*, but for the pleasure there is in novelty. To give you some idea of the small progress of the drama through all *Italy*, I need only repeat, that I have never yet seen there one play consisting of five acts; and that the joy it affords arises from mistaking one word for another, blunders, indelicate jokes, &c. At *Paris*, *Harlequin* is allowed some freedoms, which, I believe, would hardly be suffered in a *London* theatre (however *Frenchmen* may value themselves on the elegance of their taste,) but then the *Parisians* have the resource of another theatre, where both tragedy and comedy may be said to flourish almost to perfection; whereas *Harlequin* and the other *Italian* characters of *Punch*, *Don Fastidio*, *Pantaloon*, &c. are, in a manner, the only characters you see on the stages of this country.

[141] A box in the Pergola about a century later; from *Italian Sights* by J.J. Jarves.

(James Jackson Jarves (1818–1888) was born in Boston, Massachusetts the son of a glassmaker. After living in Hawaii in the 1840s, and founding a newspaper there, he moved to Florence where he built up an important collection of early Italian painting which he sold to Yale University in 1871.)

It is not a costly affair, you may dispense with receptions *chez vous*, but it is an unpardonable sin in the world of fashion not to be at home in the Opera. The world goes to the Opera as to a *réunion*; there they pay their visits, chat, laugh, partake of refreshments, turn the back upon the stage – in short almost drown by their conversation the music. The Opera is nothing; the assemblage of fashion everything. A box then, at the Pergola, is really an economical affair, as it saves the expense of society under one's roof; it is a most amusing one from the variety of ranks, nations and toilets there represented.

The Uffizi

[142] An early account of the Uffizi and the Studiolo of Francesco I, both seen as cabinets of curiosities; from Fynes Moryson's *An Itinerary* . . .

Piazza della Signoria . . . is the fairest and largest of all the rest, and therein is the Senators Pallace, and many stately statuas, one of a virgin taken by force, and of the ravisher beating her keeper, & treading him under his feet; another of Hercules, treading Cacus under his feet (for the Florentines beare Hercules in their great Seale); the third of David, all which are of white Marble; the fourth of Perseus, carrying in one hand the head of Medusa upon his Shield, and treading the bulk of her body under his feet, curiously wrought in brasse. In the same Market-place is a most faire Fountaine set round about with faire statuaes of brasse, and in the midst thereof, the statuaes of a Giant, and of three horses, almost covered with water, all wrought in white marble, do power the waters out of their mouthes into the Cesterne. In the corner of this market place is the Senators Pallace, so called, because the Senate was wont to meete there in time of the free State, but now it is the Dukes pallace, & the second that he hath within the Citie. Therein I saw a Cat of the Mountaine, not unlike to a dog, with the head of a black colour, and the back like an hedghog, a light touch wherof gave a very sweet sent to my gloves. Here they shewed us (as they use to shew to curious strangers) the Dukes Treasure (as they cal it) namely, vessels of gold and silver, Roses hallowed by the Pope (which these Princes hold for rich presents); many chambers and galleries, having a sweet prospect upon the Arno, and adorned with pictures and statuaes, notable for the matter, art, and price; a most faire looking glasse; a Theater for Comedies; one table of Porphery valued at five hundred Crownes; another of Jasper stone, valued at foure hundred Crownes, a table then in the workmans hands unperfected, the Jewels wherof they valued at fiftie thousand Crownes, and the workmanship at twelve thousand Crownes. Moreover, they shewed us the pictures of the Popes of the house of Medici; rich swords and hats, and a lather of silver to mount into the Coach; and many notable antiquities; and certaine birds of India, with many other beautifull things, which they use to shew to curious strangers, and for the same expect some reward of them in curtesie. Among other things, I wondered to see there the picture of Elizabeth our famous Queene: but the Duke of Florence much esteemed her picture, for the admiration of her vertues, howsoever the malitious Papists had long endevoured to obscure her fame, especially in those remote parts, whose slaunders God turned to her greater glory. Here they did shew us the great Dukes study, called Il studiol' del gran Duca, in which wee did see most faire pictures; two chests of Christal guilded over; divers statuaes, not of brasse, but of mixt mettals, shining here like silver, there like gold; a cup of Amber, a little Mountaine of pearles, wrought together by the hands of Duke Francis; a Pyramis of Pearles as they grow in oyster-shels; two knives set with Jewels, and a third Indian knife; a naile halfe turned into gold by Torneser an Alchumist, the other part still remaining Iron; a piece of gold unpolished, as it was digged out of the Mines; two pictures of Flemings, whereof one was valued at five hundred, the other at eight hundred Crownes; a clock of Amber; a piece of Amber falling upon a Lizard, and retaining the lively forme thereof; a stone called Vergoara that cureth poyson; the head of a Turke all of pure gold; a most beautifull head of a Turkish woman; a Table of gold, and of Jasper stone, and other Jewells, among which one Emerald of a perfect greene colour, was highly valued, being round, and almost as big as an egge, for they that kept it, reputed it worth one hundred thousand Crownes.

[143] The Grand-ducal collections in the Palazzo Vecchio and the Uffizi are also seen as a sequence of cabinets; from Richard Lassels's 1654 manuscript *Description of Italy*.

Going from hence you may visit the Gallery of the Great Duke in the old pallace. At the entrance into it, you presently cast your eye upon the two pictures of the two Queens of the Medicean familie, Katherine and Marie of Medices; both Queens and both Queen mothers of ffrance. Then turning, you see a long wide gallerie adorned below with heads and statues upon pedestals; and above with the true pictures of the famousest men in latter ages for learning and soldiery, and made by prime hands. Among the statues you may observe that of Scipio Africanus (which pleased me the best) and the habit of the Romans in his time. Having thus gazed a while at every one of these pictures, and complimented, by a particular taking notice of every one of them, the worthy Heros they represent; you will presently be lett into the great Cabinets which are joined to this Gallery. In the first whereof they will shew your Lordship the Tabernacle of S. Lorenzo's Chappel which I spoke of even now. Having seen it thrice and vewed it exactly (as I did) you will perchance be of my opinion that this Tabernacle cometh the nearest of any thing in the world, to the makeing an amends to our Saviour Christ for his ill nights lodgeing in Bethleem when he was born in a Stable. The whole composition and materials of this great Tabernacle being nothing but pretious stones set to together with art and skill as rare as the materials, I can neither describe it sufficiently nor admire it enough.

In the second Cabinet theyle shew you two Tables of inestimable valew, in which are expressed to life birds and flowers in their severall colours, and all this by severall pretious stones mosaically sett together. In the same Cabinet you see a German Cabinet of Ebeny beset with pretious stones on the outside; and within the histories of the Ghospel curiosly expressed to life in severall squairs of ivory sett here and there. Within it is showne the passion of our Saviour and the twelve Apostles curiosly cut in Amber. It was the present of the Duke of Bavaria to this Great Duke [*Ferdinand II*]; and valewed by him to be worth two hundred thousand crownes. And I was pleased to heare he valewed it so high: for its hansome for the receiver to valew things high; and for the givers to prize them low.

In a third Cabinet they will shew you a world of curiosityes together. The head of an Emperour cutt in one Turkie stone as big as a great peachstone. The naile half iron, half gold by Alchimy. The great cabinet full of ancient meddals of gold, and beset with rich stones. Some originals of Hans Holbain a famous paintre. A sett or cabinet of curious glasses. The sett of curious cupps in Ivory. The picture of a bird in curious mosaicall worke, by the same hand that made Paulus Quintus his picture which you will see in the Pallace of Burghesi in Rome. The Unicorns horne. The pillar of Allebastre curiously wrought, with a world of other Princely rarities.

From thence they will lead you to the Armorie in the same pallace, where your Lordship will be delighted to see divers

sortes of armes and habits of severall people and Princes: as the
K. of China's habit; Charles the greats sword; and the like: with a
loadstone holding up a greater peice of iron then itself.

Thence returning thorough the long Gallery againe they will
lead you into the *Guarderoba*, a great squaire and high roome full
of high and great cubbords, in which thorough strong wyar
grates youle see the great Dukes plaite. There are twelve of these
cubbords, and all filled up to the topp with plait desked up in
ordre. In one of these cubbords there is a whole service of gold:
that is Dishes, plaites, store, spoones, forkes, &c all of pure gold.
The rest are sylver, and of severall sortes for all uses. In an other is
shewne a saddle and furniture for a horse, of gold besett with
Turkie stones, diamonds and pearles: with stirrops of gold,
bridle, and trappings sutable, all being present[s] sent to the
Great Duke by the Great Turke (if I remember well.)

In fine, in an other Cubbord is seene a curious Antipendium
for an Altar, all of gold, with the pictures of S. Charles of
Borromaeus in the midst of it, of curious ennammel and
diamonds.

[144] An early nineteenth-century view of the development of the Uffizi; from *Letters on Italy* by Antoine Laurent
Castellan.

It was this prince [*Cosimo I*] who first conceived the idea of the
Gallery which now contains the Museum Florentinum, and
which has been carried to such a degree of magnificence by his
successors. This vast edifice owes its origin to a design of uniting
the ancient palace of the Republic to the Palazzo Pitti. Vasari
executed this beautiful and useful work. The corridor, which
passes over a bridge and through a part of the city, leading from
the old palace to the habitation of the sovereign, was built in
1564, in the space of five months.

But this gallery became insufficient to contain all the objects of
art which increased so rapidly. The Grand Duke Francis
continued the labours of his predecessor; and, on the scite of some
of the neighbouring houses, he added to the gallery some
magnificent halls. The ceiling of one of these halls was covered
with mother-of-pearl. And yet this cabinet is more ornamented
by the beautiful objects it contains.

The Grand Duke Francis considerably augmented the collection of medals, and added all the antiques he could procure.

In 1552 he received twenty-six marble statues, which had been in the Vatican; but which that scrupulous pontiff, Pius V. dismissed, from a principle of religion; but not wishing them to be transferred into ecclesiastical hands, he had refused them to Ferdinando de Medici, on account of his being a cardinal. Amongst these statues were the seven muses, without the least traces of any part of the figures having been restored.

The Cardinal Ferdinando, the brother of the Grand Duke, had got possession at Rome of the villa and gardens of the Medici. Here a second Museum was established, which was fated one day to increase the richness of that of Florence. It is sufficient to mention the Venus de Medici, and the statues of Niobe and her children, to appreciate the value of this collection. In 1569 the two brothers divided between them the collection of the bishop of Pavia, consisting of fifty-nine statues.

Cosmo II. who had bad health, did not contribute much to the embellishment of this gallery. But, in the long reign of his successor Ferdinando II. many additions were made to it. The Cardinal Leopold, the brother of Ferdinando, formed a rich and numerous collection of pictures and sketches, which, to their beauty, added the merit of antiquity. They extended as far back as the restoration of the arts and the time of the Greek painters. The cardinal also possessed a collection of medals, cameos, &c. Cosmo III. added many pictures to the museum.

The Genius of the house of Medici, ere totally extinguished, seemed to wish to establish its rights to the gratitude of men by some durable monument. Giovanni Gastone, the last scion of this illustrious family, commenced the magnificent description of this gallery, which is known by the name of the Museum Florentinum.

The new sovereigns of Tuscany, princes of the house of Lorraine, contributed to the embellishment and completion of this admirable collection. In the year 1762, however, it was on the point of being totally destroyed by a fire, which burst out with great violence. It lasted many hours, extending its ravages into the western corridor, and consuming a considerable part of the building. The fire arose in a chimney which had been imprudently constructed over the *logge de Lanzi*; and it was fortunate that the fire commenced at this extremity, where there were fewer valuable articles than on the other side; but it was extinguished with the loss of only a few of these precious objects.

Under the government of the Archduke Pietro Leopoldo, the legislator and reformer of Tuscany, the Gallery of Florence assumed a new appearance. The great fault of the gallery was a want of classification. Under his directions, many more halls were built, and a new flight of steps to ascend to them; and added to the museum the most precious ornaments of the other palaces. He likewise sent to Rome for the statues from the Villa Medicis, and more especiallly for those of Niobe and her children. By his exertions every class of objects had their distinct place, they were found without trouble, and classed so as to satisfy all tastes. He was rigorous in his selection, and admitted nothing that was not worthy of being preserved. The prince himself watched over the execution of his projects, and animated the workmen by his presence. One knows not which most to admire, – the grandeur of the enterprize, or the celerity of the execution. In 1780, in the space of one year, new buildings were added, and divided into halls; while, by this means, the communication was rendered more easy, and they were ornamented with stuccoes, gilding, paintings, and marbles; the tapestry and other drapery was renewed; the statues and pictures were placed in other situations, cleaned, or restored; whilst every thing was ranged according to the system of a library, where every volume had its own separate and distinct place. And this metamorphosis was executed in so rapid a manner, that travellers, ere they had completed the tour of Italy, as they repassed through Florence, thought they beheld a new gallery, and were full of admiration at a change which almost appeared magical.

[145] An unenthusiastic eighteenth-century response to the Venus de' Medici; from Tobias Smollett's *Travels through France and Italy*.

(The novelist Tobias Smollett (1721–1771) was born in Scotland and educated at Glasgow University. His *Travels* were based on a 1763–65 tour of Europe and first published in 1766. He died during a second residence in Italy near Livorno in 1771.)

With respect to the famous Venus Pontia, commonly called *de Medicis*, which was found at Tivoli, and is kept in a separate apartment called the *Tribuna*, I believe I ought to be intirely silent, or at least conceal my real sentiments, which will otherwise appear equally absurd and presumptious. It must be want of taste that prevents my feeling that enthusiastic admiration with which others are inspired at sight of this statue: a statue which in reputation equals that of Cupid by Praxiteles, which brought such a concourse of strangers of old to the little town of Thespiae. I cannot help thinking that there is no beauty in the features of Venus; and that the attitude is aukward and out of character. It is a bad plea to urge that the antients and we differ in the ideas of beauty . . . Others suppose, not without reason, that this statue is a representation of the famous Phryne, the courtesan of Athens, who at the celebration of the Eleusinian games, exhibited herself coming out of the bath, naked, to the eyes of the whole Athenian people.

[146] An ecstatic reaction to the same Venus in 1789; from *Travels in France and Italy . . .* by Arthur Young.

(Arthur Young (1741–1820) was perhaps the greatest writer on agriculture of all time. On his third and last journey to France in 1789 he continued into Italy as far as Florence, returning home via Paris where he witnessed the beginnings of the revolution.)

After all I had read and heard of the Venus of Medicis, and the numberless casts I had seen of it, which have made me often wonder at descriptions of the original, I was eager to hurry to the *tribuna* for a view of the dangerous goddess. It is not easy to speak of such divine beauty with any sobriety of language; nor without hyberbole to express one's admiration, when felt with any degree of enthusiasm; and who but must feel admiration at the talents of the artist that thus almost animated marble? If we suppose an original, beautiful as this statue, and doubly animated, not with life only, but with a passion for some favoured lover, the marble of Cleomenes is not more inferior to such life, in the eyes of such a lover, than all the casts I have seen of this celebrated statue are to the inimitable original. You may view it till the unsteady eye doubts the truth of its own sensation: the cold marble seems to acquire the warmth of nature, and promises to yield to the impression of one's hand. No thing in painting so miraculous as this. A sure proof of the rare merit of this wonderful production is its exceeding, in truth of representation, every idea which is previously formed; the reality of the chisel goes beyond the expectancy of imagination; the visions of the fancy may play in fields of creation, may people them with nymphs of more than human beauty; but to imagine life thus to be fashioned from stone, that the imitation shall exceed, in perfection, all that *common* nature has to offer, is beyond the compass of what ordinary minds have a power of conceiving. In the same apartment there are other statues, but, in the presence of Venus, who is it that can regard them? They are, however, some of the finest in the world, and must be reserved for another day. Among the pictures, which indeed form a noble collection, my eyes were riveted on the portrait of Julius II. by Raphael, which if I possessed, I would not give for the St John, the favourite idea he repeated so often. The colours have, in this piece, given more life to canvas than northern eyes have been accustomed to acknowledge. But the Titian! – enough of Venus; – at the same moment to animate marble, and breathe on canvas, is too much. – By husbanding the luxury of the sight, let us keep the eye from being satiated with such a parade of charms; retire to repose on the insipidity of common objects, and return another day, to gaze with fresh admiration.

[147] A refreshingly open-minded response to Titian's Venuses in the Uffizi; from Hippolyte Taine's *Italy*.

I pass twenty others to reserve the last look for Titian's two Venuses. One, facing the door, reclines on a red velvet mantle, an ample vigorous torso as powerful as one of Rubens' Bacchantes, but firmer – an energetic and vulgar figure, a simple, strong, unintellectual courtesan. She lies extended on her back, caressing a little cupid naked like herself, with the vacant seriousness and passivity of soul of an animal in repose and expectant. The other, called 'Venus and the Dog', is a patrician's mistress, couched, adorned and ready. We recognize a palace of the day, the alcove fitted up and colours tastefully and magnificently contrasted for the pleasure of the eye; in the background are servants arranging clothes; through a window a section of blue landscape is visible; the master is about to arrive. Nowadays we devour pleasure secretly like stolen fruit; then it was served up on golden salvers and people sat down to it at a table. It is because pleasure was not vile or bestial. This woman holding a bouquet in her hand in this grand columnar saloon has not the vapid smile or the wanton and malicious air of an adventuress about to commit a bad action. The calm of evening enters the palace through noble architectural openings. Under the pale green of the curtains lies the figure on a white sheet, slightly flushed with the regular pulsation of life, and developing the harmony of her undulating forms. The head is small and placid; the soul does not rise above the corporeal instincts; hence she can resign herself to them without shame, while the poesy of art, luxury and security on all sides comes to decorate and embellish them. She is a courtesan, but also a lady; in those days the former did not efface the latter; one was as much a title as the other and, probably, in demeanour, affection and intellect one was as good as the other.

[148] A more complex American Protestant response to the second of these pictures, the Venus of Urbino: from Mark Twain's *Innocents Abroad*.

(Mark Twain was the pseudonym – derived from a Mississippi pilot's warning call – of Samuel Langhorne Clemens (1835–1910). *Innocents Abroad* (1869) established his reputation as an author but his two greatest books *Tom Sawyer* and *Huckleberry Finn*, both drawn from childhood experiences, were published later, in 1876 and 1884 respectively.)

You enter the Uffizi and proceed to that most-visited little gallery that exists in the world – the Tribune – and there, against the wall, without obstructing rag or leaf, you may look your fill upon the foulest, the vilest, the obscenest picture the world possesses – Titian's Venus. It isn't that she is naked and stretched out on a bed; no, it is the attitude of one of her arms and hand. If I ventured to describe the attitude, there would be a fine howl; but there the Venus lies, for anybody to gloat over that wants to; and there she has a right to lie, for she is a work of art, and Art has its privileges. I saw young girls stealing furtive glances at her; I saw young men gaze long and absorbedly at her; I saw aged, infirm men hang upon her charms with a pathetic interest. How I should like to describe her, just to see what a holy indignation I could stir up in the world just to hear the unreflecting average man deliver himself about my grossness and coarseness, and all that. The world says that no worded description of a moving spectacle is a hundredth part as moving as the same spectacle seen with one's own eyes; yet the world is willing to let its son and its daughter and itself look at Titian's beast, but won't stand a description of it in words. Which shows that the world is not as consistent as it might be.

[149] An early description of Botticelli's 'The Birth of Venus'; from Walter Pater's *The Renaissance*.

(Walter Pater (1839–1894) spent most of his life in Oxford where he was educated at Queen's College and elected Fellow of Brasenose. His *Studies in the History of the Renaissance* were first published in 1873. The essay on Botticelli originally appeared in 1870, thus several years after Crowe and Cavalcasselle's detailed account but before Ruskin first mentions him in print.)

What is strangest is that [*Botticelli*] carries this sentiment into classical subjects, its most complete expression being a picture in the *Uffizii*, of Venus rising from the sea, in which the grotesque emblems of the middle age, and a landscape full of its peculiar feeling, and even its strange draperies, powdered all over in the Gothic manner with a quaint conceit of daisies, frame a figure that reminds you of the faultless nude studies of Ingres. At first, perhaps, you are attracted only by a quaintness of design, which seems to recall all at once whatever you have read of Florence in the fifteenth century; afterwards you may think that this quaintness must be incongruous with the subject, and that the colour is cadaverous or at least cold. And yet, the more you come to understand what imaginative colouring really is, that all colour is no mere delightful quality of natural things, but a spirit upon them by which they become expressive to the spirit, the better you will like this peculiar quality of colour; and you will find that quaint design of Botticelli's a more direct inlet into

Greek temper than the works of the Greeks themselves even of the finest period. Of the Greeks as they really were, of their difference from ourselves, of the aspects of their outward life, we know far more than Botticelli, or his most learned contemporaries; but for us long familiarity has taken off the edge of the lesson, and we are hardly conscious of what we owe to the Hellenic spirit. But in pictures like this of Botticelli's you have a record of the first impression made by it on minds turned back towards it, in almost painful aspiration, from a world in which it had been ignored so long; and in the passion, the energy, the industry of realisation, with which Botticelli carries out his intention, is the exact measure of the legitimate influence over the human mind of the imaginative system of which this is perhaps the central subject. The light is indeed cold – mere sunless dawn; but a later painter would have cloyed you with sunshine; and you can see the better for that quietness in the morning air each long promontory, as it slopes down to the water's edge. Men go forth to their labours until the evening; but she is awake before them, and you might think that the sorrow in her face was at the thought of the whole long day of love yet to come. An emblematical figure of the wind blows hard across the grey water, moving forward the dainty-lipped shell on which she sails, the sea 'showing his teeth,' as it moves, in thin lines of foam, and sucking in, one by one, the falling roses, each severe in outline, plucked off short at the stalk, but embrowned a little, as Botticelli's flowers always are. Botticelli meant all this imagery to be altogether pleasurable; and it was partly an incompleteness of resources, inseparable from the art of that time, that subdued and chilled it. But his predilection for minor tones counts also; and what is unmistakable is the sadness with which he has conceived the goddess of pleasure, as the depository of a great power over the lives of men.

I have said that the peculiar character of Botticelli is the result of a blending in him of a sympathy for humanity in its uncertain condition, its attractiveness, its investiture at rarer moments in a character of loveliness and energy, with his consciousness of the shadow upon it of the great things from which it shrinks, and that this conveys into his work somewhat more than painting usually attains of the true complexion of humanity. He paints the story of the goddess of pleasure in other episodes besides that of her birth from the sea, but never without some shadow of death in the grey flesh and wan flowers. He paints Madonnas, but they shrink from the pressure of the divine child, and plead in unmistakable undertones for a warmer, lower humanity. The same figure – tradition connects it with Simonetta, the mistress of Giuliano de' Medici – appears again as Judith, returning home across the hill country, when the great deed is over, and the moment of revulsion come, when the olive branch in her hand is becoming a burthen; as *Justice*, sitting on a throne, but with a fixed look of self-hatred which makes the sword in her hand seem that of a suicide; and again as *Veritas*, in the allegorical picture of *Calumnia*, where one may note in passing the suggestiveness of an accident which identifies the image of Truth with the person of Venus. We might trace the same sentiment through his engravings; but his share in them is doubtful, and the object of this brief study has been attained, if I have defined aright the temper in which he worked.

Via de' Bardi

[150] The bankruptcy of the Bardi and the destruction of their street; from George Eliot's *Romola*.

The Via de' Bardi, a street noted in the history of Florence, lies in Oltrarno, or that portion of the city which clothes the southern bank of the river. It extends from the Ponte Vecchio to the Piazza de' Mozzi at the head of the Ponte alle Grazie; its right-hand line of houses and walls being backed by the rather steep ascent which in the fifteenth century was known as the Hill of Bogoli, the famous stone-quarry whence the city got its pavement – of dangerously unstable consistence when penetrated by rains; its left-hand buildings flanking the river and making on their northern side a length of quaint, irregular pierced façade, of which the waters give a softened loving reflection as the sun begins to decline towards the western heights. But quaint as these buildings are, some of them seem to the historical memory a too modern substitute for the famous houses of the Bardi family, destroyed by popular rage in the middle of the fourteenth century.

They were a proud and energetic stock, these Bardi; conspicuous among those who clutched the sword in the earliest world-famous quarrels of Florentines with Florentines, when the narrow streets were darkened with the high towers of the nobles, and when the old tutelar god Mars, as he saw the gutters reddened with neighbours' blood, might well have smiled at the centuries of lip-service paid to his rival, the Baptist. But the Bardi hands were of the sort that not only clutch the sword-hilt with vigour; but love the more delicate pleasure of fingering minted metal: they were matched, too, with true Florentine eyes, capable of discerning that power was to be won by other means than by rending and riving, and by the middle of the fourteenth century we find them risen from their original condition of *popolani* to be possessors, by purchase, of lands and strongholds, and the feudal dignity of Counts of Vernio, disturbing to the jealousy of their republican fellow-citizens. These lordly purchases are explained by our seeing the Bardi disastrously signalized only a few years later as standing in the very front of European commerce – the Christian Rothschilds of that time –

undertaking to furnish specie for the wars of our Edward the Third, and having revenues 'in kind' made over to them; especially in wool, most precious of freights for Florentine galleys. Their august debtor left them with an august deficit, and alarmed Sicilians made too sudden demand for the payment of deposits, causing a ruinous shock to the credit of the Bardi and of associated houses, which was felt as a commercial calamity along all the coasts of the Mediterranean. But, like more modern bankrupts, they did not, for all that, hide their heads in humiliation; on the contrary, they seemed to have held them higher than ever, and to have been among the most arrogant of those grandees who under certain noteworthy circumstances, open to all who will read the honest pages of Giovanni Villani, drew upon themselves the exasperation of the armed people in 1343. The Bardi, who had made themselves fast in their street between the two bridges, kept these narrow inlets, like panthers at bay, against the oncoming gonfalons of the people, and were only made to give way by an assault from the hill behind them. Their houses by the river, to the number of twenty-two (*palagi e case grandi*), were sacked and burned, and many among the chief of those who bore the Bardi name were driven from the city.

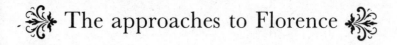 The approaches to Florence

[151] A mid-sixteenth-century view of Florence and its environs; from Sir Thomas Hoby's *Travels and Life . . . written by himself.*

(The half-brother of the then more famous diplomat Sir Philip, Thomas Hoby (1530–1566) travelled twice through Italy and eventually achieved more lasting fame with his translation of Castiglione's *Cortegiano*. Part of his travel account was plagiarized from Leandro Alberti's *Descrittione di tutta Italia* of 1550 (there being few other sources available at this date) but much else is based on first-hand observation.)

This faire citie of Florence is built upon the river Arno, which runneth through it; and the river is passed over by iiij bridges in iiij sundrie places. It is compassed on the east and the northe side with pleasant hilles full of frutefull trees. On the west side yt hathe a verie bewtifull plaine so full of faire houses that yt appearethe a farr of a great towne as farr as Prato. Yt is named Valdarno. When yt was a commune welthe the armes of the citie was a red lilie in a white feelde, but now yt is under Duke Cosmus de Medicis, second Duke of yt, which mainteynethe all virtue in yt. Within Florence is the faire church called Santa Maria del fiore, all of marble; in the toppe of yt is the marvelous peece of worke called the Cupula, worthie to bee seen of all travellars. Without this church there is a rounde temple dedicated to Saint Jhon Baptist, which in times past was the temple of Mars, with gats of brasse, within the which is a faire vessell made of riche stones where children are christened. Abowt this vale it was that Hannibal lost one of his eyes riding throwghe the marishes, as Lyvie makethe mention.

In this countreye here growethe a wyne called Torbiano di Toscano, which is reckoned among the plesant and delicate wines of Italye. In this citie I remayned vj or vij dayes with Mr Christopher Alen.

[152] A nineteenth-century view of the approach to Florence; from *Letters from Italy and Switzerland* by Felix Mendelssohn.

(Felix Mendelssohn-Bartholdy (1809–1847) set off, with Goethe's encouragement, on a tour of Italy in 1830, having already begun his career as a composer and performer. He married in 1836, but already showed symptoms of the illnesses which finally killed him at the age of 38.)

My driver pointed out a spot between the hills, on which lay a blue mist, and said 'Ecco Firenze!' I eagerly looked towards the place, and saw the round dome looming out of the mist before me, and the spacious wide valley in which the city is situated. My love of travel revived when at last Florence appeared. I looked at some willow-trees (as I thought) beside the road, when the driver said, 'Buon olio', and then I saw that they were hanging full of olives.

My driver, as a genus, is undoubtedly a most villainous knave, thief, and impostor; he has cheated me and half-starved me, and yet I think him almost amiable from his enthusiastic animal nature. About an hour before we arrived in Florence he said that the beautiful scenery was now about to commence; and true it is that the fair land of Italy does first begin then. There are villas on every height, and decorated old walls, with sloping terraces of roses and aloes, flowers and grapes and olive leaves, the sharp points of cypresses, and the flat tops of pines, all sharply defined against the sky; then handsome square faces, busy life on the roads on every side, and at a distance in the valley, the blue city.

So I drove confidently into Florence in my little open carriage, and though I looked shabby and dusty, like one coming from the Apennines, I cared little for that. I passed recklessly through all the smart equipages from which the most refined English ladies looked at me; while I thought it may one day actually come to pass that you, who are now looking down on the *roturier*, may shake hands with him, the only difference being a little clean linen and so forth. By the time that we came to the *battisterio*, I no longer felt diffident, but gave orders to drive to the Post, and then I was really happy, for I received three letters . . . I was now quite delighted, and as we drove along beside the Arno, to Schneider's celebrated hotel, the world seemed once more a very pleasant world.

[153] The eccentric Sir George Sitwell buys Montegufoni; from *Great Morning* by Osbert Sitwell.

My dearest Osbert,

You will be interested to hear that I am buying in your name the Castle of Acciaiuoli (pronounced Accheeyawly) between Florence and Siena. The Acciaiuoli were a reigning family in Greece in the thirteenth century, and afterwards great Italian nobles. The castle is split up between many poor families, and has an air of forlorn grandeur. It would probably cost £100,000 to build today. There is a great tower, a picture-gallery with frescoed portraits of the owners, from a very early period, and a chapel full of relics of the Saints. There are the remains of a charming old terraced garden, not very large, with two or three statues, a pebblework grotto and rows of flower-pots with the family arms upon them. The great saloon, now divided into several rooms, opens into an interior court where one can take one's meals in hot weather, and here, over two doorways, are inscriptions giving the history of the house, most of which was rebuilt late in the seventeenth century as a 'house of pleasure'. The owners brought together there some kind of literary academy of writers and artists. All the rooms in the Castle have names, it seems, as the Sala of the *Gonfalonieri*, the Sala of the *Priori* – twelve of the Acciaiuoli were *Gonfalonieri* and twelve, I think, *Priori*, – the Chamber of Donna Beatrice, the Cardinal's Chamber, the library, the Museum. There seem to have been bathrooms, and every luxury. We shall be able to grow our own fruit, wine, oil – even champagne! I have actually bought half the Castle for £2,200; the other half belongs to the village usurer, whom we are endeavouring to get out. The ultimatum expires today, but I do not yet know the result. The purchase, apart from the romantic interest, is a good one, as it returns five per cent. The roof is in splendid order, and the drains can't be wrong, as there aren't any. I shall have to find the money in your name, and I do hope, my dear Osbert, that you will prove worthy of what I am trying to do for you, and will not pursue that miserable career of extravagance and selfishness which has already once ruined the family. – Ever your loving father,

GEORGE R. SITWELL

[154] The Medici villas; from the life of Michelozzo
Michelozzi in Vasari's *Lives* . . .

It was also from Michelozzo's design and with his advice that
Cosimo de' Medici made the palace of Cafaggiuolo in Mugello,
giving it the form of a fortress, with ditches surrounding it, and
arranged the farms, ways, gardens, fountains in wooded groves,
aviaries, and other requisites of a country house. Two miles from
the palace he made a convent for the bare-footed friars of St
Francis, in a place called il Bosco, which is a fine work. In like
manner he made many various improvements at Trebbio, as
may be seen. Two miles from Florence he made the palace of the
villa di Careggi, which was a rich and magnificent structure.
Michelozzo brought water to it in the fountain which may be
seen there at the present time. For Giovanni, the son of Cosimo
de' Medici, he made another magnificent palace at Fiesole, the
foundations being dug in the sides of the hill, at a great expense,
but not without great advantage, as he utilised the basement for
the vaults, larders, stables, butteries and other convenient
things. Above, besides the usual chambers, halls and other
apartments, he made some for books and others for music; in fine,
in this building Michelozzo displayed to the full his ability as an
architect. The building, besides what I have said, was so
excellently constructed that it has never stirred a hair's breadth.
When it was completed, he built above it, at Giovanni's expense,
the church and convent of the friars of St Jerome, on the very top
of the hill.

[155] Galeazzo Maria Sforza, the 15-year-old son of the
Duke of Milan, is entertained by the Medici at their villa at
Careggi in 1459; from a letter in the Archivio di Stato di
Milano translated by Rab Hatfield in *The Three Kings and
the Medici.*

I went to Careggi, a most beautiful palace belonging to the same
Cosimo, which I was able to inspect thoroughly; and it pleased
me wonderfully; and I was no less impressed by the neatly kept
gardens – which truly are too delightful to describe – than by the
worthy construction of the house itself, which has no less rooms
and kitchens and halls and furnishings of every kind than those

which are found in any of the splendid palaces in the city itself; and I dined together with all of the above [*most of the Medici, Sigismondo Malatesta, and several other lords from the Romagna*] – except for Giovanni di Cosimo, who seemed not to want to sit at my table nor even eat, so intent was he on seeing that everyone was served properly. After dinner (the lord Messer Sigismondo having gone away immediately) I went with the rest of the company to a room to hear songs accompanied on the guitar by a Maestro Antonio, whom I believe Your Excellency must – if not know – at least have heard of . . . (he sings the praises of Tiberius, etc.). After listening to this I came upon a group of ladies in festive dress and beautiful for sure, among whom there were the wife of Piero, that of Giovanni, one of Piero di Cosimo's oldest daughters, the wife of Pierfrancesco, and a young lady of the Strozzi who – if she is not the most beautiful woman in this city – at least there are few who surpass her; and there were also a number of peasant girls; and in that place they all danced in the Florentine fashion, with jumps and changes of place, all nicely executed.

[156] Cosimo I's patronage of Tribolo at Castello; from Vasari's *Lives* . . .

I persuaded Duke Alessandro to recall Michelagnolo and the others from Rome to finish the sacristy begun by Clement, and I proposed to give him work at Florence. But the duke was assassinated by Lorenzo di Pier Francesco de' Medici [*6 January 1537*], a circumstance that prevented this project, and caused the despair of artists. When Tribolo heard of the duke's death, he wrote sorrowing letters of comfort to me, advising me to go to Rome, as he understood I wished to do, to leave the court and pursue my studies, and that he would fall in with what I should arrange. But as it happened this was not necessary, as on Sig. Cosimo de' Medici becoming duke, who routed his enemies at Monte Murlo in his first year, quiet was established. The duke used then to frequent the villa of Castello, rather more than two miles from Florence, where he began gradually to build quarters for himself and the court, being incited by Maestro Piero da S. Casciano, reputed a master of merit and a devoted servant of Signora Maria, the duke's mother, and the builder and servant of Sig. Giovanni. He resolved to satisfy a long-cherished desire to bring water to that place. Accordingly an aqueduct was begun to bring water from the hill of Castellina, about a quarter of a mile from Castello, the work progressing bravely with many labourers. But the duke perceived that Piero did not possess invention or design equal to the task of preparing a work that could later on receive decoration, such as the site and the water required, and one day, when he was speaking of the matter there, M. Ottaviano de' Medici and Cristofano Rinieri, Tribolo's friend and an old servant of Signora Maria and the duke, praised Tribolo as being a man well fitted for such a task. The duke therefore gave Cristofano a commission to fetch him from Bologna.

The villa of Castello is situated at the roots of Monte Morello, below the villa of Topaia, which is half-way up. In front of it the plain slopes gradually to the River Arno for a mile and a half, and at the point where the mountain begins is the palace built with good design by Pier Francesco de' Medici. Its principal front faces south over an extensive swamp, with two large lakes filled with water from an ancient Roman aqueduct built to bring water from Valdimarra to a vaulted reservoir at Florence, so that it possesses a delightful view. In the middle of the lakes is a bridge twelve braccia broad, leading to an avenue of the same width, covered by mulberry-trees along its whole length. . . . I will speak of the fountain and of the Arno which Tribolo did. The river holds a vase to its side, and leans on a lion with a lily in its claws, the vase receiving its water from a hole in the wall, behind which la Falterona was to be. As the long basin is exactly like that of Mugnone, I will say nothing except that it is a pity that such a beautiful work is not in marble. Continuing his conduit, Tribolo brought the water from the grotto under the orange garden, and the next one to the labyrinth, which it encircled, and in the middle he made the water-spout. He then united the waters of Arno and Mugnone under the level of the labyrinth in bronze channels, finely devised, filling the pavement with slender jets, so that by turning a tap all those who come to see the fountain are sprinkled, and escape is not easy . . . He next began the fountain of the labyrinth, making marine monsters encircling the base, in marble, so carved with their tails intertwined that it is a unique work of its kind. He then did the marble basin, first carried out at Castello, with a large marble bas-relief, from the villa of Antella, brought by M. Ottaviano de' Medici from Giuliano Salviati. Before making the basin Tribolo did some cherubs dancing, to decorate this, holding festoons of marine objects beautifully carved. He also gracefully executed the cherubs and masks for spouting water, and proposed to erect a bronze statue three braccia high on the top, to represent Florence, to which the waters of Arno and Mugnone flow. For this figure he had made a fine model, which was to wring water out of its hair. After bringing the water to the first quadrangle of thirty braccia beneath the labyrinth, he began the great fountain. This was octagonal, and devised to receive all the waters mentioned into the first basin, from the labyrinth and from the main conduit as well. Each of the eight sides forms a step of $\frac{1}{5}$ a braccia high, and at each angle is a projection with a corresponding one on the steps, which rise to the height of $\frac{2}{5}$ at the angles, so that the middle point of the steps is indented, giving them a quaint appearance, but very convenient to mount. The rim of the fountain is shaped like a vase, and the body of it is round. The pedestal is octagonal and continues in this shape almost up to the button of the tazza, forming eight pedestals on which are seated eight cherubs of life-size, in various attitudes, with entwined arms and legs, forming a rich ornament. The tazza, which was round and 8 braccia across, discharged water evenly all round into the octagonal basin, like a fine rain. Thus the cherubs are not touched, and seem to be playing and avoiding the bath in a charmingly childish manner, an idea unequalled for its simple beauty.

[157] An enthusiastic early description of Tribolo's work in Cosimo I's garden at Castello; from William Thomas's *Historie of Italie* . . . (1549)

Thre myles without the citee, the Duke hath made a garden at a little house that was his fathers. Wherin is a laberinth or mase of boxe full of Cypre trees, having in the middest one [of] the fairest conduite of white marble, that ever I sawe: besides that it hath dyvers other conduites, and suche conveighances, that in maner every flowre is served with renning [sic] water: and al the chanels are of white marble so fayre, that it is in my iudgement at this presente, one of the excellentest thynges in all Europe.

[158] An Elizabethan visits the completed gardens of Castello in 1594; from Fynes Moryson's *An Itinerary* . . .

Thence we rode in our returne to Florence, to another Pallace of the Dukes, called Il Castello, being two miles distant from Florence: in the Garden whereof wee did see a faire Oke, called la Quercetta, to the top whereof we ascended by staires, and there with the turning of a cock, the water sprung up on all sides. There is a Fountaine, or a statua of a woman, made of mixt mettall (richer then brasse, called vulgarly di Bronzo,) and this statua shed water from all the haires of the head, and there be seates which cast out water when they are set upon. Here in another Cave are divers Images of beasts of Marble, curiously wrought, namely, of Elephants, Camels, Sheepe, Harts, Wolves, and many other beasts, admirable for the engravers worke. Here our guide slipped into a corner, which was only free from the fall of waters, and presently turning a cock powred upon us a shower of raine, and therewith did wet those that had most warily kept themselves from wetting at all the other fountaines. This Garden was full of pleasant hills and shades of Cipresse trees, and had three Cesternes of Marble to keepe water.

[159] A late sixteenth-century love-nest-cum-hunting-lodge, from unpublished chapters of Fynes Moryson's *An Itinerary* . . . in *Shakespeare's Europe* edited by Charles Hughes.

Among many Uccellami which I have seen I will describe one, belonging to a Florintyne gentleman named Bondelmonte lying neere St Casciano. Upon a hill somwhat large but not very high, and of easy ascent, this place of delight was planted, where first upon the rising of the hill upon one syde was alitle howse built, having a pleasant prospect, on the one syde towardes the lower groundes fitt for the sporte of Birding, on the other syde towardes the hill. At the one end this howse had a Beddstead fitted with Cushions of lether, and being narrowe it had a Cubbard which drawne out inlarged it for a bedfellowe if neede were. The rest of the house coulde not well receave above six persons. The insyde was curiously paynted, but with Lascivious pictures of naked wemen with divers postures to wanton daliance. It had a litle table hunge up against the wall, under which was a most obscene picture of a Satyre and a naked woman. And neere it was a Cubbard, wherein the gentleman had Pasta Reale, Ciambelini, and like delicate kindes of bread, with other Junketts, and a bottle of white Muskadyne, to intertayne his Mistres or other frendes. From this house on both sydes and rounde about the hill, were planted hedges being like Battlements, and the Arbours like towers and Bulwarkes, all which were hunge with lymed twiggs, and in the Arbours were Cages of divers birdes, with Sparrowe Hawkes and Owles tyed neere them, whose least stirring made the birdes Cry, which made flying birdes come and fall upon the lymed twiggs. Upon the greene plott before the house, and within the hedges, divers netts were spread, and living birdes tyed to stickes, and within the house satt the gentleman governing all this sporte, by diverse ropes lifting up the stickes and birdes, which fluttering and Chirpping made flying birdes fall among them, and with other ropes drawing the netts when any birdes fell within their Compasse.

[160] The Villa Gamberaia; from Harold Acton's *Memoirs of an Aesthete* (1948)

[*Léon Bakst*] was very enthusiastic about Tuscan gardens and was making a careful study of the Villa Gamberaia. This belonged to two retired ladies, Princess Ghika and Miss Blood, who cultivated their garden as Voltaire proposed in *Candide*, without heeding the outer world.

The villa, a mellow Tuscan country house of modest proportions with projecting eaves, stands on a high ridge above the village of Settignano with an unrivalled view of the valley of the Arno, and the garden is a perfect example of *magnum in parvo*, a great effect on a small scale.

Between the house and a high retaining wall crowned with statues and old stone vases, a long bowling green runs towards a balustrade at one end with hills and valleys melting into the distance, and in the opposite direction towards a grotto for sculptured lovers in a framework of shells and coloured pebbles, guarded by a grove of the slimmest, blackest cypresses. To the south there is an oblong water garden with four symmetrical tanks of water-lilies and a fountain with a boy bestriding a dolphin in the middle. Owing to this profusion of water there is a greater variety of flowers than in most Tuscan gardens. A tall clipped hedge screens the garden along its length and a circular arcade rounds it off with stone benches between arches of yew. Here are sheltered walks on so many different levels and with so many surprising effects that even the opium smoker must forget his pipe. Behind the wall flanking the bowling green there is a mysterious terraced wood and a grotto garden which is surely the most beautiful of its kind, a rococo jewel of formal rockery surmounted by a balustrade with busts and vases, and with balustraded flights of steps topped by stone obelisks, leading to a lemon garden and another grove of ilexes and cypresses where you may rest from the summer glare. All this may sound vast but it does not occupy much space. The whole plan is highly concentrated, fastidious and versatile. I write in the present tense, for Gamberaia is still alive to me though the Germans have nearly destroyed it. The house is just a blackened shell . . . And I wonder what happened to the water-colours Bakst painted in the garden.

[*The Villa Gamberaia has since been painstakingly restored and the gardens may be visited by appointment.*]

[161] The Horner sisters describe the Villa Stibbert; from *Walks in Florence* by Susan and Joanna Horner.

A lane to the right, winding up a short but steep ascent, leads to the Villa Stibbert. All the undulating land between the Via Vittorio Emanuele and the Via Bolognese bears the name of Mont' Ughi, from a certain Captain Ugo, who left Rome some time in the twelfth century in quest of adventures, or to make his fortune. Arriving with his band of armed followers in the vicinity of Florence, he wasted the whole country, and, finally, established himself on this height, where he built his castle, and where, in modern days, an English gentleman, Mr Stibbert, has converted two farmhouses into a beautiful villa. The story of Ugo is preserved in a fresco beneath a Loggia adjoining the house, painted by the Florentine artist Bianchi. From this Loggia a beautiful view may be obtained of hill and valley richly cultivated, which once was devastated by the robber chieftain. The little chapel beside the Loggia is supposed to occupy the site of Ugo's Castle, and within its walls lie buried the remains of the celebrated engraver Raffaelle Morghen, who died in 1833 . . .

The grounds round the Villa Stibbert combine English taste for order with the usual elegance of the Italian garden, consisting of terraces decorated with lovely busts amidst the luxuriant growth of a southern vegetation. Within the villa there is a most rare and remarkable collection of armour, which Mr Stibbert allows to be seen on certain days to those who can obtain a card of admission through his personal friends.

Descending a few steps from the entrance hall into a vast saloon with a vaulted ceiling, the visitor finds himself surrounded by figures of men in various postures, and of horses with their riders in full armour. They represent different periods of Italian and German history. Numerous swords and other weapons, horses' bits of singular construction, banners, &c., decorate the walls, which are painted with coats of arms and other devices in a low tone of colour. Some precious relics are under glass on tables in the middle of the room. In the centre is a horse and man fully equipped for the tournament; to the right a red-bearded figure wears the armour of the Emperor Maximilian, the *letzte Ritter* of the Germans; he has on a kilt of crimson and green velvet striped with black and gold, the Austrian colours; and broad ribbons of crimson and green are crossed over his breast.

One very rich coat of mail inlaid with gold belonged to a Visconti of Milan. In a recess to the left, a rider comes forth clad in the armour of one of the Guadagni family. Six cavaliers, three on each side, guard the farther entrance to this saloon. Three are Saracens in fine chain armour, carrying round shields, and with the horsetail for a banner; the other three cavaliers are European.

The room beyond contains many valuable and curious examples of Japanese and oriental armour, and has likewise two figures on horseback, the horses being decorated with gilt horns.

A second magnificent hall, lighted from above, contains the picture Gallery, and a richly-decorated boudoir is painted and adorned with flowers in relief, after the taste of the Louis Quinze period.

[162] Two English Royalists in exile visit the Grand Duke Ferdinand II at Poggio a Caiano; from Sir John Reresby's *Travels and Memoirs* . . .

Ten miles from Florence the duke hath another country-house, called Poggio-Achaiano, which another gentleman and myself took the opportunity of seeing while his highness was there. The house is nothing so considerable in itself, as in its situation, standing betwixt several hills on one side, covered with vines and olive trees, and a valley divided into many walks by rows of trees, leading different ways; one leads to a park where the Great Duke had made a paddock-course, by the direction of signior Bernard Gascoigne, an Italian, who having served our late king in his wars, carried the pattern from England.

There we found the duke diverting himself in the morning, who, after his return to dinner, according to his usual civility to strangers, sent us two dishes of fish (being Friday) and twelve bottles of excellent wines, to our inn.

Near to this house is another park [*Artimino*] the largest in Italy, or rather a chace, said to be thirty miles in compass.

[163] The extraordinary gardens and waterworks of Pratolino in the late sixteenth century; from Sir Robert Dallington's *Survey of the Great Dukes State of Tuscany*

Having gazed your fill upon the beauties of this Towne, if for varieties sake, and your better recreation, you will walke abroade into the *Villa per spasso*, as the *Italian* saith; you shall have there in view, so many, and such goodly Pallaces, for the space of six or seaven miles compasse, as (they say) would make one other *Florence*. But above all, the great Dukes Pallace of *Pratolino*, built by his brother *Francesco*, is the most admirable, not for the Pallace it selfe, or manner of the building; for there are many can match it, if not excell it: But for the exquisite and rare invention of Water-workes, wherein it is excellent, and thought to exceede *Tivoli* by Rome, so much in this kinde commended. The house it selfe is built in forme of a *Romaine* T, the head of the letter which is the front of the house, being in length seaventy paces, & the other part fifty foure: the roomes for offices of Court, and lodgings are seaventy, whereof these are all of one bignesse, forme, and furniture: with three goodly halles richly furnished, running along the middest of the Pallace, from the one end to the other, and the one opening into the other, so as according to the winde or sunne, he may give his intertainment for the best ease of them he feasteth: It is seated betweene two high hilles, upon a third lower then they, from which hilles yee descend some quarter of a mile, by a way set with quick-set [*hedge*], & kept after our English fashion: yee mount up to the *Terreno* of the Front by twelve staires, very faire of Stone, directly whereupon, at the head of a Garden set round with Statues of the Muses in a ground sencibly ascending, is seene a huge Giant cut out of the maine Rock, with all his parts, as armes, hands, legges, and feete, symmetrical to his head, wherein may stand a dozen men: In it are kept Pigeons; the loovers whereat they come in and out, are his eares; the windowes which give light to the roome, are his eyes. Out of his mouth falleth into a very fine poole, all the water that serves the worke on the other side the [*sic*] Pallace, among which are many sights yeelding very great content, as *Noes Arke* with all kinds of beasts, *Hercules* fighting with a Dragon, Birds artificially singing, organs musically playing, showers of Raine plentifully downe powring, and infinite sort of such devise, more delightsome to be seene then pleasant to be discoursed of. To conclude, the devise so good, the workmanship so rare, and the charge so great, as it is said constantly that it cost Duke *Francesco* three hundred thousand Crownes.

[164]   The best and last (c.1819) description of the magnificent gardens of Pratolino just before their almost total destruction; from Antoine Laurent Castellan's *Letters on Italy*.

Amongst the numerous and magnificent palaces of the sovereigns of Tuscany, that of Pratolino is acknowledged to be most worthy of the traveller's attention. The hand of nature had prepared the elements, that of the artist had only to reduce them to shape and symmetry. The forests which covered the ground, needed only the axe in certain parts, or to be formed in others into avenues. The thick tufts of trees, when pierced by winding path-ways, were transformed into retired asylums and inextricable labyrinths. On all sides fountains sparkled up which did not demand the human hand to guide them. Their waters were either collected in vast basins, or flowed through channels open to the air, or forcing their way through canals from which they sprung in jets, they then fell in cascades, carrying along into every part their freshness and the gentle murmur of their motion.

These woods composed of firs, laurels, and other ever-green trees, seemed the asylum of perpetual spring. To provide for the pleasures of the chace and angling, the park was stocked with wild animals, and the waters were filled with fish of every species. The gardens were under the management of experienced gardeners, who transplanted thither the rarest trees and flowers, and brought to perfection the fruits of all nations. In short this retreat called to mind the delicious abodes which the voluptuous emperors of Rome retired to, in pursuance of the counsels of Epicurus, to lay down the purple and to crown themselves with the roses of pleasure. . . .

The grottos of Pratolino are situated in that part which is exposed to the south. They occupy the level ground beneath the terrace which surrounds the castle, and serves it as a base. You descend by a double staircase, in the form of a horse-shoe, to an esplanade in front of the grottos, which forms a second terrace lower than the first. On the side of the gardens it is cut off precipitately, on account of the declivity of the ground, but the lateral extremities are on a level with the grass plot.

The distribution of the grottos, although they are unequal in size and grandeur, is remarkable for the advantages which have been taken of the situation in which they have been constructed. They are all of them vaulted, and rest on beautiful columns of marble. One certainly cannot too much admire the brilliancy of the interior decoration, which is nearly the same through them all. The walls and the vaulted roofs are ornamented with stalactites, madrepores, marine plants, corals, shells, and mother-of pearl; and all those objects are mingled with paintings in Mosaic. Everywhere one sees statues of marble or of bronze, which cast streams of water into basins of marble or of gilded lead. These waters, by secret passages, flow beneath the pavement, and escape into the gardens, where they are again applied to a thousand different purposes.

Amongst the statues, many are to be attributed to celebrated artists, and are no less remarkable for their composition than their execution. The most beautiful have been transported to

Florence; yet, notwithstanding, there are several left worthy of observation.

The Grotto of the Deluge is the first the stranger arrives at: it is so called from the quantity of water which flows in it, not only from the ceiling, but from the walls, and even from the pavement. When you enter it, you are completely in the power of the fountain players, who can inundate you without the possibility of your avoiding it, for the fountains bar the passage, and even reach you on the esplanade; the pavement of which, constructed like that of the grotto – of small round stones of various colours, and arranged in compartments, so as imitate Mosaic work, is pierced by innumerable holes, through which a multitude of little spouts of water issue.

It may be added, that we may not have again to return to this subject, that every sort of surprise, and all arts of deceit, are used to entrap the curious. – Sometimes the commodious seats which invite them to repose themselves break with their weight, and duck them in an unexpected bath: – sometimes a ladder is placed as if it led to some curious object, but scarcely have you placed your foot on the first step, when a catch goes off, and unmasks a fountain, which rushes direct into your face: – sometimes, when you are least expecting it, a marine monster, or some other strange figure, rises, – rolls its eyes on you, opens its mouth, and covers you with a flood of water.

In a colder climate this sort of amusement would prove somewhat inconvenient. It is, however, foreseen; no one is exposed to it against his will, and you may avoid it by proper precautions.

The Grotto of the Samaritan is one of the most curious, from the numerous mechanical inventions of Buontalenti, which force the water into action. There is a sort of theatre, in which several complicated movements successively take place. The cave represents a hamlet composed of huts intermingled with trees. – The door of a house opens, and a beautiful village girl comes out, carrying a vase, and approaches one of the fountains to draw water. – Her movements are very natural, and her body possesses a kind of suppleness and grace. She arrives at the fountain, fills her vase with water, places it again on her head, and returns towards the cottage; not, however, without frequently turning round her head to gaze at a shepherd seated near, who seems to admire her, and who attempts to prevail on her to stay and listen to his music. On the sides of the theatre, a blacksmith opens his shop, and is seen busily employed with his workmen in the labours of the forge: – a miller, also, carries sacks of grain to a mill, the mechanism of which is most complete. – In the distance is heard the sound of horns and the barking of dogs, and we are entertained with the representation of a hunt: many wild animals run across the bottom of the stage, pursued by a pack of hounds and hunters. – In the foreground, birds, perched in the branches, pour forth their song; and swans and ducks are seen sporting in the waters. . . .

The grotto of Cupid, the fountain of Esculapius, the urns, the tombs, and the statues, which people these woods with recollections, attest the respect of the Medici for the precious monuments of art and antiquity – here rises Mount Parnassus, with the statues of Apollo and the Muses; Pegasus is bounding from the summit of the mountain, whence also a limpid stream starts, the sound of which is mingled with the notes of a musical instrument, which is played by water – there rise fountains, ornamented with groups of statues, representing fabulous personages, or scenes from common life. . . .

Such are the gardens of Pratolino, such is the vast enclosure fenced in by a curtain of impenetrable forests, where Francesco de Medici forgot fame and honour in the lap of pleasure. The seductive Bianca Capello was the queen of these solitudes; frequently armed with the symbols of Diana, and surrounded like her with her nymphs, she traversed the woods to the sounds of horns and warlike music; more frequently, however, in the diviner habit of the queen of love, she wandered through these paths with her lover, consecrating the places which witnessed their delights, with monuments, alas! more durable than their happiness.

Having now given some account of the palace and gardens of Pratolino, I shall proceed to say something of that extraordinary work the Colossus of the Apennines. In front of the castle I have said there lies an open space of ground about 300 feet in length, and 100 in breadth; this piece of ground is bordered on each side by lofty fir trees and beeches, the trunks of which are hidden by tufts of laurels, in which are placed niches for statues; the middle of it is covered with turf, and farther on a piece of water extends itself in the shape of a half-circle, behind which rises the colossal statue of the Apennines.

'The Colossus of the Apennines' – Giambologna's giant in the
gardens of Pratolino; by Stefano della Bella

Rising from an elevated and apparently irregular base, to
which you arrive by two flights of steps which follow the
semicircular bend of the basin, this statue at first appears to be a
pyramidal rock, on which the hand of man has rudely attempted
to execute the project which the statuary intended to work on
Mount Athos, and which Alexander had the proud wisdom to
reject; but on a second view we recognize the genius of a pupil,
and worthy rival of the great Michael Angelo.

John of Bologna, inspired by the writings of the ancients,
executed in this work, the idea which they formed, and have
transmitted to us of their Jupiter Pluvialis, a name much more
applicable to this figure than that of the Colossus of the
Apennines, which has been attributed to it one knows not why.
The style is grand, and the character of the head is perfectly
suited to the subject; his bushy temples brave the storm, and
seem covered with a hoar frost; his hair descends like icicles upon

his large shoulders, and the locks of his beard resemble stalactites. In order to add to the extraordinary effect of this Colossus, a sort of crown is placed on his head formed of small *jets d'eau* which fall upon his shoulders, and rolling over the whole figure make it sparkle in the rays of the sun.

The position is good, setting and bending forward, the God rests one hand on a rock, whilst the other presses the head of a marine monster, which spouts a large volume of water; although by this position much of his height is lost, his head still overtops the trees, and standing off from the blue heavens almost seems to touch the clouds; it would be difficult to imagine a more picturesque and perfect composition in all its proportions; when you gaze on it you perceive no enormous disparity with the objects around, so well does it harmonize with all that surrounds it, and you only conceive an idea of its real magnitude, by comparing it with the groups of passengers, which, when seen at a certain distance, resemble pigmies: if we suppose this giant standing up, it would not be too much to say, that he would be an hundred feet in height.

In the interior of the body there are several apartments, and in the head there is a beautiful chamber, to which the eye-balls serve as windows; the extremities are constructed of a coarse laying of stones; the trunk is formed of bricks covered with mortar or cement, which has acquired the hardness of marble, but which when fresh must have been easily worked, and capable of taking the requisite impressions.

It is said that many of the pupils of John of Bologna who were employed on this work, when they came to execute figures of ordinary dimensions, found that in their giant labours they had lost their exactness of eye and skill of hand.

The untenanted Pratolino is now a melancholy spectacle; the vast apartments, the long galleries, formerly ornamented with pictures or rich hangings, now only display the nakedness of uncovered walls; the mosaic pavements are covered with dust, and the wind sobs through the broken casements. This beautiful place, now almost forgotten, attracts only the traveller, whose affection for the arts prompts him to search for them in the midst of the ruins, which the hand of time and the negligence of man have accumulated.

[165] The Franciscan Monastery in Fiesole; from *Yester-days of an Artist-Monk* by Dom Willibrord Verkade OSB.

(Jan Verkade (1868–1946), after studying in Amsterdam, moved to Paris in 1891 where he entered the circle of Gauguin and Sérusier. Influenced by them to paint in Brittany, Verkade soon became an influential member of the Pont Aven school. After converting to Catholicism, he moved first to Italy and later to Beuron where he became a Benedictine monk.)

I passed the Feast of the Ascension (May 11, 1893) with the Franciscans in Fiesole, and on that occasion finally received permission to reside in the cloister on the height. Sérusier returned to France. The harmonious beauty of Italy did not appeal to him. He preferred the severer beauty of Brittany. My landlord in the *Via Taddeo* was sorry to see me go, but in a niche of his dwelling I left a large picture of the Madonna and Child, my first mural painting. . . .

The Franciscan cloister of Fiesole is rather extensive, having been at different times enlarged. The little courtyard with its well forms the nucleus around which in a quadrangle the church and the original cloister are situated. At the time I was there, the little ancient cloister, which is now evacuated, and has been made accessible to travellers, including women, was the residence of the clerics, that is to say, of the brothers who are preparing themselves for the priesthood by the study of theology. To this little courtyard there is now joined a much larger one with decorative arcades and a simple well. This courtyard is enclosed on the southern side by the apartment of the clerics, on the western side by the refectory and library, on the north by the steward's rooms and on the east by the tailor's shop and a large refectory for visitors. Above the steward's rooms and the dining-hall for guests is a second story with projecting galleries, which furnish access to a row of guest-rooms of the most primitive character.

Here I was now located. My cell, therefore, faced the north, and from my window I had a magnificent view of the grove of cypresses and the sombre Apennines. *Monte Senario* rose, clearly defined, from the mountain-chain, with the mother-cloister of the Servites on its summit. The furniture of my room consisted of a large bed, almost as broad as it was long, a wash-stand, a *prie-*

dieu, a small table and a straw-chair. The walls were white-washed and the floor was paved with red bricks. No one lived in this story except the porter of the cloister and myself. From the open passageway before my cell I could sometimes discern a young monk behind the little window of a cell in the clerics' residence, but otherwise I at first saw very little of the cloister's community, except in the recreation hours, when the fathers and brothers assembled under my window, or took a walk through the little wood. But little by little I came into more intimate relations with them and was known as 'Giovanni' or, as the clerics called me 'Gianni', for whom perhaps today there is still preserved a friendly recollection high up on the hill of Fiesole.

[166] A Welsh poet is driven 'pazzo' by the summer heat in a villa in the hills near Scandicci (1947); from *The Collected Letters of Dylan Thomas*, edited by Paul Ferris.

I have met many of the young intellectuals of Florence, who are rarefied and damp: they do not write much but oh how they edit! They live with their mothers, ride motor-scooters, and translate Apollinaire . . . I am awfully sick of it here, on the beautiful hills above Florence, drinking chianti in our marble shanty, sick of vini and contadini and bambini, and sicker still when I go, bumpy with mosquito bites, to Florence itself, which is a gruelling museum. I loved it in Rome, felt like Oppenheim on the Riviera, but we have been here, in this villa, two months and I can write only early in the morning, when I don't get up, and in the evening, when I go out. I've wanted to write to you, and have longed for a letter from you. We're coming back, some brown as shit, some bleached albino, one limp and carmine, all broke, early in August. Will you be in London, or visiting? I do hope we see each other often this autumn. I am told the bitter's better, and I will be writing a filmscript to buy same. We really do have an enormous swimming pool, (into which I have been only once, by mistake), and our own vineyard, olives, mosquitoes, and small Italian mice with blue chins. I have written a longish poem which I'd like to send you when it is typed by an Italian professor of English in Florence. I asked the professor about Elba, where we thought of going, and he said – it was the first remark I heard him make – 'Plenty di fish-dog'. He translates Henry James and

Virginia Woolf. Give my love to May and yourself. Write when you can, before August if possible, and tell me where, if you're in London, as you said, last time we met, you might be, I can write. Now I am going out to the cicadas to shake my legs a bit.

In the very opposite of haste,
Dylan

❧ Life, Customs and Morals ❧

[167] England's role in the decline of pre-Medicean banking in Florence; from Fernand Braudel's *Civilization and Capitalism: 15th–18th Century*

In the Florence of the *Duecento* and *Trecento*, credit was something central not only to the entire history of the city, but to that of her rivals among the Italian towns, not to say the whole Mediterranean or the Western world. It is in the context of the revival of the European economy from at least the twelfth century that we must view the establishment of the great merchant banking houses of Florence. They were borne on the current which was to place Italy ahead of the rest of Europe for centuries on end: in the thirteenth century, Genoese boats were sailing the Caspian Sea, Italian travellers and merchants were reaching India and China, the Venetians and Genoese had occupied the vital points on the Black Sea; there were Italians looking for Sudanese gold in North African ports, while others had scattered to France, Spain, Portugal, the Netherlands and England. And wherever they went, Florentine merchants bought and sold spices, woollens, hardware, metals, cloth, silkstuffs – but most of all they trafficked in money. . . .

The greatest achievement of the Florentine firms was undoubtedly the conquest of and ascendancy over the far-off kingdom of England. In order to reach their position of influence here, they had to supplant the Jewish moneylenders, the merchants of the Hanseatic ports and the Low Countries, to overcome the stubborn resistance of native English traders, and they also had to shoulder aside some Italian competitors. The Florentines took the place of the pioneering Riccardi – the Lucchese merchants who had financed Edward I's conquest of Wales. A little later, it was the Frescobaldi of Florence who were lending Edward II money for his wars against Scotland; and the Bardi and Peruzzi subsequently acted as Edward III's backers in his moves against France in the opening stages of what was to be the Hundred Years' War. The triumph of the Florentines lay not only in holding the purse strings of the kings of England, but also in controlling sales of English wool which was vital to continental workshops and in particular to the *Arte della Lana* of Florence.

But the English venture ended in 1345 with the fall of the house of Bardi – 'a colossus with feet of clay' as it was called, but a colossus all the same. In that dramatic year, Edward III owed huge sums of money both to them and to the Peruzzi (900,000 florins to the Bardi and 600,000 to the Peruzzi) – a sum out of all proportion to the capital these firms actually owned, proof that they had made their gigantic loans with money from their own depositors – in a proportion of about 1 to 10. The crash when it came ('the most serious in the entire history of Florence' according to the chronicler Villani) was a heavy blow to the city because of the other disasters which accompanied it. As much as Edward III defaulting on his debts, the real villain was the recession which divided the fourteenth century in half, with the Black Death following on its heels.

Florence's fortune as a *banking* city now declined before the rising star of *trade* in both Genoa and Venice. And it was Venice, the queen of trade, which emerged triumphant after the Chioggia war in 1381. The Florentine experiment in what was evidently a forerunner of modern banking, did not survive the international economic crisis. Florence retained her trade and industry; and even revived her banking sector in the fifteenth century. But she never again played such a pioneering indeed world-leading role. The Medici were not the Bardi.

[168] The Black Death; as described by Boccaccio in his introduction to the *Decameron* (1358).

(Giovanni Boccaccio (1313–75) was a cosmopolitan Tuscan who trained first to be a merchant, then a canon lawyer but eventually through success as a man of letters became a diplomat. He had probably started the *Decameron* when he first met Petrarch in 1350. Henceforth he turned increasingly to scholarly Latin works, eventually retiring to his native Certaldo where he died.)

... one thousand three hundred and forty eight years had passed since the fruitful Incarnation of the Son of God when, in the worthy city of Florence, the most noble in all Italy, there arrived the most deadly pestilence, which, either because of the movements of the heavenly bodies or because our sinful deeds had provoked the righteous wrath of God to send it among mortals by way of corrective punishment, had started some years earlier in the East whence, having taken innumerable lives, it spread wretchedly and relentlessly without respite from place to place towards the West.

Against it no amount of ingenuity or man-made measures could prevail, though quantities of rubbish were cleared from the city by specially appointed officials and entry was denied the sick and much advice was circulated in order to safeguard health. Neither were humble supplications directed to God (not once but on numerous occasions in formal processions and other ways) effective, for in the early spring of the said year its grievous effects began to reveal themselves in a ghastly and incredible manner. It didn't manifest itself as it had done in the East where whoever started to bleed from the nose would inevitably die, but, in male and female alike, it began with swellings either in the groin or armpits, some of which grew to resemble a common apple, others an egg, some large, others small, all of which the common people called *gavoccioli*. And from the two said parts of the body, the said deadly *gavocciolo* would spread at random to every part, the disease soon altering its quality manifesting itself in black or bruise-like blotches which appeared on the arms and thighs, in some cases large but sparsely distributed, in others very small but frequent. And just as the *gavocciolo* had from the first been a sure sign of imminent death so these also spelled the same fate for whoever they afflicted. Neither doctors' advice nor the power of medicine had any effect . . .

And what made this plague even more virulent was that the afflicted had only to be in the company of the healthy for the latter to become infected in the same way as fire consumes dry or oily substances when they are nearby. Still more evil was the fact that not merely speaking or treating with the infected gave healthy people the disease or caused their death, but the mere touching of the clothes or of any other thing which had been touched by those with the disease seemed to infect one with it. It is extraordinary to hear what I have to say, so much so that if it had not been witnessed by my own and many others' eyes I would hardly believe it let alone record it in writing even if I had heard it from a trustworthy person. I say that the plague I am describing was so virulent in its spread from one to another that very often it did not merely spread from one human being to another but even from something which belonged to an infected man or one who had died of the disease to a non-human animal, contaminating it and killing it very quickly. Among other things

I witnessed, as I have said, with my own eyes, I saw one day that the rags of a pauper who had died of the disease had been thrown out into the public street, where they were discovered by two pigs. As they are wont to, the pigs first with their snouts and then with their teeth took them and shook them against their cheeks. In no time, after rolling over as if they had been poisoned, they were dead, lying stretched out on the evil rags.

Such things and worse provoked various fears and fantasies in those who remained alive and almost all reacted rather cruelly by fleeing in disgust from the infected and their possessions, believing they would thus preserve their own health. And there were some, who warned that a moderate life-style and the avoidance of every excess would give considerable protection. These formed little groups and lived apart from everyone else enclosing themselves in houses in which there were no infected persons, and so as to live healthily and temperately consumed the most delicate foods and best wines, avoiding every luxury, and refraining from speaking with outsiders or from hearing any news of the dead or diseased and diverting themselves with music and whatever other pleasures they could conjure up. Others taking an opposite view, that the surest medicine for so much evil was to drink heavily and enjoy things, went around singing and making merry and satisfying every appetite they could, laughing and ridiculing whatever might happen.

[169] Slavery in early Renaissance Florence; from Iris Origo's 'The Domestic Enemy'.

Of the 357 slaves [*on an official list of slaves sold in Florence between July 1366 and 2 March 1397*] 274 were Tartars, thirty Greeks, thirteen Russians, eight Turks, four Circassians, five Bosnians or Slavs, one Cretan and the rest 'Arabs' or 'Saracens'. And of these at least the Greeks, Russians, Circassians, and Bosnians were almost all Christians. The other interesting point is the very large preponderance of female slaves: 329 of them are women or little girls, and of the twenty-eight males only four are over sixteen.

Youth seems to have been the foremost requisite in both sexes: thirty-four of the girls in the Florentine list are under the age of twelve, and eighty-five more between twelve and eighteen, while only six are over thirty. The most popular age, in short, was immediately after puberty – and it was then that slaves fetched the highest prices. Thus in Florence, at the end of the fourteenth century, a child under the age of ten generally cost only twenty-five or thirty florins, and there is a record of one little girl sold in 1414 to a Ser Bonaiuto, 'with all her defects visible and invisible,' for only twenty florins. But a girl aged ten to fifteen cost anything between thirty and forty florins: and one between fifteen and twenty-five, forty-five or fifty florins, while sometimes a handsome girl of fifteen (such as a fine Circassian) might fetch as much as sixty-five florins. Boy slaves under twelve, at about the same date, were worth about twenty-five florins, and boys up to eighteen, between twenty-seven and thirty-seven florins . . .

The sumptuary laws of Florence – which already forbade any maidservant to wear the high-soled shoes (*pianelle*) then in fashion, or a train to her gown – decreed that 'all slaves, nurses and maids born outside the territory of Florence' might wear 'neither cotes nor dresses nor sleeves of any kind, in any bright colours,' but must be dressed in coarse grey *romagnolo* wool 'of natural colour,' with a little cape of black cloth. 'On no account' might they have a silk gown or a belt adorned with gold or silver. On their heads they might wear only 'a linen towel with black stripes,' and on their feet 'no soled hose or *pianelle*,' but wooden clogs with black straps.

. . . not only a man's immediate descendants, but every relative living under the same roof and eating the same bread – aunts and uncles and cousins and cousins' children, down to the most remote ties of blood – all these constituted the *casato*, as it had the Roman *gens*, and was often extended to include also all dependents and servants. 'And let them all warm themselves,' wrote Alberti, 'at the same fire, and sit at the same table.'

In these great organisms there was a place not only for wives, but concubines, not only for sons, but bastards. Many a young bride, arriving in her new home, might find among the maidservants of the house some who were her husband's concubines and others who were his sisters, and not a few respectable house-holders, in reporting the members of their household to the tax-collector, would quite frankly include their illegitimate children and, later on, remember them in their wills.

To enter such a household, even as a slave, was to become part of the *famiglia*, and it is quite plain that, in this respect, slaves were treated just like any other servant. This is, indeed, why too much indignation about their legal status is out of place. True, a slave was subject to his master's *potestas puniendi*; he could be beaten and whipped, according to the statutes of most cities, with impunity; but so, we must remember, could the householder's own wife and children. The slave, if domestic chastisements did not prove sufficient, could be put – at his master's request – in prison; but so could his master's sons. 'If he does not obey you well,' wrote Lapo Mazzei about his much-loved son, Piero, to Simone d'Andrea, the manager of the firm in which Piero was working, 'beat him like a dog, and put him in prison, as if he were your own.' . . .

The records of the law-courts give a glimpse into a dark domestic under-world so violent that only laws of an equal stringency, perhaps, could have kept it in check at all. Many of the slave-owning households must have been divided into two camps, with sullen, resentful, half-savage slaves on one side, and on the other, suspicious, and often extremely nervous masters. And, indeed, their fears were natural enough. In a period in which poison was a common weapon, who was in a better position to administer it than a slave? And who was more likely than these dark strangers to possess the secrets of witchcraft? Certainly the Grand Council of Venice was of this opinion, for on 28 October 1410, it passed a law approving the questioning by torture of all such slaves or servants as were discovered 'making charms or herbs' or placing them 'in the food or on the persons of their master' . . . And in Florence, on 20 August 1379 a female slave who had put some nitrate of silver into an enema which she administered to her master who then died in agony, was sentenced by the Capitano del Popolo to be placed in an open cart and drawn through the streets of Florence, while the population watched her flesh being torn to pieces with red-hot pincers until she reached the place of execution, where she was burned alive.

[170] A Carmelite monk turned painter (Fra Filippo Lippi) has to be confined due to his uncontrollable lust for the opposite sex, but eventually succeeds in abducting a young nun and marrying her; from Vasari's *Lives* . . .

It is said that Fra Filippo was so lustful that he would give anything to enjoy a woman he wanted if he thought he could have his way; and if he couldn't buy what he wanted, then he would cool his passion by painting her portrait and reasoning with himself. His lust was so violent that when it took hold of him he could never concentrate on his work. And because of this, one time or other, when he was doing something for Cosimo de Medici in Cosimo's house, Cosimo had him locked in so that he wouldn't wander away and waste time. After he had been confined for a few days, Fra Filippo's amorous or rather his animal desires drove him one night to seize a pair of scissors, make a rope from his bed-sheets and escape through a window to pursue his own pleasures for days on end. When Cosimo discovered that he was gone, he searched for him and eventually got him back to work. And after that he always allowed him to come and go as he liked, having regretted the way he had shut him up before and realizing how dangerous it was for such a madman to be confined. Cosimo determined for the future to keep a hold on him by affection and kindness and, being served all the more readily, he used to say that artists of genius were to be treated with respect, not used as hacks . . .

Subsequently, he was asked by the nuns [*of the Carmelite convent at Prato*] to paint the altarpiece for the high altar of Santa Margherita, and it was when he was working at this that he one day caught sight of the daughter of Francesco Buti of Florence, who was living there as a novice or ward. Fra Filippo made advances to the girl, who was called Lucrezia and who was very beautiful and graceful, and he succeeded in persuading the nuns to let him use her as a model for the figure of Our Lady in his painting. This opportunity left him even more infatuated, and by various ways and means he managed to steal her from the nuns, taking her away on the very day that she was going to see the exposition of the Girdle of Our Lady, one of the great relics of Prato. This episode disgraced the nuns, and Francesco, the girl's father, never smiled again. He did all he could to get her back, but either from fear or some other reason she would never leave Fra Filippo; and by him she had a son, Filippo, who became, like his father, a famous and accomplished painter.

[171] Crime and punishment in 1500; from Luca Landucci's *Diario Fiorentino*.

24th February. A Sienese physician, of the house of Belanti of Siena, was murdered by three men, sent (it was said) by Pandolfo Petrucci, who fell upon him from the butcher's shop which is at the corner of the Via Ghibellina next to the *Stinche*. One was caught by the people at the time, and another was caught in the evening, being found in the neighbourhood of Sant' Ambrogio; the third fled and escaped, having acted, it was said, with great cunning, for after he had struck the first blow, he exclaimed to the others: 'Strike him!' and took to his heels and left them, so that the people noticed them only and let him go. It was said that he had betrayed them.

26th February. They were hung at the *Canto delle Stinche* [*Corner of the Prison of the Stinche*],where they had committed the crime. They went on the executioner's cart, being tortured most cruelly with red-hot pincers all through the city; and here at Tornaquinci the brazier for heating the pincers broke. There not being much fire left, and it not sparkling properly, the *Cavaliere* shouted at the executioner, and made him stop the cart, and the executioner got out and went for charcoal to the charcoal-burner, and for fire to Malcinto the baker, and took a kettle for a brazier, making a great fire. The *Cavaliere* kept crying all the time: 'Make it red-hot!' and all the people were desirous that they should be tortured without pity. The very boys were ready to assassinate the executioner if he did not do his work well, hence they [*the condemned men*] shrieked in the most terrible way. And all this I saw here at Tornaquinci.

[172] Renaissance snow-sculpture; from Luca Landucci's *Diario Fiorentino*.

13th January [*1510*]. It began to snow in Florence and all through the district, and it snowed four days running without stopping, so that it was half a *braccio* deep all over Florence; and it froze, so that it lasted in the city till the 22nd, when it snowed again on the top of this, becoming a *braccio* deep in many places. A number of most beautiful snow-lions were made in Florence by good masters; amongst others there was a very large and fine one next to the *campanile* of Santa Maria del Fiore, and one in front of Santa Trinità; and many nude figures were made also by good masters at the Canto de' Pazzi; and in Borgo San Lorenzo a city with fortresses was made, and many galleys; and so on, all over Florence.

23rd January. The snow began to melt and soften, so that such a mess was made in all the streets, that one could not get along or go about to do one's business; for one or two days there was no means of crossing the streets without making gangways; and therefore I record it.

[173] Florentine fashions in the early 1530s; recorded by the continuator of Luca Lunducci's *Diario Fiorentino*.

In the year 1529 the custom of wearing hoods began to go out, and by 1532 not a single one was to be seen; caps or hats being worn instead. Also, at this time, men began to cut their hair short, everyone having formerly worn it long, on to their shoulders, without exception; and they now began to wear a beard, which formerly was only worn by two men in Florence, Corbizo and one of the Martigli.

At this time also hose [*here intending short breeches*] were begun to be made in two pieces, which had formerly been made all in one, and without a seam; now they slashed them up everywhere, and put silk underneath, letting it project at all the slashes.

[174] Cosimo I eulogized as a Machiavellian Prince by a contemporary visitor to Florence; from William Thomas's *Historie of Italie . . .*(1549).

This Duke Cosmo sued first to marrie with the wife of Duke Alexander the emperours daughter, but the bishop of Rome that nowe is, purchaced hir (to his no small coste) for his sonnes sonne, Duke Octavio. For the whiche there hath ben mortall hate betwene Duke Cosmo and the bishop. And beyng thus prevented, the Duke to obteigne the more stay towardes the emperour, maried the doughter of *Don Diego di Tolledo*, Vice Re of Naples, by whose meane he hath redeemed the Cittadella of the emperour, for the summe of 400000 duckates, and is nowe absolute lorde and kynge within himselfe.

He hath divers faier children by his wyfe, and loveth hir so well, that in maner he never goeth abrode (unlesse it be to churche) without hir, and is reputed to be a very chaste man. He is learned and wyse, he useth fewe wordes, and is neverthelesse in his owne tounge eloquente. In the administration of iustice he is so sincere, that syns the tyme of his reigne, whiche is nowe above .x. yeres, I have not hearde, that he hath pardoned any person condemned to die. He hath restreigned the Vice of Sodomie (which heretofore reigned more in Florence than elsewhere in Italy) with paine of death: and hath broughte his astate to suche quietnesse, as it hath not ben this .300. yeres past: so that Florence may well saie, that in hym she hath founde hir longe desired libertee. For though he absolutely hath the whole revenewes to his owne use, yet the suretee that the Florentynes have in their owne thynges (whiche heretofore they never had) is muche more worthe to theym, than the common revenew was beneficiall to the citee.

Finally the vertue of this Duke Cosmo, besides the worthinesse of his Dominion, hath brought hym in suche reputacion, that he is now numbred as one of the rarest princes of our tyme, and feared also, as one in whom there be hydde thynges of greatter moment than the rule of that onely astate.

[175] Michel de Montaigne dines with the Grand Duke Francesco I and Bianca Cappello in November 1580; from his *Journal du Voyage en Italie.*

Messieurs [*Charles*] d'Estissac and de Montaigne dined with the Grand Duke as he calls himself. His wife was seated in the place of honour, the Duke next to her, next to the Duke the Duchess's sister-in-law together with her husband, the Duchess's brother. According to the Italians this Duchess is beautiful; she has an agreeable and imposing face, a large bust and breasts the way they like them here. She certainly seemed capable of having bewitched this prince and of being able to maintain his devotion long-term. The Duke is a stout dark man of my height, large-limbed and very courteous in his manner and facial expression, always passing through the crowds of his people without a hat, which is a fine thing. He has the bearing of a healthy man of about forty. On the other side of the table sat the Cardinal [*Ferdinando*] and another youth of eighteen years [*Don Giovanni dei Medici*], both brothers of the Duke. Drink is brought to the Duke and his wife in a basin in which there is an uncovered glass full of wine and another full of water. They take the glass of wine and pour back into the basin whatever they don't require, refilling their glasses with water from the other glass, which they then replace in the basin which the cupbearer holds for them. The Duke takes a fair amount of water; she almost none.

[176] A French philosopher visits the Florentine prostitutes in 1581; from Michel de Montaigne's *Journal du Voyage en Italie*.

In the end I had to admit that Florence deserved the title *la bella*.

    That day I went alone for amusement's sake to see those women that let anyone see them who wants to. I saw the most famous: nothing very special. Their lodgings are gathered together in a particular part of the city and are therefore disdained and moreover in a wretched condition. They are certainly not to be compared with the Roman or Venetian whores either for beauty, grace or dignity. If any of them wishes to live outside this area, she must be of little account and must practise some other trade to disguise her true one . . . Just as the Roman and Venetian whores display themselves at their windows for their lovers, so these do so at the doors of their houses, offering themselves to the public at the appropriate hours; and there you see them, some with more company, some with less, arguing and singing in the street in groups.

[177] An English traveller visits Giambologna's workshop (next door to his house in Borgo Pinti), in 1594; from Fynes Moryson's *An Itinerary* . . .

In the house of John Bolena a Flemming, and an excellent engraver [*i.e. sculptor*], I did see yet unperfected a horsemans statue of brasse, fifteen els high, the belly of the horse being capable of 24 men, whereof foure might lie in the throat; and this horse was made as going in the high way, putting forward the neere foot before, & the farre foot behind, & standing upon the other two, which statua was to be erected to Duke Cosimo, being valued at 18. thousand crownes. Also another foot statua of white marble, which was to be erected to Duke Ferdinand then living.

[178] Wine, silk, and the late-sixteenth-century diet and economy; from Sir Robert Dallington's *Survey of the Great Dukes State of Tuscany* (1605).

The Vine which without comparison is the greatest commoditie of *Tuscany*, if not of *Italy*, hath these uses. Of the Grape they feed, of the iuyce they make Wine; of the shreddings they make small bundles, like our Fagots of gaule in *Cambridge*, & sell them for two *quatrini* a peece for firing: of their leaves feed their Oxen, or else dung their land; & lastly of the stones they feed their Pigions, which after the Vintage they riddle out of the Grape being dryed, and these they sell at 20. *soldi* the *Staio*.

There are divers sorts of Grapes, the names of such as I remember are these; *Uva Canaiola*, good either to eate or for Wine; *Passerina* a small Grape, whereof Sparrowes feed, good onely for Wine; *Trebbiana* the best sort of white Grapes for Wine, whereof they make their *Vin Trebbiano*, *Zibibbo*; these are dryed for Lent: *Moscatello* with a taste like Muske, not for wine, but to eate: *Uva grossa* not to eate, but for Wine; *Raverutta*, of it selfe neither to eate, nor for Wine, but a few of these put among a great vessell of Wine, giveth it a colour, for which use it onely serveth: *San Columbana* and *Rimaldesca* a very delicate Grape, either for Wine or to eate; *Lugliola* which hath his name of the moneth of Iuly wherein it is ripe, better to eate then for Wine; and lastly *Cerisiana*, named for the taste it hath like a Cherry, better for Wine then to eate.

They have also as many names for their Figs, the best are the *Brugiotti*, which being needlesse to recount, as also to stand thus particularly upon all the rest, I will omit to speake: only in a word I will speak of the Mulberry, for that the mention thereof draweth consequently therewithall the discourse of the Silke-worme, which being another of the greatest commodities of *Tuscany* I may not forget.

In the two moneths of May and Iune this worme laboureth, the rest of the yeare they be onely seedes kept in some warme & close places, where they may neither be indangered by cold nor thunder, for either of these destroyeth them. When she hath wrought her selfe into a bottome, they put it into warme water to finde the end thereof, but if they would preserve the worme for seed, then they finde the end without putting the bottome into water (for this killeth the worme) which being found, and wound upon a Cane, they suffer the worme to lye upon a wollen cloath, till growing to a Flie it engender with another, whereof come infinite seeds, which are as is said, kept close all the yeare till the beginning of May, when they are laide in the Sunne and so hatched, but for want of heate, and to have of them betimes, the women will hatch them in their bosomes. So soone as they be wormes they have of Mulberie leaves given them, whereof they onely feed, to which purpose are daily great store of trees planted: the leafe is sold at foure *quattrini* the pound. Of this sort of trees the great Duke hath planted such plenty along the banckes of *Arno*, and about the Ditches of townes and other publick places, as it is probably iudged they will within these few yeares be annually worth thirty thousand Duckets. And whereas heretofore the Silkeworkers of *Florence*, besides their owne, were usually wont to buy from *Naples*, *Lombardie* and *Greece*, so much silke as yearely amounted to three hundred thousand Duckets, it is now thought that shortly they shall have enough of their owne; for yee shall observe that they of *Siena* are richer in lands than they of *Florence*, and therefore trade lesse in all Mechanicall professions: *I saulsi ricchi d'entrada, i fiorentini ricchi per industria*: which is the reason that the *Florentines* exceed the other so farre herein: insomuch as it is thought here are yeerly made of *Florence* Rashes to the worth of two Millions of Duckets, & of Silkes and Cloathes of gold and silver, to the value of three millions; hence grew this Axiome of *Aristotle*, *The more barbaraine the soyle, the more rich the Citie:* as he observed by *Athens* in *Greece*, and we finde by *Norremburg* in *Germanie*. Good reason they of *Florence* have to encrease this commoditie, by all possible meanes, without the which I see not how they should be able (not exhausting in few years their estates) to be relieved with the necessarie commodities of other countries: as Corne from *Sicilia*, Leather from *Barbaria*, Tinne, Lead, Hearing, Chaviar, and other such provision from England, & from divers other places other things as needfull: their State not having any Marchandize to spare, except a little Alume to countervaile this great charge withall. So that their helpe is an industrious paine-taking in the making of these silkes, their clothes of gold and silver, their Rashes, and painting of Leather for Hangings (a trade much used among them) howbeit the matter it selfe comming from *Spaine* and other countries, whereupon they worke, and onely the workmanship their owne, the advantage can be but small. . . .

Concerning Herbage, I shall not need to speake, but that it is the most generall food of the *Tuscan*, at whose table a Sallet is as ordinary, as Salt at ours; for being eaten of all sorts of persons, & at all times of the yeare: of the rich because they love to spare; of the poor because they cannot choose; of many Religious, because of their vow, of most others because of their want: it remaineth to beleeve that which themselves confesse; namely, that for every horse-load of flesh eaten, there is ten cart loades of hearbes and rootes, which also their open Markets and private tables doe witnesse, and whereof if one talke with them fasting, he shall have sencible feeling.

[179] *Bella figura* and the decline of Florentine intelligence in the sixteenth century; from Sir Robert Dallington's *Survey of the Great Dukes State of Tuscany.* (1605)

And yet . . . I cannot beleeve without some good reason, that the *Florentine* generally hath such a perlous wit, & such a subtill conceit, I would sooner subscribe he had a subtill dyet: for as hath before beene said, I am of that *French-mans* minde, that could not finde where that great witt lay, whatsoever either by *Macciavell* his report in his historie, or in his person may to the contrary be alleadged. I have heard of some *English* Gentlemen, whose abode hath beene there longer, and therefore their experience greater, & meanes also very good to entertaine conversation, that the *Florentine* will be very affable and ready to observe us with all possible complement, so long as we will consort him to the *Bardello,* & give his loose and lascivious discourse the hearing, which is ever of his Mistrisse, if not of a worse theame: But if at any time we offer the occasion of any better talke, & would discourse with him about some matter of pollicie, or historie, or Art, or such like, he straight shakes us off with a shrug of the shoulder, *actū est, scilicet*, we have lost our companion: in this onely wise that he will not talke because he cannot. For who will thinke that this people which do all things *alla mostra* [*for show*], and speakes alwayes *alla grande* (witnesse their great houses and small furniture of the one, their great words and small matter of the other) would be squeamish of their knowledge if they had it, that have such *quintessence* of termes to grace it? Indeed I verily thinke, that when the *Florentine* was Lord and Patrone of *Pisa, Pistoia, Volterra, Arezzo*, and those other Citties, that then he had wit. But now I see not why we should not say of him, as we use to doe of young unthrifts, that were left rich, and have foolishly spent or lost it (*They were well if they had had wit to keepe it*) I dare say, that if *Macciavell* were againe living, and should see them, that were wont to rule a state, now not to bring a few Lettice from their *Villa*, but at the gate to toll for them he would unsay that which he formerly said, and sweare they had no witte. . . .

As for their aptnesse to learn, whereof this author speaketh, if he meane mechanicall Artes, it is not seene in their shoppes, where yee shall almost have nothing hansomly done, except workes in cloath of golde and silver. And as for their liberall Sciences, it is not seene in their Schooles, where in one Universitie yee shall scarse finde two that are good *Grecians*, without the which tongue, they holde in our Schooles in England a man never deserveth the reputation of learned. Indeed it cannot be denyed, that in two faculties this towne hath had famous men in Painting and Poetry: and I verily thinke that herein *Italy* generally excelleth. And no marvaile, when all their time is spent in Amours, and all their churches deckt with colours. . . . this people lives much discontented, as appeareth by their daily and great, (but Private) complainings: having fresh in their mindes their former libertie, and heavie on their backes their present yoake. That this State is like a body which hath lately taken Phisick, whose humours are not yet well setled, or as a stomack weakned so much by purging, as there is now nothing left but melancholy. Concluding of this people, as of a person that lives alwayes under the hands of a Phisition, *Qui sub Medicis vivit, misere vivit.*

[180] The use of forks in late-sixteenth-century Florence; from Fynes Moryson's *An Itinerary* . . .

From morning to night the Tables are spread with white cloathes, strewed with flowers and figge leaves, with Ingestrars or glasses of divers coloured wines set upon them, and delicate fruits, which would invite a Man to eat and drink, who otherwise hath no appetit, being all open to the sight of passengers as they ride by the high way, through their great unglassed windowes. At the Table, they touch no meate with the hand, but with a forke of silver or other mettall, each man being served with his forke and spoone, and glasse to drinke. And as they serve small peeces of flesh (not whole joints as with us), so these peeces are cut into small bits, to be taken up with the forke, and they seeth the flesh till it be very tender. In Summer time they set a broad earthen vessel full of water upon the Table, wherein little glasses filled with wine doe swimme for coolenese.

[181] Grand-ducal interference in matters of criminal justice and the punishment for throwing an Englishman in the Arno; from Sir Robert Dallington's *Survey of the Great Dukes State of Tuscany* (1605).

There is also in *Florence* the *Gl'Otto di guardia e balia*, an office of great authoritie, for these onely give sentence of life and death, and iudge in criminall causes, these have their place only foure moneths. In this office the Prince hath alwayes a Secretary, a *Beneplacito*, his name now in place, is *Buoninsegni*, who ever goeth to his Highnesse [*Ferdinando I*] to enforme him of the matters in the Court, before they be by the *Otto* determined, and this office hath intelligence of all matters in all criminall Courts in the state, by whom the Courts have directions from the Prince before they proceed, to the iudgement or execution of the malefactor.

An instance of this we had this Ianuary last past [*1596*], which I the rather remember to make knowne, what care his Highnesse hath to give our countrey good satisfaction, of whom all English Gentlemen receive very gracious favours, as to be admitted to the presence at any *Veglia*, Revells, or other time of extraordinary sight, also to have the priviledge to weare Armes, and other such like. An *English* Gentleman was by a base groome of the house where he lodged, throwne into the *Arno*, for the money he was supposed to have in his lodging; the offender, upon suspition being apprehended, and receiving the *Strappado* divers times, and in the highest degree, notwithstanding persisted obstinately in the deniall. The lawe is there that except he confesse the fact he cannot be executed, how pregnant so ever the presumption be against him; insomuch it was thought he should have beene discharged: whereupon the court sent to his Highnesse for direction; he returned them order to use all manner of torments which possible, or in any cases that court could inflict, and if yet he would not confesse to torture him till he dyed. According to this commission they gave him the *Sveglia*, a kinde of torture, where having received a drinke to procure sleepe, the Torturers ever when he noddeth whip him with small plummets, he sitteth bare upon an Yron like the back of a knife, and hott Brickes under his feete to burne him, if he would ease himselfe that way. It is reported he endured this also, till they came to give him *L'Arco* the Bowe, at which he confessed. This done he is carried before the court, there freely to say whether he confessed for feare of torment, or that it is the very truth he said: if he avowe it, they proceed to iudgement, if otherwise, he is returned to the torture; for this is the onely way to proceed as is before said, how apparent soever the matter be, unlesse it be proved by two witnesses. As for witnesse, it is there hard to be had, being holden a dishonourable thing to be a witnesse, or an enformer, a *Spia*, as they terme it. Insomuch as if an offence be committed in the streets in the view of divers Gentlemen, though they were not of the action, no nor of the company, notwithstanding they shall have the *Strappado* to confesse the matter, which rather then doe, they will suffer. So that to have the *Strappado*, in *Florence* is no disparagement, except the cause make it so. But to returne to this matter which I have of purpose remembered, to make it appeare how these courts even in small matters receive directions from the Prince. After this fellow had avouched to the Court that he did the fact, they sent againe to his Highnesse to know how they should proceed. He returned, that the malefactor should loose his right hand at the doore where was the Gentlemans lodging, and from thence to be drawne to the place of Execution, there to be hanged and quartered, which was accordingly performed.

[182] The 14-year-old Robert Boyle visits a Florentine brothel with his tutor and gets chased by two bisexual friars; from *An Account of Philaretus during his Minority* – an autobiography.

(The Hon. Robert Boyle (1627–1691) the chemist and natural philosopher, was educated at Eton and by private tutors, including the Huguenot, Marcombes, who in 1641 accompanied Robert and his brother to Italy. After the Restoration, Boyle helped found the Royal Society, which was partly inspired by the Florentine Accademia del Cimento.)

Florence is a city, to which nature has not grudged a pleasing situation, and in which architecture had been no niggard either of cost or skill, but had so industriously and sumptuously improved the advantages liberally conferred by nature, that both the feat and buildings of the town abundantly justify the title the *Italians* have given it of *Fair*. Here *Philaretus* [*Boyle*] spent much of his time in learning of his governor (who spake it perfectly) the *Italian tongue*, in which he quickly attained a native accent, and knowledge enough to understand both books and men; but to speak and express himself readily in that language was a skill he ever too little aspired to acquire. The rest of his spare hours he spent in reading the modern history in Italian, and the new paradoxes of the great star-gazer *Galileo*, whose ingenious books, perhaps because they could not be so otherwise, were confuted by a decree from *Rome*; his highness the Pope, it seems, presuming, and that justly, that the infallibility of his chair extended equally to determine points in philosophy as in religion, and loth to have the stability of that earth questioned, in which he had established his kingdom. Whilst *Philaretus* lived at Florence, this famous *Galileo* died within a league of it, his memory being honoured with a celebrating epitaph, and a fair tomb erected for him at the public charges; but before his death, being long grown blind, to certain friers (a tribe, whom for their vices and impostures he long had hated) that reproached him with his blindness, as a just punishment of heaven, incensed for being so narrowly pried into by him, he answered, that he had the satisfaction of not being blind, till he had seen in heaven what never mortal eyes beheld before. But to return to *Philaretus*, the company of certain Jewish rabbins, who lodged under the same roof with him, gave him the opportunity of acquainting himself with divers of their arguments and tenets, and a rise of further disquisitions in that point. When carnaval was come (the season, when madness is so general in *Italy*, that lunacy does for that time lose its name) he had the pleasure to see the tilts maintained by the Great Duke's brothers, and to be present at the gentlemen's balls. Nor did he sometimes scruple, in his governor's company, to visit the famousest *Bordellos*, whither resorting out of bare curiosity, he retained there an unblemished chastity, and still returned thence as honest as he went thither, professing, that he never found any such sermons against them, as they were against themselves; the impudent nakedness of vice clothing it with a deformity description cannot reach, and the worst of epithets cannot but flatter. But though *Philaretus* were no fuel for forbidden flames, he proved the object of unnatural ones; for being at that time in the flower of youth, and the cares of the world having not yet faded a complexion naturally fresh enough, as he was once unaccompanied diverting himself abroad, he was somewhat rudely pressed by the preposterous courtship of two friers, whose lust makes no distinction of sexes, but that which its preference of their own creates, and not without difficulty and danger forced a scape from those gowned Sodomites, whose goatish heats served not a little to arm *Philaretus* against such people's specious hypocrisy, and heightened and fortified in him an averseness for opinions, which now the religieux discredit as well as the religion.

[183] Florentine gentry in the time of Ferdinando II; from Richard Lassels's 1654 manuscript *Description of Italy*.

As for the Gentry in Florence, its dyed in graine. That is, its both rich and new bredd. Belle lettere have allwayes been much cherished here. And the Academie of witts called *della Crusca* have helpd to polish the Italian tongue exceedingly, yet the gentry here hold it no disgrace to have a ship at Sea, and a back warehouse, with a faithfull servant and a countbooke at home, whiles they vapor it at Court, and in their Coaches. This makes them hold up their noble familyes by the chinn, and not onely preserves them from sincking, but allso makes them Swimm in a full Sea of honour by being able to buy offices for their children in

Princes Courts, whereby they come to greatest preferrements: whither when they are come, no man questioneth the way they came thither: whether by water, or by Land: by traffic or by sword: by the Count-book or the army. If the French gentry would follow this way, they might have shoes and stockings for their children (which some of them in the country want to my knowledge) whereby to keep their noble blood warme in winter.

The language of Florence is pure: but in their bookes, not in their mouths, They do so choake it in their throats, it is allmost quite drowned there; and doth not recover it self againe, till it come to Rome, where *Lingua Toscana in Bocca Romana*, is a most charming language, and fit onely to word a man to death withall.

[184] A circumcision in a house in the Jewish ghetto; from Richard Lassels's manuscript *Voyage of Italy* (1664).

I saw here [*at Rome*] a *marage*, and at Florence, a *circumcision*, which passed thus. Upon the eighth day after the woman was bought to bed, the neighbours and kindred were invited to the Circumcision. They came to the chamber of the lyeing in woman, and there the women as fine as they could make themselves, fell a danceing to two fidlars, and danced the common dances used in Italy: but none danced but women, and no women appeared there but marryed women. The mother of the child sits up in her bed finely dresed, and sees all this danceing for an houre; till at last the men come to circumcise the child. They do it for the most part in the next roome, if the house be capable of it. I confesse its a bloody spectacle and able to make a man heartily thank God that he is a Christian. Really if the child could speak and wish I beleeve he would rather wish the greatest curse in the world, that is, to be a woman, than to be a man upon such termes.

[185] Lady card-players in the mid-seventeenth century; from Richard Lassels's *Voyage of Italy* (1670).

I saw also here divers Pallaces of Noblemen upon occasion of their *Festine*. For it is the Custom here in Winter, to invite the

Chief *Ladies* of the Town (Married Women onely) to come to play at Cards in Winter Evenings for three or four hours space; and this one night in one Pallace, another night in another Pallace. Thither the *Ladies* go, and find the House open to all Comers and Goers both *Ladies* and Gentlemen, that are of any garb. In every Chamber the Dores are set open, and for the most part you shall see eight, or ten Chambers on a floor, going out of one another, with a square Table holding eight Persons, as many Chairs, two Silver Candlesticks with Waxe lights in them, and store of lights round about the room. At the hour appointed, Company being come, they sit down to play, a *Cavalier* sitting between every *Lady*, and all the Women as fine in Cloths and Jewels, as if they were going to *Ball*. The Dores of all these Rooms being open, the Light great, the Women glittering, and all glorious, you would take these Pallaces to be the *Enchanted Pallaces of the Old King of the Mountains*. Any Gentlemen may come into these Pallaces and stand behind the Gamesters, and see both how modestly they play, and how little they play for. In the mean time there's a Side Chamber alwayes open for Gentlemen to go into, and refresh themselves with Wine standing in snow, or with Limonade, or some such Cooling Drinks, which are also offered to the *Ladies*. In a great Room below, at the entrance of the Pallace, there is a long Table for Gamesters that love to play deep, that is love to play only for money.

[186] Carnival in 1755; from letters written by Robert Adam to his family in Edinburgh, published by John Fleming in *Robert Adam and his Circle in Edinburgh and Rome*.

(Robert Adam (1728–1792), second son of the leading Scottish architect of his day, ran the family building business for a while before travelling to Italy and Dalmatia in order to improve his professional knowledge and contacts. On his return he transferred his architectural practice to London, and within three years was appointed Architect of the King's Works, in which position he revolutionized British architecture.)

'You cannot conceive what a scene of madness and distraction among all ranks of people reigns at this place during the Carnival,' he began. 'The fun began at first with decency – a play one night an opera another and a ball the third. At these were masked the genteelest people in town who visited one another and enjoyed those little frolics their disguise entitles them to and spent the evening in calm and decent mirth. But as the days began to decrease and the end of the Carnival approached the spirit rose in proportion. Every mortal masked, from a Marquis to a shoe-black traversing the streets from morning to night. Coaches were filled equally with Princes and Killovy men; Harlequin was postillion, a Devil the coachman, whilst three or four monstrous figures loaded the back of the coach. Then began the Corso. This is a procession of all the equipages in the country and town who go to the great square, ride round making a tour through some of the streets of the town, return to the square again – one set going, another coming – by which means those acquainted with the coach they meet, pop their heads out, say a witty thing and take them in again. This solemn procession, with our best coach &ca., we used to parade in for two or three hours, that is from 3 to 6 o'clock, when night called us to other amusements.

'Next morning after this series of sports they began anew with greater vigour than ever, and now they went out at ten in the morning. Men, women and children, high and low, met at the Grand Duke's Gallery, the place of rendezvous, where, under cover of the piazzas, they walked up and down for three hours, there being booths for selling all toys, places for all regales and refreshments, and room for much wit and criticism on taste in masking and other things the consequence of this frenzy. In this pleasant entertainment we were occupied till we had just time to get home to dinner, dress and go to the Corso again at three o'clock.'

[187] Cosimo III; from *Some Observations made in Travelling through France, Italy, &c. in the years 1720, 1721, and 1722* by Edward Wright.

(Edward Wright's two-volume *Observations* . . . was first published in 1730, almost a decade after the journey he describes. Developing the tradition established by Richard Lassels and the Richardsons, Wright paid particular attention to sculpture, architecture and painting in his book.)

The people of Florence are very highly tax'd ; there is an imposition laid upon every thing they either wear or eat: And to keep the People in awe, and restrain them from entering into any seditious Discourses, there were when we were there, Spies in all Companies; by which his Royal Highness was acquainted with every thing that passed; and the Cannon in the Castle, which were pointed towards the City, were always ready charg'd in case of any popular Insurrection. His Royal Highness was about eighty Years old when we were there: His State of Health was then such as would not allow his going abroad; but whilst he could do that, he visited five or six Churches every day. I was told he had a Machine in his own Apartment, whereon were fix'd little Images in Silver, of every Saint in the Calendar. The Machine was made to turn so as still to present in front the Saint of the Day; before which he continually perform'd his Offices. His hours of eating and going to bed were very early, as was likewise his Hour of rising. He never came near any fire; and at his coming out of his Bedchamber, had an adjacent Room warm'd only by the Breath of such Attendants as were to be always ready there against his rising. His zeal was great for gaining Proselytes to the Romish Church; and he allow'd considerable Stipends to some of our Nation, that had been brought over by that expedient.

[188] The cicisbeo; from *Letters from Italy, in the years 1754 and 1755, by the late Right Honourable John Earl of Corke and Orrery*.

How shall I spell, how shall I paint, how shall I describe, the animal known by the title of a *Chichisbee?* [*Cicisbeo*]. You will not find the word in any dictionary. The etymology is not as yet made known to me. It so totally abrogates one of the chief characteristics of the *Italians*, jealousy, that, unless I had seen innumerable instances of its power in that particular, scarce your own testimony could have found credit with me. The *Chichisbee* is a man with many of the privileges of a husband, and all the virtues of an eunuch. He is an appendix to matrimony. Within a week after her nuptials, a young lady makes choice of her *Chichisbee*. From that moment she never appears in public with her husband, nor is ever imprudent enough to be seen without her *Chichisbee*. He is her guardian, her friend, and her gentleman-usher. He attends her in a morning as soon as she is awake. He presents to her chocolate before she rises. He sets her slippers; and, as soon as his morning visit is over, he withdraws where he pleases. The lady admits him not to dinner. The husband only has that honour. In the afternoon he returns to attend her in her visits. His assiduity must be remarkable; his punctuality must never waver. When she sees company at home, he is to hand her from one end of the room to the other, from chair to chair, and from side to side. If she enters into a particular discourse with another person, the *Chichisbee* retires into a corner of the room with the lap-dog, or sits in the window teaching the macaw to speak *Italian*. If the lady sits down to play, it is the duty of the *Chichisbee* to sort her cards. The husband (believe me, I entreat you, if you can,) beholds their familiarities, not only contentedly, but with pleasure. He himself has the honourable employment of a *Chichisbee* in another house; and in both situations, as *husband* and *chichisbee*, neither gives, nor receives, the least tinct of jealousy.

[189] The Casino, opera and ballet at the end of the eighteenth century; from John Moore's *A View of Society and Manners in Italy*.

Society seems to be on an easy and agreeable footing in this city. Besides the conversazionis which they have here, as in other towns of Italy, a number of the nobility meet every day at a house called the Casino. This society is pretty much on the same footing with the clubs in London. The members are elected by ballot. They meet at no particular hour, but go at any time that is convenient. They play at billiards, cards and other games, or continue conversing the whole evening, as they think proper. They are served with tea, coffee, lemonade, ices, or what other refreshments they choose; and each person pays for what he calls for. There is one material difference between this and the English clubs, that women as well as men are members.

The company of both sexes behave with more frankness and familiarity to strangers, as well as to each other, than is customary in public assemblies in other parts of Italy.

The Opera at Florence is a place where the people of quality pay and receive visits, and converse as freely as at the Casino above mentioned. This occasions a continual passing and repassing to and from the boxes, except in those where there is a party of cards formed; it is then looked on as a piece of ill manners to disturb the players. I never was more surprised, than when it was proposed to me to make one of a whist party, in a box which seemed to have been made for the purpose, with a little table in the middle. I hinted that it would be full as convenient to have the party somewhere else; but I was told, good music added greatly to the pleasure of a whist party; that it increased the joy of good fortune, and soothed the affliction of bad. As I thought the people of this country better acquainted than myself with the power of music, I contested the point no longer; but have generally played two or three rubbers at whist in the stage-box every opera night.

From this you may guess, that, in this city, as in some other towns in Italy, little attention is paid to the music by the company in the boxes, except at a new opera, or during some favourite air. But the dancers command a general attention: as soon as they begin, conversation ceases; even the card-players lay down their cards, and fix their eyes on the Ballette. Yet the excellence of Italian dancing seems to consist in feats of strength, and a kind of jerking agility, more than in graceful movement. There is a continual contest among the performers, who shall spring highest. You see here none of the sprightly, alluring gaiety of the French comic dancers, nor of the graceful attitudes, and smooth flowing motions of the performers in the serious opera at Paris. It is surprising, that a people of such taste and sensibility as the Italians, should prefer a parcel of athletic jumpers to elegant dancers.

[190] The Florentine prisons in the reign of Pietro Leopoldo (the 1780s); from *The State of the Prisons in England and Wales with preliminary Observations and an account of some foreign prisons and hospitals* by John Howard.

In Florence there are two prisons. In the great *Prison, Palazzo degl'Otto*, were only twenty prisoners. Six of them were in the *secrete* chambers, which are twenty-one strong rooms. None of the prisoners were in irons. They had mattresses to lie on. Their bread was good. In the torture chamber, there was a machine for decollation, which prevents that repetition of the stroke which too often happens when the axe is used.

In the other *Prison, Delle Stinche*, there are five doors to pass before you come to the court. The opening of the first is three feet wide, and four feet nine inches high, with an inscription over it, *Oportet misereri*, (We ought to be compassionate.) In this prison were forty-two men and fourteen women. Debtors were not separated from criminals. In one room were eight who paid for their beds. The bread was good: the daily allowance to each, fifteen ounces. None were in irons. The chaplain has apartments, and resides in the gaol. – This prison has something similar to the plan I proposed. A wall surrounds three sides of it; but being very high, and only eleven feet and a half distant, renders the prison too close.

[191] The Carnival in 1829; from James P. Cobbett's *Journal of a Tour in Italy*.

(The less vivid son of the more famous William, James P. Cobbett published his *Journal of a Tour in Italy* in 1830, the same year as his father's *Rural Rides* appeared in print. Together with his brother John he later edited his father's political works.)

We arrived here this afternoon at a very interesting moment. We are at the hotel called the *Nuova-York* (New York); and, just as we got there, the carriages of the Royal Family were coming by, with the Grand Duke and his Duchess in full state, followed by a long train of carriages, through a crowd of what, I should think, exhibited the carnival in *sufficient* perfection. The street in which our hotel stands forms a part of what is called the 'corso,' or course; and it seems that it is the custom in Italian cities to have an established *corso*; that is, some particular line of streets, through which to drive during the fashionable hours of the day, or on state occasions. Perhaps there never was any thing more inconsistent than the simultaneous appearances, upon this occasion, made by the sovereign and his subjects; the one having so much majestic dignity, and the other so much of the farcical. The equipage of the Grand Duke, the carriages, horses, liveries, were all really grand and princely; every thing about it was of a piece. The foot-passengers, of all degrees, were standing, walking, running, huddling about, in the greatest confusion, and a large part of them wearing masks and dresses of the most outrageously ridiculous kinds. It seemed as if the assemblage at some masquerade, to which men and women of all degrees might receive admittance, were all at once turned onto the street, while the Grand Duke paraded along more like a man going to be crowned, than like a participator in such a fantastical exhibition. Among those who are strangers to such a scene as this, there are some people so sedate that they would regard the sight as a mere novel absurdity; and it does not, to be sure, exactly correspond with any kind of jollity known in *our* country. Yet, if there were nothing else to make one sympathise with these people in their carnival, there is one thing that ought to make us do so: there is such a display of thorough *good humour* in the thing . . . it is mirth worked up almost to a frenzy. All those of the common people that can afford it, get some sort of carriage to ride in, a cart, or wagon, or something or other on wheels. They stick up a parcel of large green branches of trees around the carriage; and, dressed themselves in ludicrous masquerade, all standing on end in the thing crammed full, brandishing boughs in the faces of other passengers whom they meet, they go roaring along like so many madmen.

[192] A nostalgic comparison between Grand-ducal and post-Risorgimento Florence; from *Old Time Travel* by Alexander Innes Shand.

(Alexander Shand (1832–1907), admitted to the Scottish bar in 1865, became a prolific contributor to *The Times*, *Blackwood's Magazine* and the *Saturday Review*. In 1893 he was appointed British commissioner at the Paris exhibition. *Old Time Travel* (published in 1903) was subtitled: *Personal reminiscences of the Continent forty years ago compared with experiences of the present day*.)

Florence was the brightest of Italian cities, Naples not excepted. The city of the factions and street fights, the birth-place of the Renaissance, and the centre of light and leading under the Medicis, was lively as ever five-and-forty years ago, and intellectual to boot. When the rest of Italy was groaning under foreign rule, under the abuses of the Papal *régime* and the brutalities of the Neapolitan Bourbons, Florence was flourishing under the beneficent rule of its Grand Dukes. Always volatile and prone to *émeutes* and revolution, the Florentines welcomed the annexation to Piedmont, though they had sent few soldiers into the battlefield. In 1860 I happened to drive into Florence on the very day when the fall of the dynasty was finally recognised. Our carriage crossed the Piazza della Signoria when the workmen were taking down the Grand Ducal arms from the façade of the Uffizi Palace. Recognising our nationality, they turned to grin and wave their hands, in assurance of English sympathy with their liberation. In the evening there were fireworks in the Cascine, and the lights of brilliant illumination were flashed back from the bosom of the Arno. Well, the Florentines have had their will; they have seen their city crowned the capital, and then abandoned; and perhaps, like the Milanese, they have come to realise that they have changed King Log for King Stork. They were always liberally inclined, and they are still tolerably loyal, but the taxation has increased six-fold since they sent Leopold II on his travels. He had ample private revenues, and spent them freely, and nothing could be pleasanter than his cultured little court, where all were welcomed who came decently introduced.

[193] D.H. Lawrence compares socialism and fascism in Florence; from the 1924 Epilogue of *Movements in European History* by 'Lawrence H. Davison'.

(The Epilogue to D.H. Lawrence's pseudonymously published school textbook was excluded from all editions prior to 1971.)

In Italy, in Florence, there was the same lingering ease and goodwill in 1919 as before the War. By 1920 prices had gone up three times, and socialism was rampant. Now we began to be bullied in every way. Servants were rude, cabmen insulted one and demanded treble fare, railway porters demanded large sums for carrying a bag from the train to the street, and threatened to attack one if the money were not paid. The train would suddenly come to a standstill in the heat of the open country: the drivers had gone on strike for a couple of hours . . . If in the country you asked at a cottage for a drink of wine, worth a penny, the peasant would demand a shilling, and insult you if he did not get it.

This was all pure bullying. And this was socialism. True it was the bad side of socialism, the hatred of 'superiors' or people with money or education or authority. But socialism it was.

Such socialism made itself enemies. And moreover, it could not trust itself. In an old civilised country like Italy, it was bound to cave in.

In the summer of 1920 I went north, and Florence was a state of continual socialistic riot: sudden shots, sudden stones smashing into the restaurants where one was drinking coffee, all the shops suddenly barred and closed. When I came back there was a great procession of Fascisti and banners: *Long Live the King* . . .

This was the beginning of Fascism. It was an anti-socialist movement started by the returned soldiers in the name of Law and Order. And suddenly, it gained possession of Italy. Now the cabs had a fixed charge, a fixed charge for railway porters was placarded in the railway stations, and trains began to run punctually. But also, in Fiesole near Florence the Fascisti suddenly banged at the door of the mayor of the village, in the night when all were in bed. The mayor was forced to get up and open the door. The Fascisti seized him, stood him against the wall of his house, and shot him under the eyes of his wife and children, who were in their night dresses. Why? Because he was a socialist.

That is Fascism and Law and Order. Only another kind of bullying.

[194] Envoi: Florence in 1844; from Charles Dickens's *Pictures from Italy*.

But how much beauty . . . is here when, on a fair clear morning, we look, from the summit of a hill, on Florence! See where it lies before us in a sun-lighted valley, bright with the winding Arno, and shut in by swelling hills; its domes, and towers, and palaces, rising from the rich country in a glittering heap, and shining in the sun like gold!

Magnificently stern and sombre are the streets of beautiful Florence; and the strong old piles of building make such heaps of shadow, on the ground and in the river, that there is another and a different city of rich forms and fancies, always lying at our feet.

Prodigious palaces, constructed for defence, with small distrustful windows heavily barred, and walls of great thickness formed of huge masses of rough stone, frown, in their old sulky state, on every street. In the midst of the city – in the Piazza of the Grand Duke, adorned with beautiful statues and the Fountain of Neptune – rises the Palazzo Vecchio, with its enormous overhanging battlements, and the Great Tower that watches over the whole town. In its court-yard – worthy of the Castle of Otranto in its ponderous gloom – is a massive staircase that the heaviest waggon and the stoutest team of horses might be driven up. Within it, is a Great Saloon, faded and tarnished in its stately decorations, and mouldering by grains, but recording yet, in pictures on its walls, the triumphs of the Medici and the wars of the old Florentine people. The prison is hard by, in an adjacent court-yard of the building – a foul and dismal place, where some men are shut up close, in small cells like ovens; and where others look through bars and beg; where some are playing draughts, and some are talking to their friends, who smoke, the while, to purify the air; and some are buying wine and fruit of women-vendors; and all are squalid, dirty, and vile to look at. 'They are merry enough Signore,' says the Jailer. 'They are all blood-stained here,' he adds, indicating, with his hand, three fourths of the whole building. Before the hour is out, an old man, eighty years of age, quarrelling over a bargain with a young girl of seventeen, stabs her dead, in the market-place full of bright flowers; and is brought in prisoner, to swell the number.

Among the four old bridges that span the river, the Ponte Vecchio – that bridge which is covered with the shops of Jewellers and Goldsmiths – is a most enchanting feature in the scene. The space of one house, in the centre, being left open, the view beyond, is shown as in a frame; and that precious glimpse of sky, and water, and rich buildings, shining so quietly among the huddled roofs and gables on the bridge, is exquisite. . . .

In this other large Piazza, where an irregular kind of market is held, and stores of old iron and other small merchandise are set out on stalls, or scattered on the pavement, are grouped together, the Cathedral with its great Dome, the beautiful Italian Gothic Tower the Campanile, and the Baptistry with its wrought bronze doors. And here, a small untrodden square in the pavement, is 'the Stone of DANTE,' where (so runs the story) he was used to bring his stool, and sit in contemplation. I wonder was he ever, in his bitter exile, withheld from cursing the very stones in the streets of Florence the ungrateful, by any kind remembrance of this old musing-place, and its association with gentle thoughts of little Beatrice!

The chapel of the Medici, the Good and Bad Angels of Florence; the church of Santa Croce where Michael Angelo lies buried, and where every stone in the cloisters is eloquent on great men's deaths; innumerable churches, often masses of unfinished heavy brickwork externally, but solemn and serene within; arrest our lingering steps, in strolling through the city. . . .

Beyond the walls, the whole sweet Valley of the Arno, the convent at Fiesole, the Tower of Galileo, Boccaccio's house, old villas and retreats; innumerable spots of interest, all glowing in a landscape of surpassing beauty steeped in the richest light; are spread before us. Returning from so much brightness, how solemn and how grand the streets again, with their great, dark, mournful palaces, and many legends: not of siege, and war, and might, and Iron Hand alone, but of the triumphant growth of peaceful Arts and Sciences.

What light is shed upon the world, at this day, from amidst these rugged Palaces of Florence! Here, open to all comers, in their beautiful and calm retreats, the ancient Sculptors are immortal, side by side with Michael Angelo, Canova, Titian, Rembrandt, Raphael, Poets, Historians, Philosophers – those illustrious men of history, beside whom its crowned heads and harnessed warriors, show so poor and small, and are so soon forgotten. Here, the imperishable part of noble minds survives, placid and equal, when strongholds of assault and defence are overthrown; when the tyranny of the many, or the few, or both, is but a tale; when Pride and Power are so much cloistered dust. The fire within the stern streets, and among the massive Palaces and Towers, kindled by rays from Heaven, is still burning brightly, when the flickering of war is extinguished and the household fires of generations have decayed; as thousands upon thousands of faces, rigid with the strife and passion of the hour, have faded out of the old Squares and public haunts, while the nameless Florentine Lady, preserved from oblivion by a Painter's hand, yet lives on, in enduring grace and youth.

Let us look back on Florence while we may, and when its shining Dome is seen no more, go travelling through cheerful Tuscany, with a bright remembrance of it; for Italy will be the fairer for the recollection.

Bibliography

ACTON, HAROLD, *Memoirs of an Aesthete*, London, 1948.

ARDITI, BASTIANO, *Diario di Firenze e di altre parti della cristianità (1574–1579)*, ed. Roberto Cantagalli, Florence, 1970. (Translated by E. Chaney)

BERENSON, BERNARD, *Italian Painters of the Renaissance*, London, 1930.

BOCCACCIO, GIOVANNI, *Il Decamerone*, ed. G. Bozzo, 2 vols, Milan, 1895. (Translated by E. Chaney)

BORSOOK, EVE, *The Mural Painters of Tuscany from Cimabue to Andrea del Sarto*, 2nd edition, Oxford, 1980.

——, 'L' Hawkwood d'Uccello et la "Vie de Fabius Maximus" de Plutarque', *Revue de l'Art*, LV, France, 1982. (Translated abridgement done by the author.)

BOYLE, JOHN, 5TH EARL OF CORK AND ORRERY, *Letters from Italy in the years 1754 and 1755 by the late Right Honourable John Earl of Corke and Orrery*, London, 1773.

BOYLE, ROBERT, 'An Account of Philaretus during his minority', in *The Works of the Honourable Robert Boyle, in six volumes. To which is prefixed the life of the author*, ed. Thomas Birch, London, 1772.

BRAUDEL, FERNAND, *Civilization and Capitalism: 15th–18th Century*, Vol II *The Wheels of Commerce*, translated by Sian Reynolds, London, 1982.

BRUCKER, GENE, *The Society of Renaissance Florence: A Documentary Study*, New York, 1971.

BRYANT, WILLIAM CULLEN, *Letters of a Traveller; or, Notes of things seen in Europe and America*, New York, 1850.

BYRON, LORD GEORGE GORDON, *Childe Harold's Pilgrimage*, London, 1819–24.

CAMUS, ALBERT, in *Reflections on Florence*, edited by Simone Bargellini and Alice Scott, Florence, 1984.

CASTELLAN, ANTOINE LAURENT, *Letters on Italy*, London, 1820.

CELLINI, BENVENUTO, *The Life of Benvenuto Cellini*, ed. and translated by Robert H.H. Cust, 2 vols, London, 1910.

CHANEY, EDWARD, '"Philanthropy in Italy": English Observations of Italian Hospitals (1545–1789)' in *Aspects of Poverty in Early Modern Europe*, ed. T. Riis, Florence-Stuttgart, 1981.

——, 'From the Alps to Anglo-Tuscany' in *Bollettino del CIRVI, III, i* (1982)

——, *The Grand Tour and the Great Rebellion: Richard Lassels and 'The Voyage of Italy' in the Seventeenth Century*, Geneva-Turin, 1985.

COBBETT, JAMES P., *Journal of a Tour in Italy*, London, 1830.

Cook's Handbook to Florence, London, 1924.

COOPER, JAMES FENIMORE, *Gleanings in Europe*, Italy, 1838.

DALLINGTON, SIR ROBERT, *A Survey of the Great Dukes State of Tuscany. In the yeare of our Lorde 1596*, London, 1605.

DICKENS, CHARLES, *Pictures from Italy*, London, 1846.

DUPATY, PRESIDENT CHARLES MARGUERITE JEAN BAPTISTE MERCIER, *Travels through Italy, in a Series of Letters; written in the year 1785 by President Dupaty. Translated from the French by an Englishman*, London, 1781.

ELIOT, GEORGE, *Romola*, London, 1863.

EUSTACE, JOHN CHETWODE, *A Classical Tour through Italy*, 3rd edition, London, 1815.

EVELYN, JOHN, *The Diary of John Evelyn now first printed in full from the manuscripts belonging to Mr John Evelyn*, ed. E.S. de Beer, 6 vols, Oxford, 1955.

FLEMING, JOHN, *Robert Adam and his Circle in Edinburgh and Rome*, 2nd edition, London, 1978.

FORSTER, E.M., *A Room with a View*, London, 1908.

GALLENGA, A., *Italy Revisited*, 2nd edition, 2 vols, London, 1876.

GAYE, GIOVANNI (ed.), *Carteggio inedito d'artisti dei secoli XIV. XV. XVI.*, 3 vols, Florence, 1839–40. (Translated by E. Chaney)

GIANFIGLIAZZI, BONGIANNI, *Will*, in the Archivio di Stato di Firenze. (Translated by Rab Hatfield)

GILBERT, CREIGHTON, *Italian Art 1400–1500, Sources and Documents in the History of Art*, Englewood Cliffs, New Jersey, 1980.

GUICCIARDINI, FRANCESCO, *History of Italy and History of Florence*, ed. John R. Hale, translated by Cecil Grayson, Chalfont St Giles, 1966.

HARTT, FREDERICK, *Florentine Art under Fire*, Princeton, 1949.

HATFIELD, RAB, *The Three Kings and the Medici: a Study in Florentine Art and Culture during the Quattrocento*, unpublished Ph.D. dissertation, Harvard University, 1966.

HAWTHORNE, SOPHIA, *Notes in England and Italy*, New York, 1869.

HOBY, SIR THOMAS, *The Travels and Life of Sir Thomas Hoby, Knight of Bisham Abbey, written by himself. 1547–1564*, ed. Edgar Powell, Camden Society (Miscellany Vol X), London, 1902.

HOLT, ELIZABETH, *A Documentary History of Art*, Vol I, New York, 1957.

HORNER, SUSAN, Manuscript diary in the library of the British Institute of Florence (1847/48).

HORNER, SUSAN and JOANNA, *Walks in Florence*, 2 vols, London, 1873.

HOWARD, JOHN, *The State of the Prisons in England and Wales with preliminary Observations, and an account of some foreign prisons and hospitals*, 4th edition, London, 1792.

HYMAN, ISABELLE (ed.), *Brunelleschi in Perspective*, Englewood Cliffs, New Jersey, 1974.

JAMES, HENRY, *Italian Hours*, London, 1909.

——(ed.), *William Wetmore Story and his Friends*, 2 vols, London, 1903.

JARVES, JAMES JACKSON, *Italian Sights and Papal Principles*, London, 1856.

KEYSLER, JOHN GEORGE (JOHANN GEORG), *Travels through Germany, Bohemia, Hungary, Switzerland, Italy, and Lorrain. Giving a True and Just Description of the present state of those countries; their natural, literary, and political History; manners, laws, commerce, manufactures, painting, sculpture, architecture, coins, antiquities, curiosities of art and nature, & illustrated with copper-plates, engraved from drawings taken on the spot. Carefully translated from the second edition of the German.* 4 vols, London, 1760.

LANDUCCI, LUCA, *Diario Fiorentino*, ed. I. Del Badia, translated as *A Florentine Diary from 1450-1516* by Alice de Rosen Jervis, London, 1927.

LASSELS, RICHARD, *Description of Italy*, 1654 manuscript in the National Library of Scotland, Edinburgh; ed. E. Chaney in *The Grand Tour and the Great Rebellion*, Geneva–Turin, 1985.

——, *The Voyage of Italy*, 1664 manuscript in the possession of E. Chaney.

——, *The Voyage of Italy*, Paris, 1670.

LAWRENCE, D.H., *Aaron's Rod*, London, 1922.

——, *Movements in European History* (1925), Oxford, 1971.

MACLEOD, JOSEPH, *People of Florence. A Study in Locality*, London, 1968.

MANETTI, ANTONIO DI TUCCIO, *The Life of Brunelleschi*, ed. Howard Saalman, translated by Catherine Enggass, Pennsylvania University Park, 1970.

MENDELSSOHN-BARTHOLDY, FELIX, *Letters from Italy and Switzerland*, translated by Lady Wallace with a biographical notice by Julia de Marguerittes, London, 1865.

MONTAIGNE, MICHEL DE, *Journal du Voyage en Italie (1580–81)*, ed. A. d'Ancona, Città di Castello, 1895. (Translated by E. Chaney)

MOORE, JOHN, *A View of Society and Manners in Italy*, 6th edition, 2 vols, London, 1795.

MORGAN, LADY SYDNEY, *Italy*, 2 vols, London, 1821.

MORYSON, FYNES, *An Itinerary written by Fynes Moryson, Gent, first in the Latin Tongue, and then translated by him into English: containing his Ten Yeers Travell through the Twelve Dominions of Germany, Bohmerland, Sweitzerland, Netherland, Denmarke, Poland, Italy, Turky, France,*

England, Scotland & Ireland. Divided into III Parts. London, 1617.

——, *Shakespeare's Europe: A Survey of the Condition of Europe at the end of the 16th Century, being unpublished chapters of Fynes Moryson's 'Itinerary' (1617)*, ed. C. Hughes, London, 1903.

ORIGO, IRIS, 'The Domestic Enemy', in *Speculum* xxx, 1955.

PATER, WALTER, *Studies in the History of the Renaissance*, London, 1873.

PIERS, HENRY, *A Discourse of H.P. his Travelles*, Bodleian Library Rawlinson MS.D. 83.

POPE–HENNESSY, JOHN, *Fra Angelico* (1952), 2nd edition, London, 1974.

PUCCI, ANTONIO, 'Proprietà di Mercato Vecchio' in *Delizie degli eruditi toscani*, ed. I di San Luigi, Florence, 1770–89, Vol VI. (Translated by Nicholas Havely)

RAYMOND, JOHN, *Il Mercurio Italico, or An Itinerary containing a Voyage made through Italy in the yeare 1646 and 1647*, London, 1648.

RERESBY, SIR JOHN, *Travels and Memoirs*, London, 1813.

ROGERS, SAMUEL, *The Italian Journal*, ed. J.R. Hale, London, 1956.

ROSS, JANET, *Italian Sketches*, London, 1887.

——, *Old Florence and Modern Tuscany*, London, 1904.

RUBINSTEIN, NICOLAI, 'The Beginnings of Political Thought in Florence', *Journal of the Warburg and Courtauld Institutes*, Vol V, 1942.

——, 'The Piazza della Signoria in Florence', in *Festschrift Herbert Siebenhüner*, eds. E. Hubala and G. Schweikhart.

RUCELLAI, GIOVANNI, *Giovanni Rucellai ed il suo zibaldone*, Vol I, *Il Zibaldone Quaresimale*, ed. A. Perosa, London, 1960. (Translated by E. Chaney)

RUSKIN, JOHN, *The Diaries of John Ruskin*, ed. J. Evans and J. Whitehouse, 3 vols, Oxford 1956–57.

——, *Mornings in Florence: being simple studies of Christian Art, for English Travellers*, Orpington, 1875–77.

SACCHETTI, FRANCO *Il libro delle Trecentonovelle*, ed. E. Li Gotti, Milan, 1946. (Translations by E. Chaney and N. Havely)

SEVERN, JOSEPH, (see *Sharp, William*)

SHAND, ALEXANDER INNES, *Old Time Travel*, London, 1903.

SHARP, SAMUEL, *Letters from Italy, describing the customs and manners of that country, in the years 1765, and 1766*, London, 1766.

SHARP, WILLIAM, *The Life and Letters of Joseph Severn*, London, 1892.

SHERER, JOSEPH MOYLE, *Scenes and Impressions in Egypt and in Italy*, London, 1824.

SITWELL, OSBERT, *Great Morning*, London, 1948.

SMOLLETT, TOBIAS, *Travels through France and Italy*, 2 vols, London, 1766.

SPENCE, JOSEPH, *Letters from the Grand Tour*, ed. Slava Klima, Montreal–London, 1975.

STEEGMULLER, FRANCIS, 'A Letter from Florence' in *Stories and True Stories*, Boston, 1972.

STENDHAL (HENRI BEYLE), *The Private Diaries of Stendhal*, ed. and translated by Robert Sage, London, 1955.

TAINE, HIPPOLYTE, *Italy*, translated by J. Durand, 4th edition, New York, 1875.

THOMAS, DYLAN, *Collected Letters*, ed. Paul Ferris, London, 1985.

THOMAS, WILLIAM, *The Historie of Italie, a boke excedyng profitable to be redde: Because it intreateth of the astate of many and divers common weales how thei have ben, & now be gouerned*, London, 1549.

TROLLOPE, THOMAS ADOLPHUS, *What I Remember*, London, 1887.

TROUBRIDGE, LADY UNA, *The Life and Death of Radclyffe Hall*, London, 1961.

TWAIN, MARK, *Innocents Abroad*, Hartford, Connecticut, 1870.

VASARI, GIORGIO, *Le Vite de' piu eccellenti pittori, scultori ed architettori*, ed. G. Milanesi, Florence, 1906. (Translated by E. Chaney)

——, *The Lives of the Painters, Sculptors and Architects*, translated by A.B. Hinds, London, 1900.

——, *The Lives of the most Eminent Painters, Sculptors and Architects*, translated by G. du C. de Vere, 10 vols, London-New York, 1912.

VERKADE, DOM WILLIBRORD, *Yesterdays of an Artist-Monk*, translated from the German by John L. Stoddard, London, 1930.

VESPASIANO DA BISTICCI, *The Vespasiano Memoirs: Lives of Illustrious Men of the XVth Century by Vespasiano da Bisticci, Bookseller*, ed. and translated by W.G. and E. Waters. London, 1926.

VILLANI, GIOVANNI, *Croniche Fiorentine*, 8 vols, Florence, 1823. (Translations by E. Chaney and N. Havely)

——, *Villani's Chronicle, being selections from the first nine books of the Croniche Fiorentine*, translated by Rose E. Selfe, ed. Philip E. Wicksteed, London, 1906.

WILDE, OSCAR, *The Letters of Oscar Wilde*, ed. Rupert Hart-Davis, London, 1962.

WITTKOWER, RUDOLF, *Gothic versus Classic: Architectural Projects in Seventeenth-Century Italy*, New York, 1974.

WOTTON, SIR HENRY, *The Life and Letters of Sir Henry Wotton*, ed. Logan Pearsall Smith, 2 vols, Oxford, 1907.

WRIGHT, EDWARD, *Some Observations made in Travelling through France and Italy &c, in the years 1720, 1721, and 1722*, 2nd edition, London, 1764.

YOUNG, ARTHUR, *Travels in France and Italy during the years 1787, 1788 and 1789*, ed. T. Okey, London, 1915.

Index

Number in *italics* refers to illustrations

GENERAL INDEX